Miller Place and Mount Sinai

Through Time

Edna Davis Giffen
and Ann M. Becker

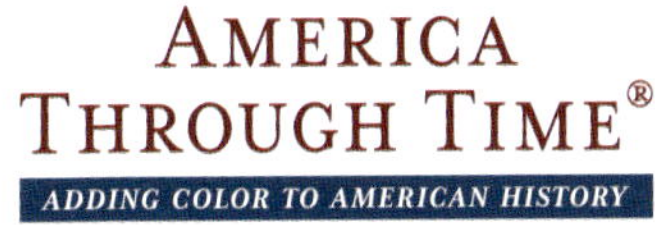

America Through Time is an imprint of Fonthill Media LLC

Fonthill Media LLC
www.fonthillmedia.com
office@fonthillmedia.com

First published 2015

ISBN 978-1-63500-035-1

Typeset in Mrs Eaves XL Serif Narrow
Printed and bound in Great Britain by CPI Group (UK) Ltd, Croydon, CR0 4YY

Connect with us:
www.twitter.com/usathroughtime
www.facebook.com/AmericaThroughTime

Introduction

Mount Sinai and Miller Place have been intertwined since the 17th century. Originally, both areas were a part of the Old Man's territory purchased by the Town of Brookhaven in 1664. By the early 18th century the term Old Man's referred to the territory from Crystal Brook Hollow to Pipe Stave Hollow, from the Long Island Sound to what today is New York State Route 25A. In 1844, legend has it that the name Old Man's was changed to Mt. Sinai when the postmaster, Charles Phillips, opened his Bible and with closed eyes, pointed with a knitting needle, landing near the name Mount Sinai. Andrew Miller and his descendants were among the most prominent members of the early community of Old Man's. Roads did not have formal names in the early days, but were described as leading from one place to another. In this case the road from Setauket, another 17th century Long Island community, to Andrew Miller's place was a main thoroughfare. Eventually "Andrew" was dropped and the area became known as Miller's Place, and in 1894, the apostrophe was dropped from the name. Both communities developed their housing and commercial developments along the north shore, close to the harbor and easy access to fresh water. Land to the south was farmed or used as wood lots.

During the colonial period, most residents were subsistence farmers who often pursued secondary occupations as carpenters, weavers, blacksmiths, and millers. Mount Sinai had a water-powered mill; and both communities had wind-powered mills in the 18th century. Cordwood was the most valuable cash commodity for local farmers and residents from the 1700s up through the late 1890s. Coastal schooners would anchor on the beach at high tide, and at low tide men from local communities would load cordwood while the boat sat on the beach. The wood went to NYC or to the brick kiln factories in the Haverstraw area along the Hudson. Both communities established schoolhouses soon after New York State set up local school districts in 1813. Starting from 1894 through the 1960s, both districts sent high school students to be educated in Port Jefferson, which operated as a regional school. Today they educate the majority of their children in each respective district, which serve elementary, middle and high school students.

Starting in the 19th century, both communities became popular with people looking for recreation and escape from the growing cities of New York and Connecticut. Hunting was a major interest due to the vast number of acres of woods and open space. By the early 20th century, the quiet and peace of the country brought more people seeking a vacation spot. Soon small summer communities arose with easy access to the waters of Mt. Sinai Harbor and Long Island Sound. Both communities buzzed with the activities of the summer crowd, but returned to the quiet of everyday life once these tourists went back to their city homes in the fall.

The communities were not immune to world events, and many young people, both local and summer residents, served their country with honor and distinction. After World War II, Long Island saw increased suburbanization and a boom in home construction. The farming communities of Mount Sinai and Miller Place were immune to the early developments of the 1950s, but by the 1960s developments began to grow within both hamlets. An explosion of development has taken place, beginning in the 1980s, resulting in the disappearance of most local farms and open space.

The history contained in this book is a brief look at what the communities once were, and how they look now – thanks to the work of local historians, there is much already known; however there is always much more to explore and discover about where we live.

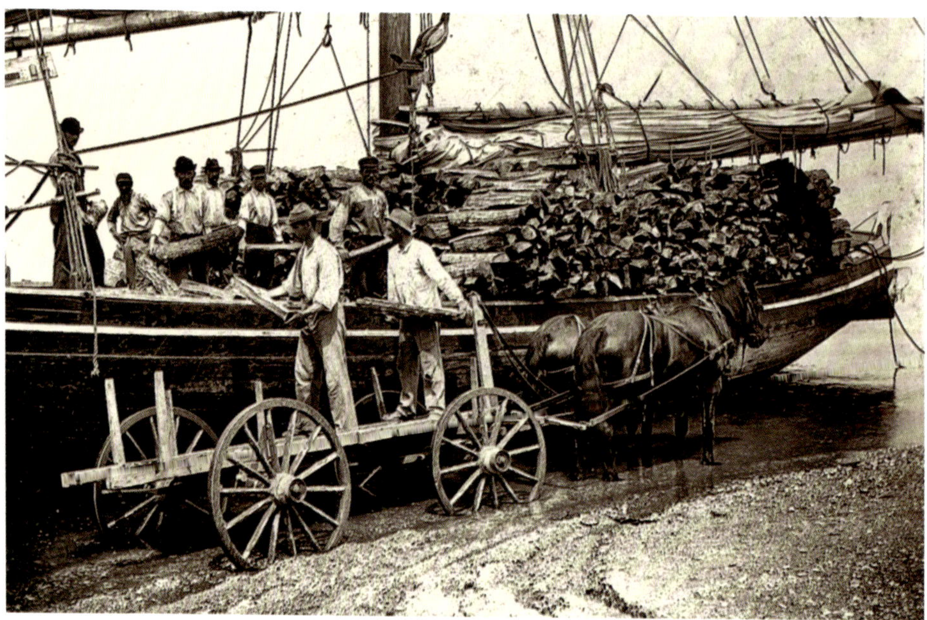

Chapter One

Historical Background

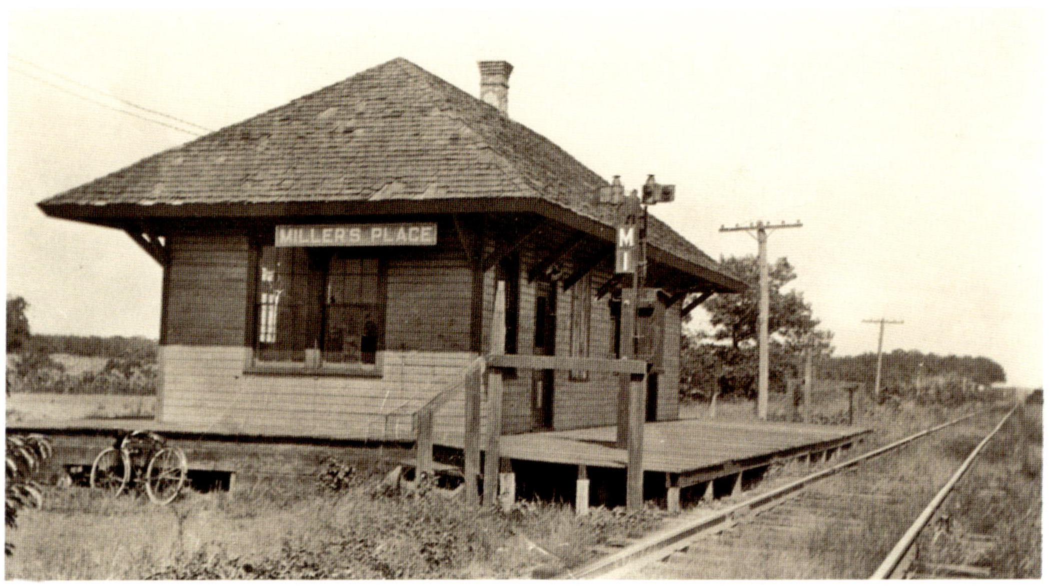

STATION: Viewed in late summer or early fall, little train activity is evident as weeds can be seen between the ties and on the outside of the tracks. Before World War I, high activity resulted in bare ground around the station and tracks. In the background note the white line over the tracks – this is the bridge taking Miller Place Road over the tracks, sometimes called Miller Place Bridge Road.

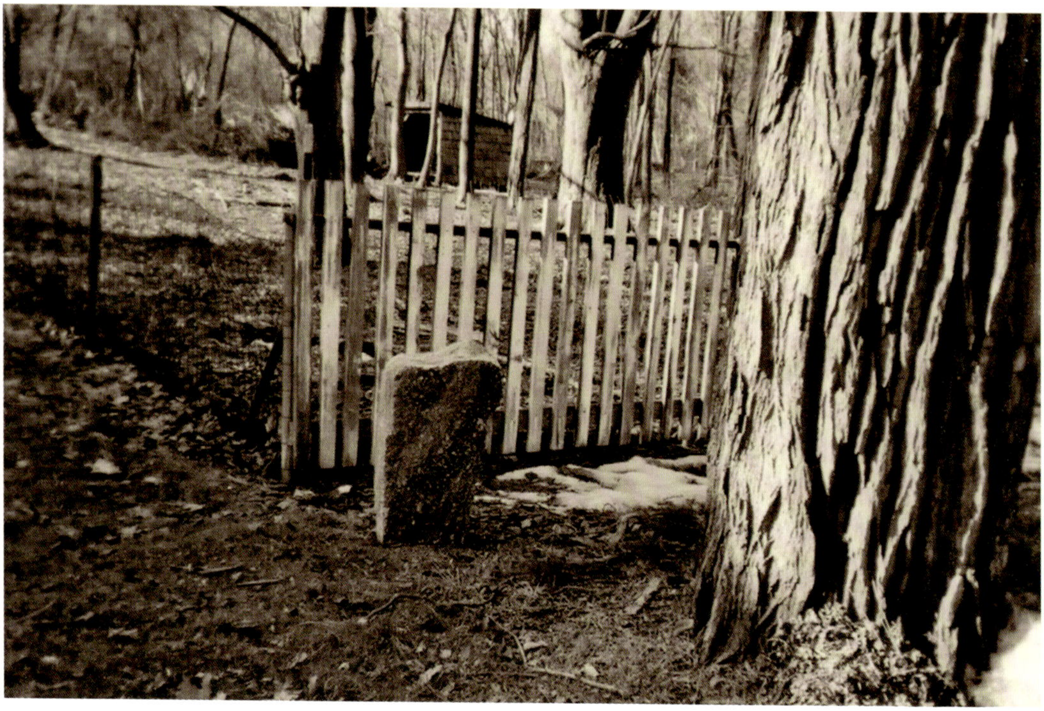

MILE MARKERS: Located on the south side of North Country Road in Miller Place and Mount Sinai designating the distance to Riverhead, the county seat. Benjamin Franklin instituted their use to standardize postal delivery and postage rates. No two stones are alike, but are noted to be vertical with flat surfaces. The writing that once graced each stone has long disappeared. The stones are exactly one mile apart.

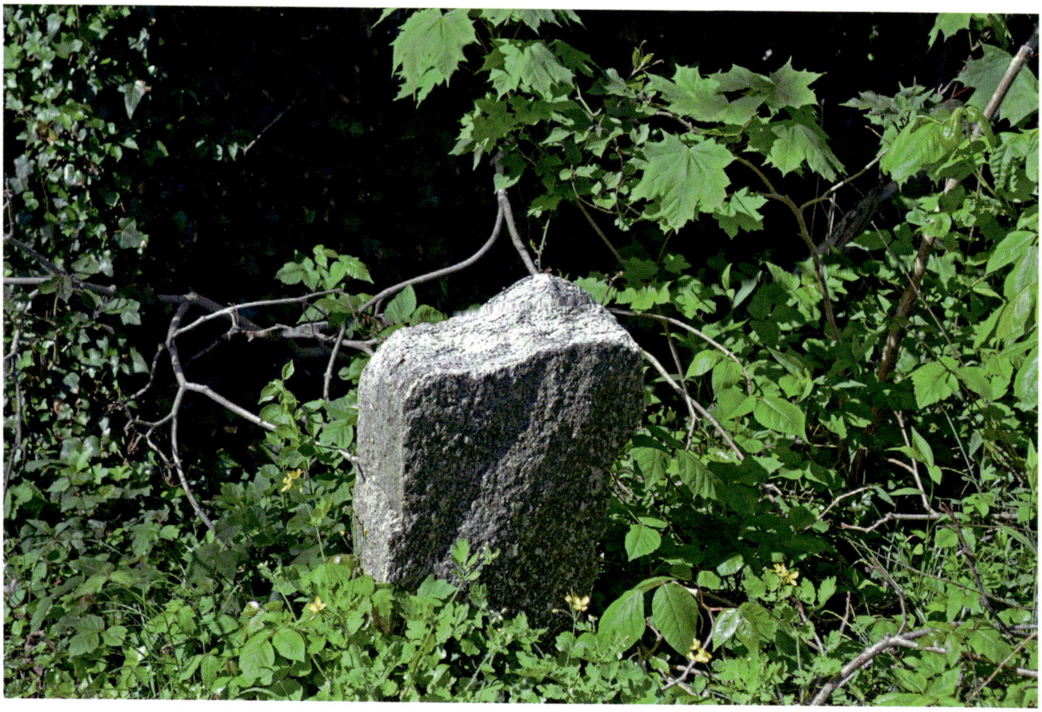

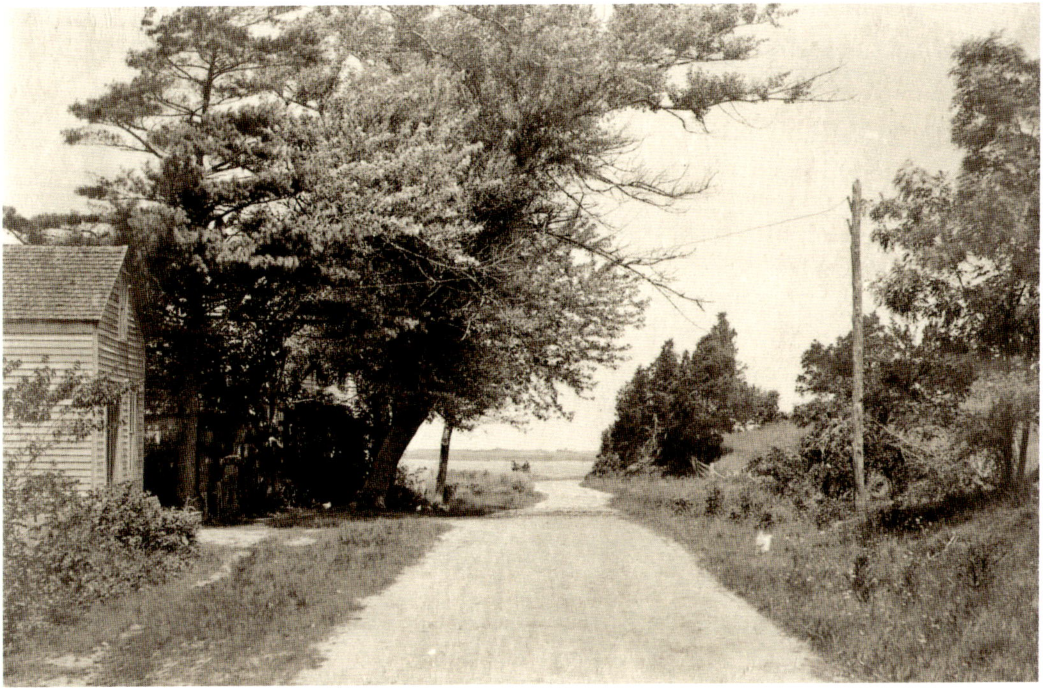

TOOKER PROPERTY: John Hutchinson established a general store on his property near the harbor on Shore Road in Mount Sinai in the early 1800s. Selah Tooker, his son-in-law, continued the store into the early 1900s where he catered to the many tourists who stayed in the boarding houses and camps on Shore Road. The building remains on the property where it was built. The two contrasting views are from the early 1900s and 2014.

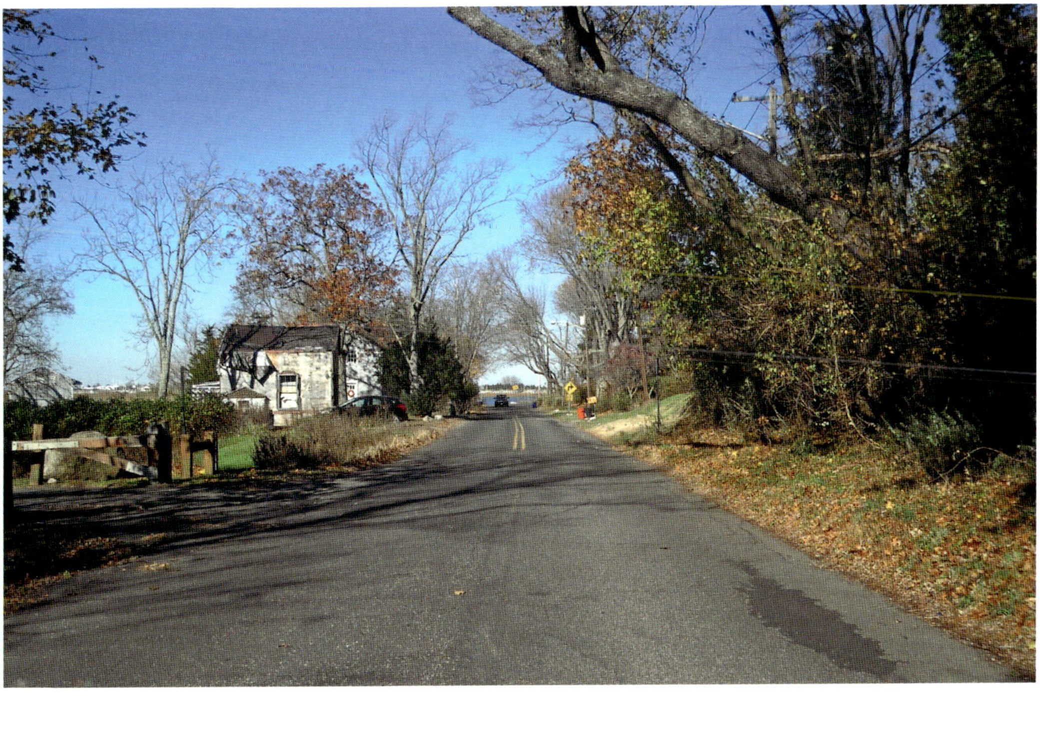

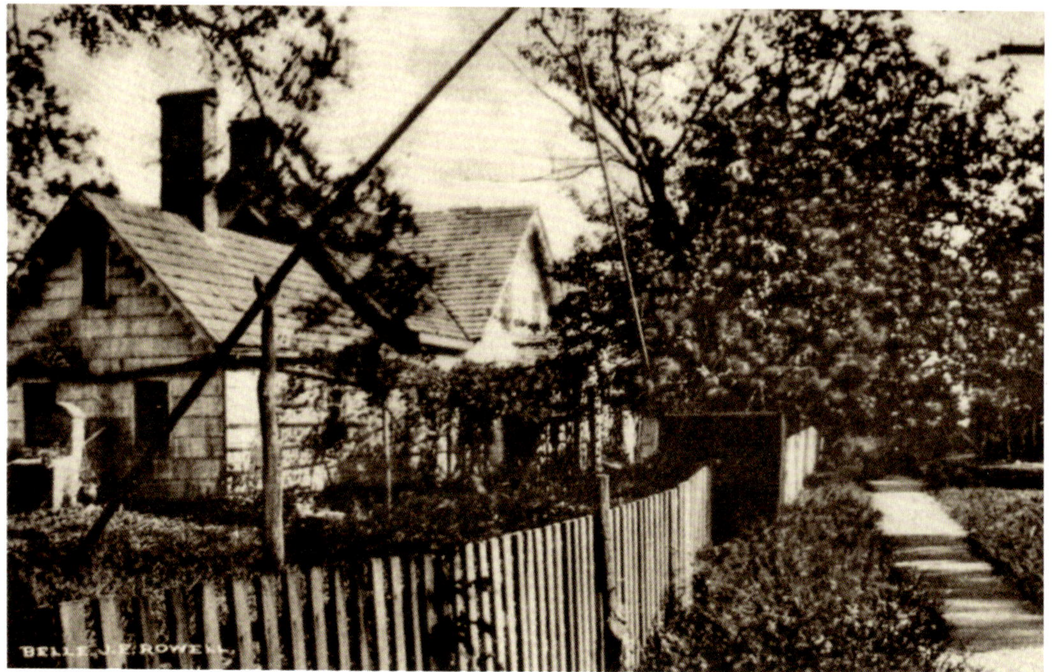

EBENEZER MILLER HOUSE: This historic Miller Place home was built about 1760, and was the site of a horrific raid during the Revolutionary War. The Miller family remained in possession of the house until 1906, when it was owned by Elizabeth and George Linkletter, who took in summer boarders. The Soma family then owned the house from 1926 through the 1980s. In her biography, actress Angelica Houston recalls visiting her grandfather at the house, which until recently served as a bed and breakfast by the name of Miller Place Ark in honor of the many girls who once summered there.

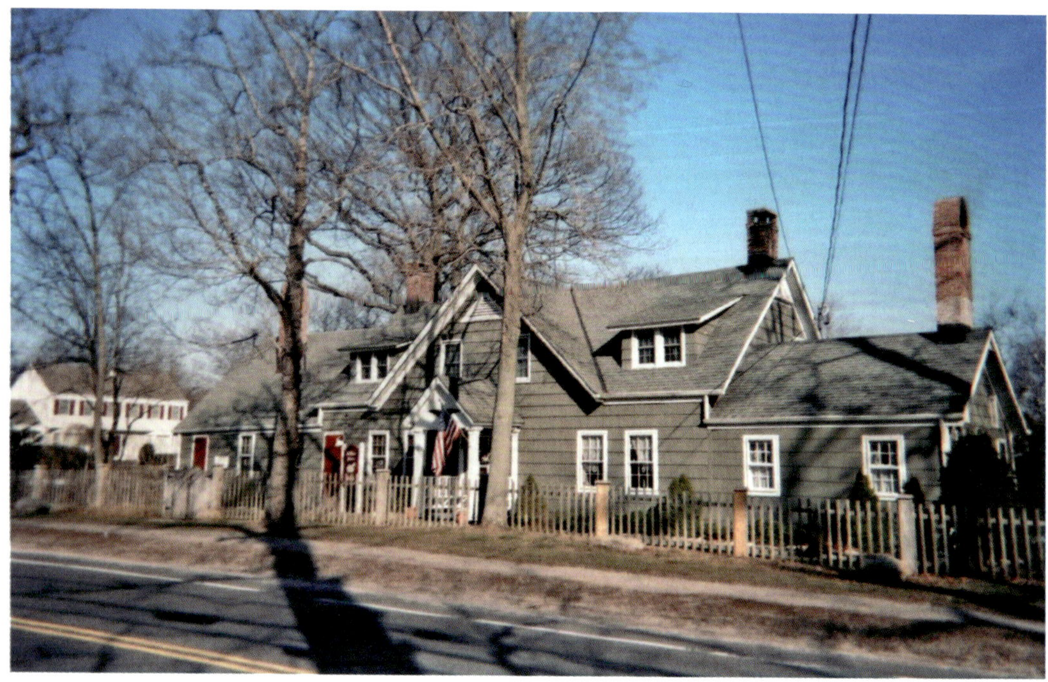

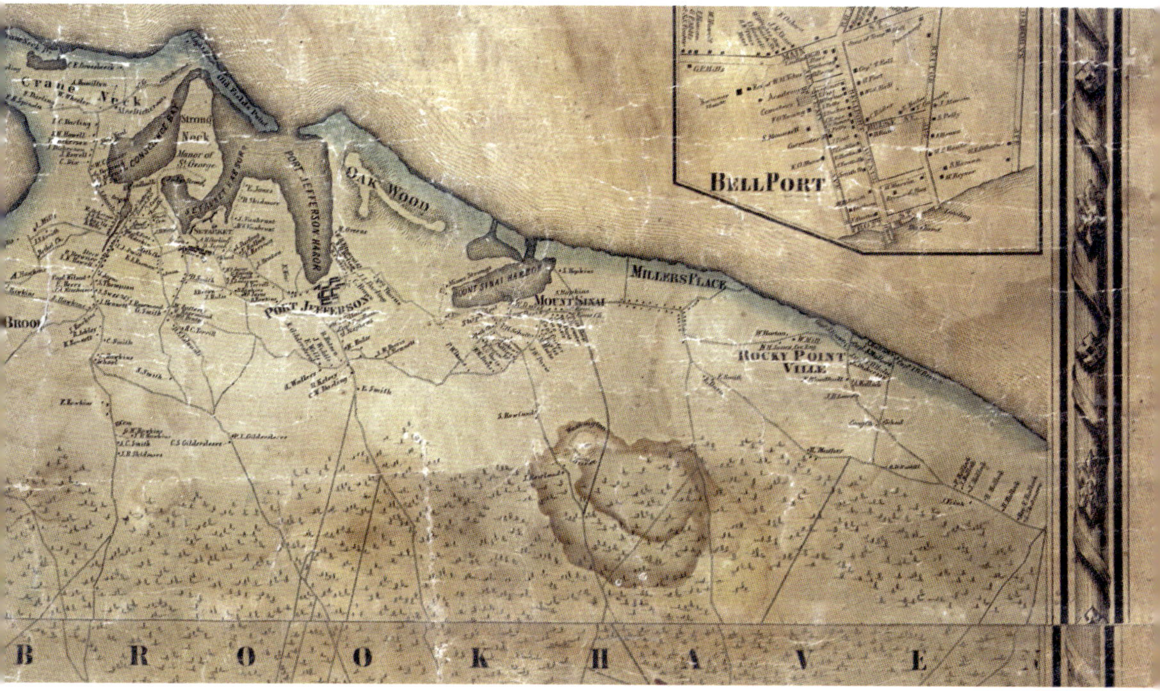

THE WASHINGTON COURSE: The Chace Map of 1858 shows the hamlets of Mount Sinai and Miller Place centered towards the northern part of the village, with vast fields and woodland to the south. A racecourse was located between Mount Sinai-Coram Road on the west side of the track and what was Hopkins Road (now Pipe Stave Hollow Road) on the east side. The aerial view shows the extensive development of the farmland that began in the 1990s. Route 25A (originally Hallock Avenue) runs parallel to the former LILCO (now the Long Island Power Authority) right-of-way, originally the site of Long Island Railroad tracks.

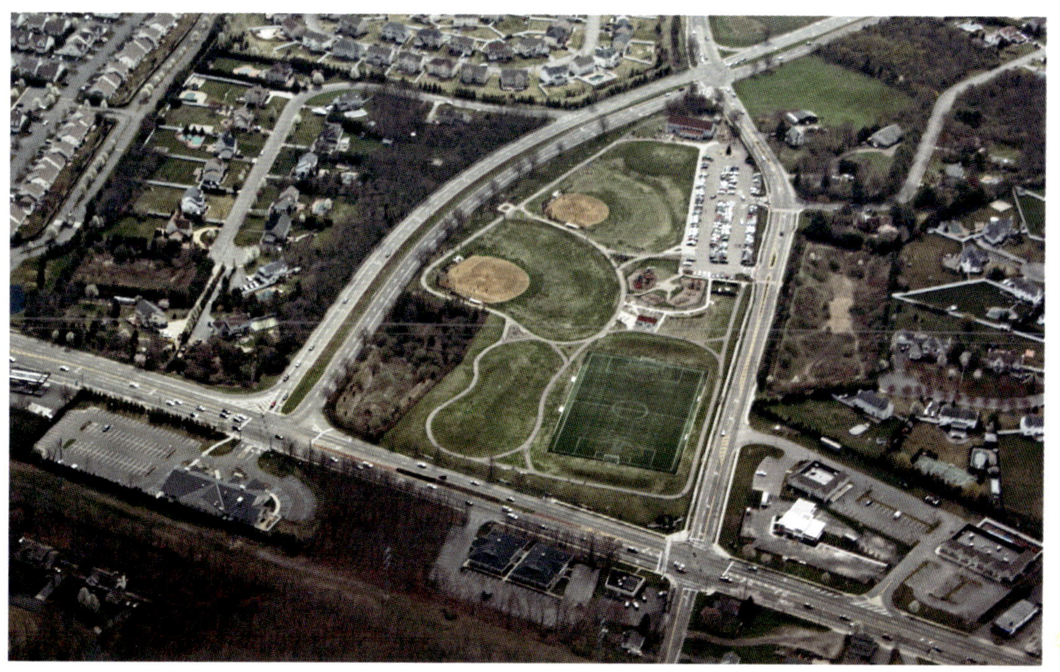

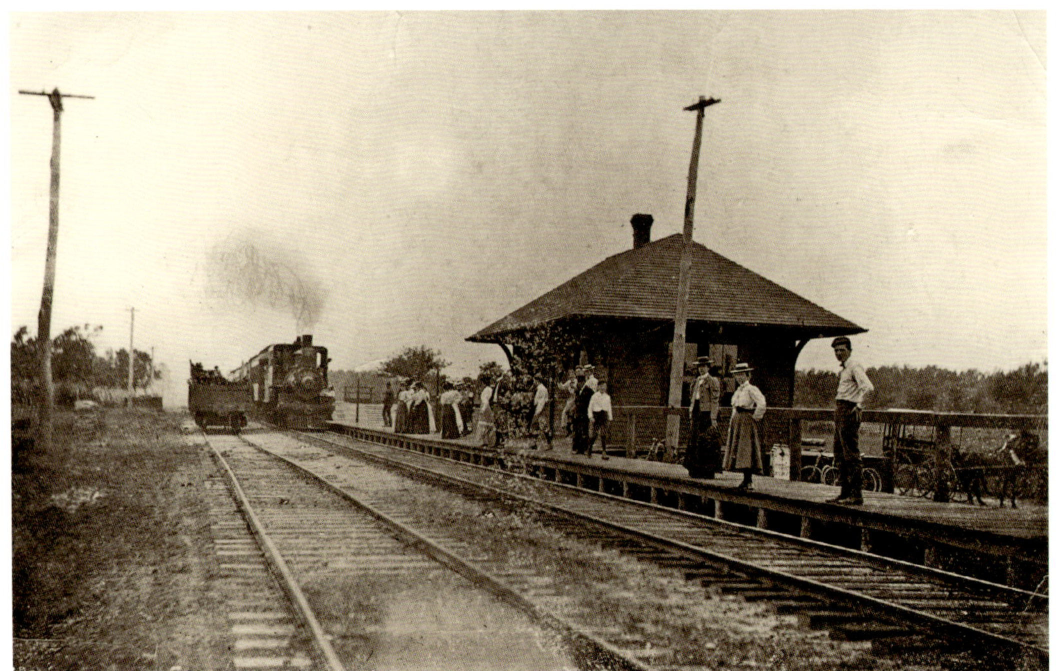

LONG ISLAND RAIL ROAD STATION: Built on the east side of Sylvan Avenue in Miller Place, near the present-day intersection of Sylvan and Echo avenues, north of what is now Route 25A, this station was built in 1894. Regular service ran from New York City through Port Jefferson and continued east to Wading River by 1893. The station burned twice, once in 1903 and again in 1934. The railroad carried passengers and freight, more in the summer than winter. The increase in the use of the automobile reduced the number of passengers, and it was abandoned in 1939.

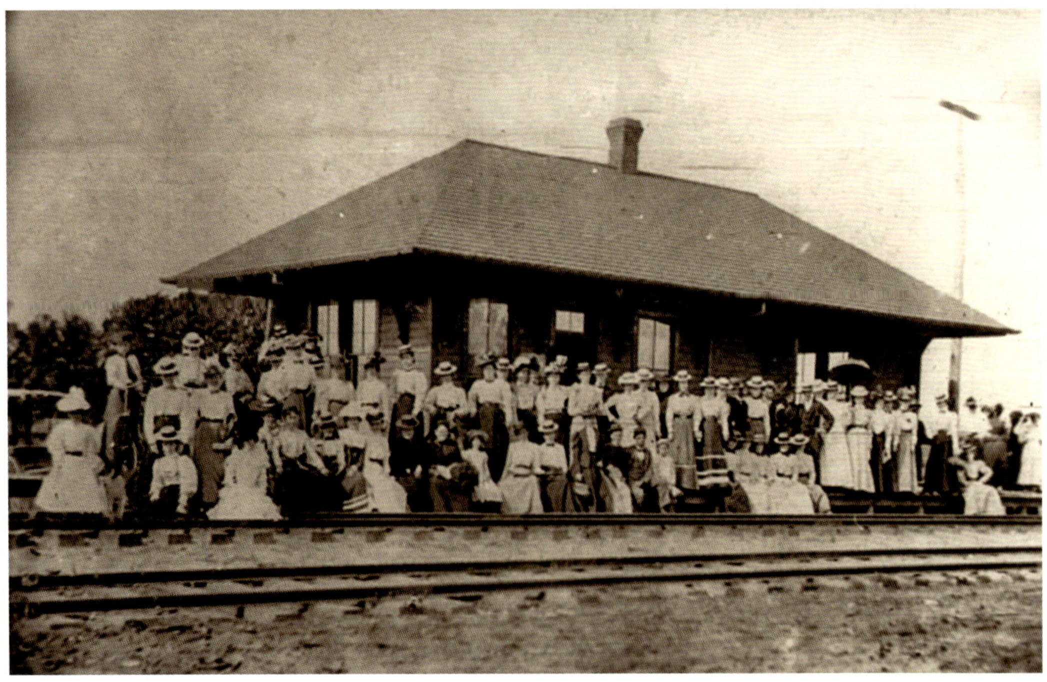

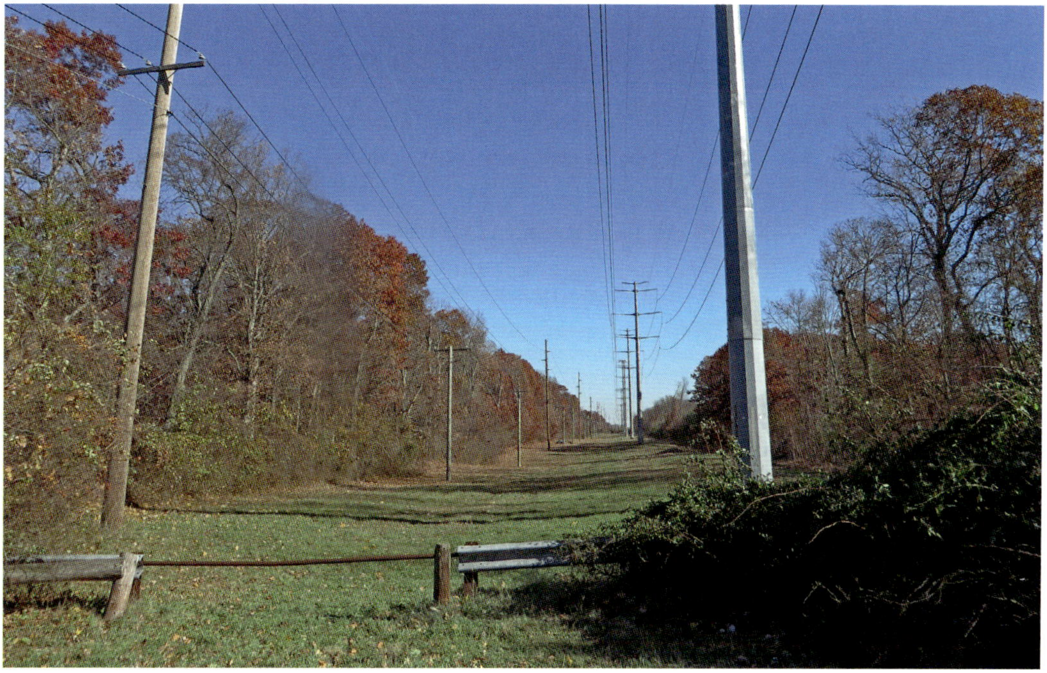

RIGHT-OF-WAY: When choosing a location, the Long Island Railroad purchased flat farmland south of the main centers of both Mount Sinai and Miller Place, avoiding the hills, valleys and swamps in both hamlets. LILCO erected high-tension lines through Mount Sinai (above) and Miller Place (below). In 2013 plans to convert this land into a public bicycle trail known as the "Rails to Trails" project, were approved between the Town of Brookhaven, Suffolk County and the Long Island Power Authority, then in charge of the property. Currently, a condominium complex sits near the site of the original train station.

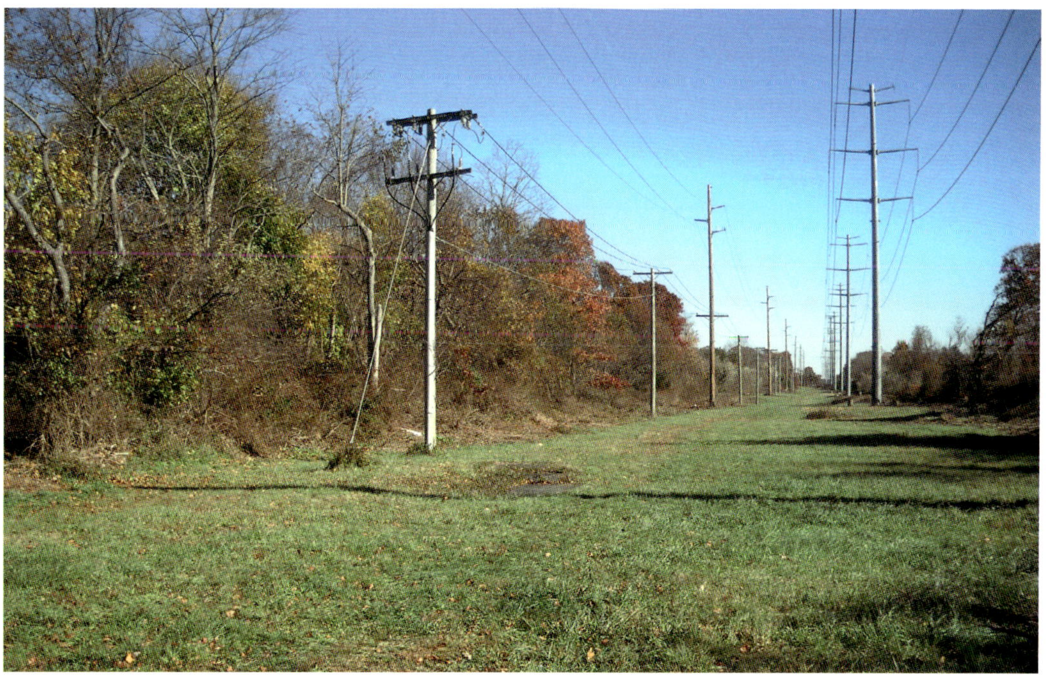

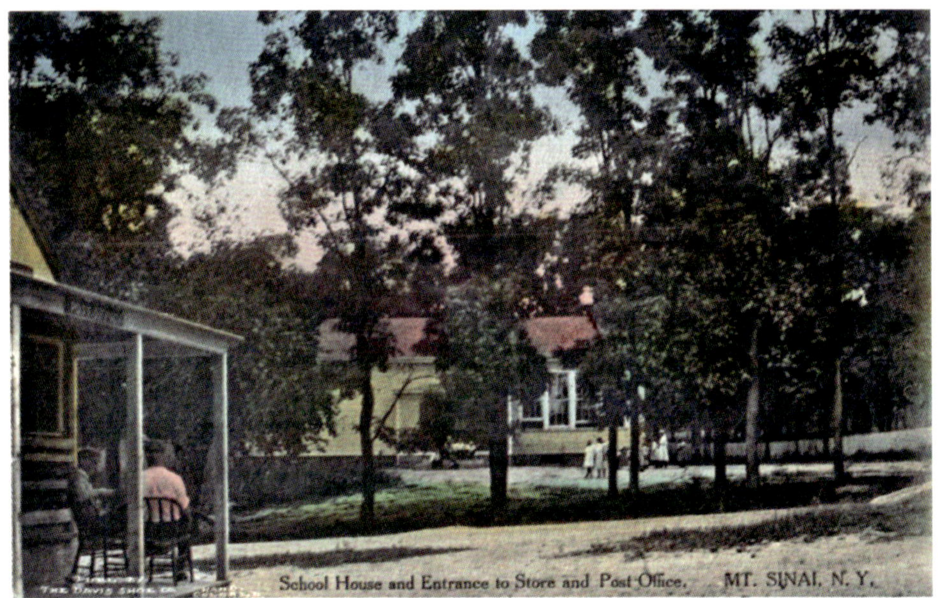

MOUNT SINAI POST OFFICE: Established in 1840, the first postmaster, Charles Phillips, operated the post office from his home. He was succeeded by his son John. John Randall served next, and in 1886 Eliza C. Randall was appointed postmaster upon the death of her husband. When she retired in 1909, Vincent R. Davis succeeded her, and moved the post office to this store on Mount Sinai-Coram Road, opposite the school. In 1916 Victor Floyd Davis became postmaster, and kept the post office and store here until 1922 when it was moved to the corner of North Country and Mount Sinai-Coram Roads. The post office continued in this location until 1975 when it was moved to its present location on Route 25A.

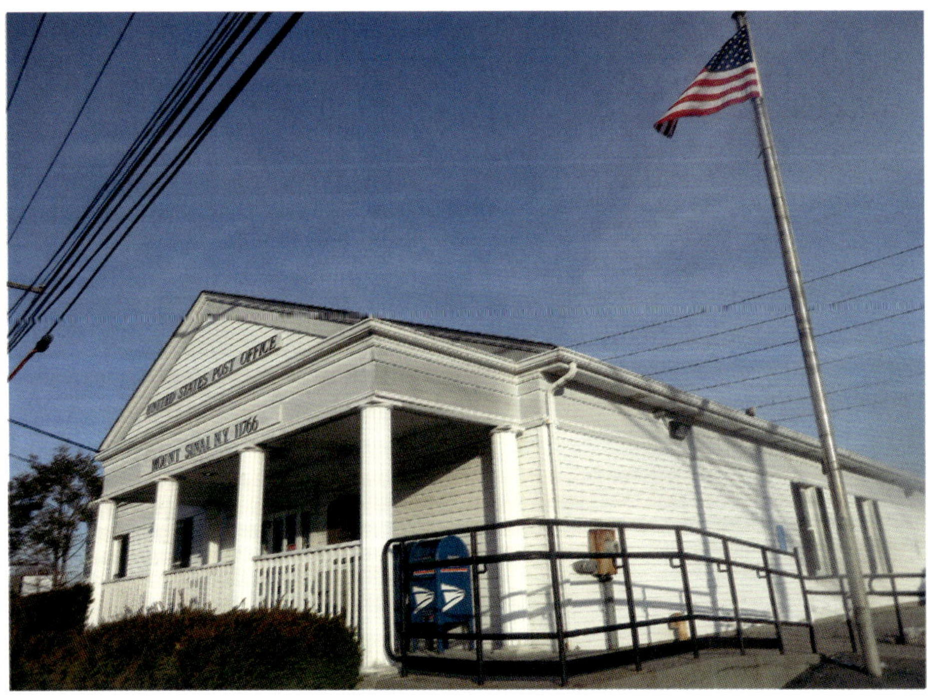

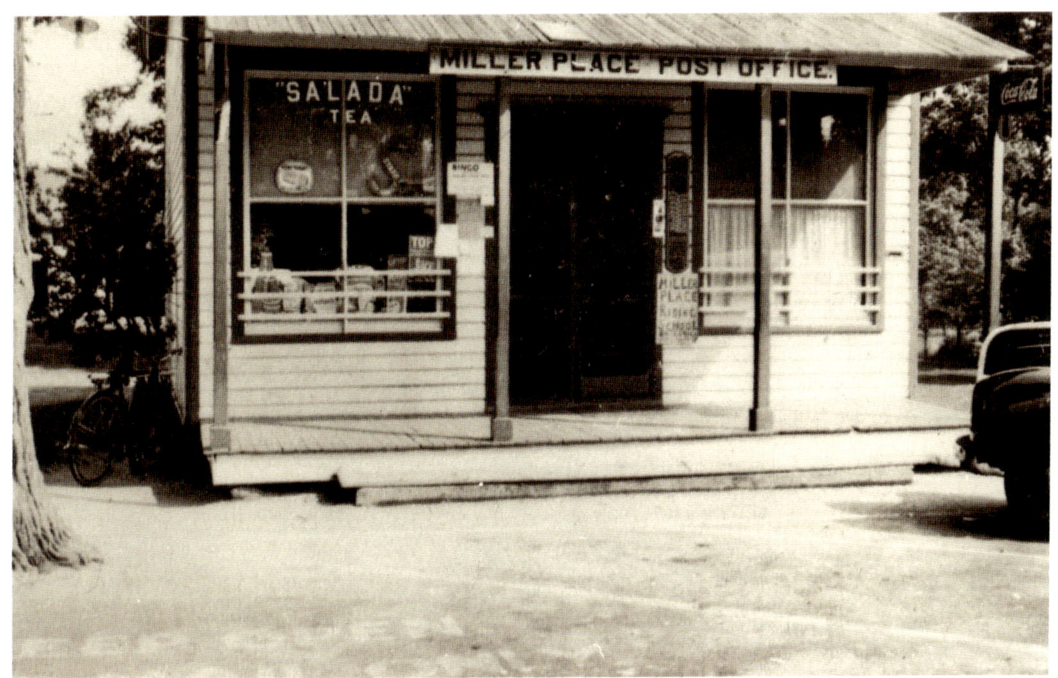

MILLER PLACE POST OFFICE: Established in 1825, in the Thomas Helme house on North Country Road, between 1849 and 1914 the post office moved thirteen times, and had eleven postmasters. In 1914 Hewlett H. Davis Sr. became postmaster and moved the post office into his general store. In 1955 the general store closed and the post office took over the entire building. In 1970 the MP post office moved to a small strip mall on the south side of Echo Avenue. In 1990 the post office moved to its present location on the north side of Echo Avenue.

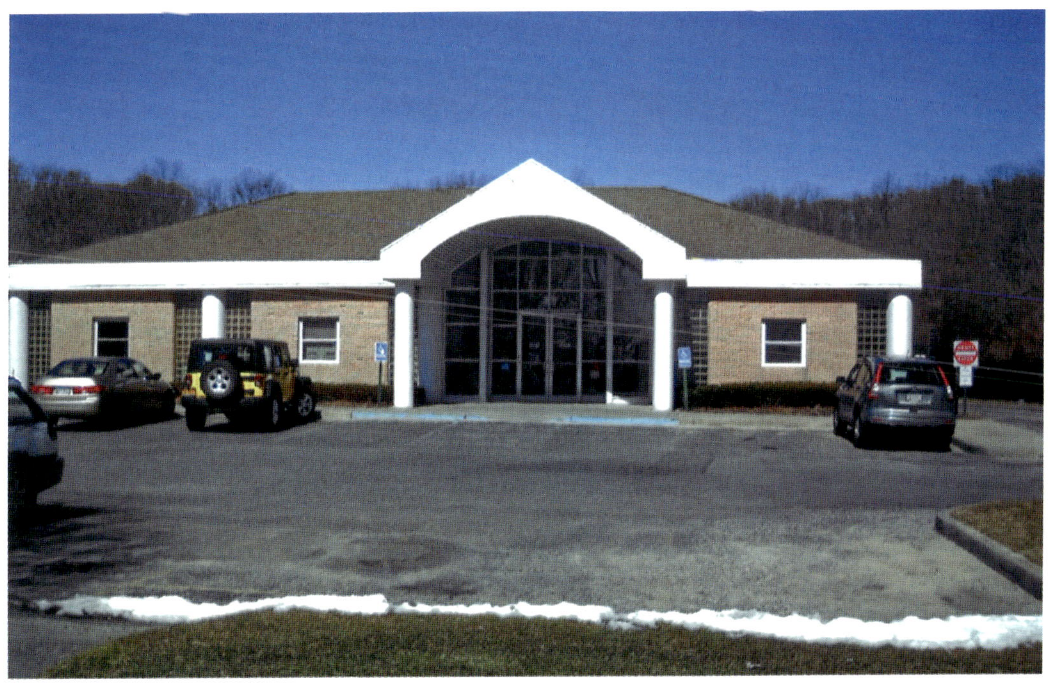

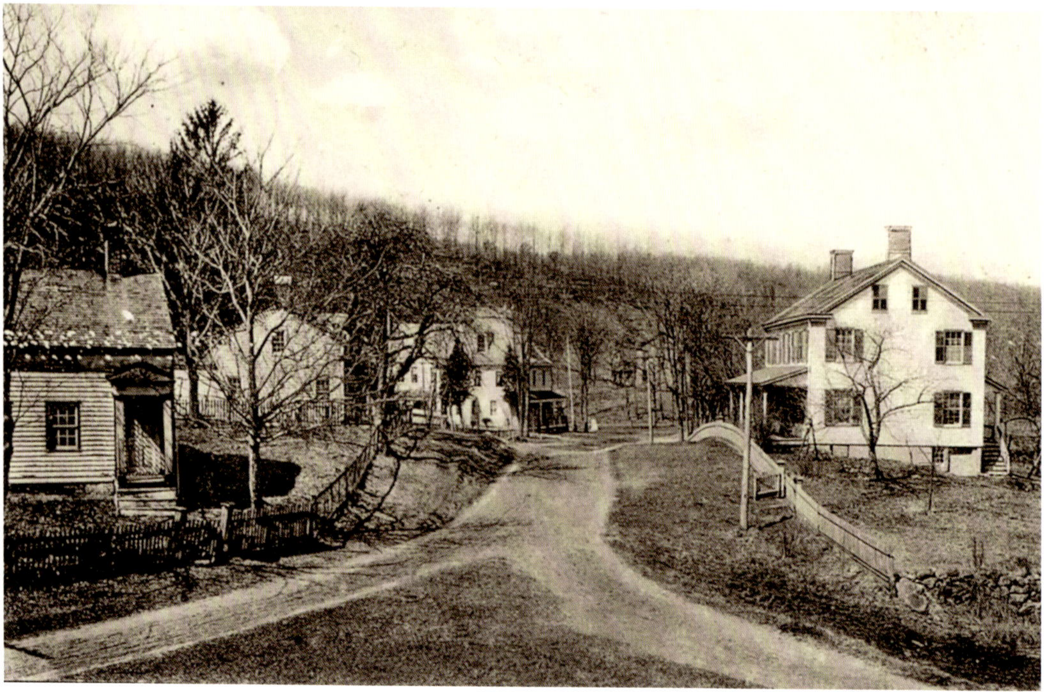

OLD POST AND SHORE ROADS: At this junction in Mount Sinai, a triangle of grass was occasionally used for community events. The most memorable one was the raising of a Service Flag in 1918 in honor of the men from Mount Sinai and Crystal Brook who served in the Great War. Direction signs were often placed in the center, but that did not occur here. As the century progressed the size of triangles grew smaller until they disappeared. This one was paved over in the late 1980s.

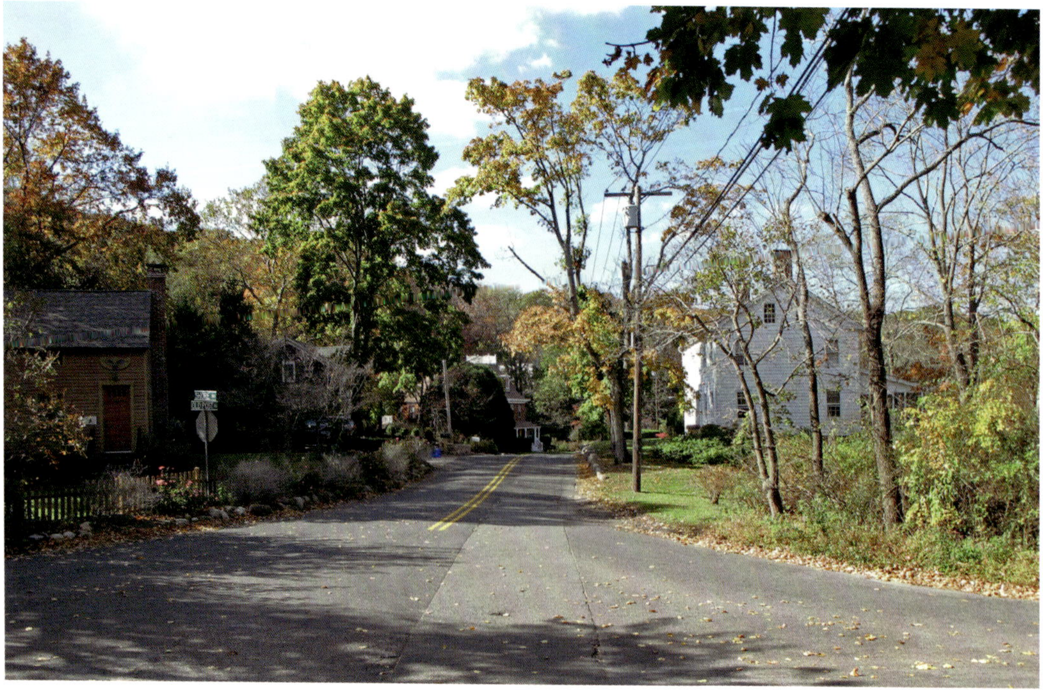

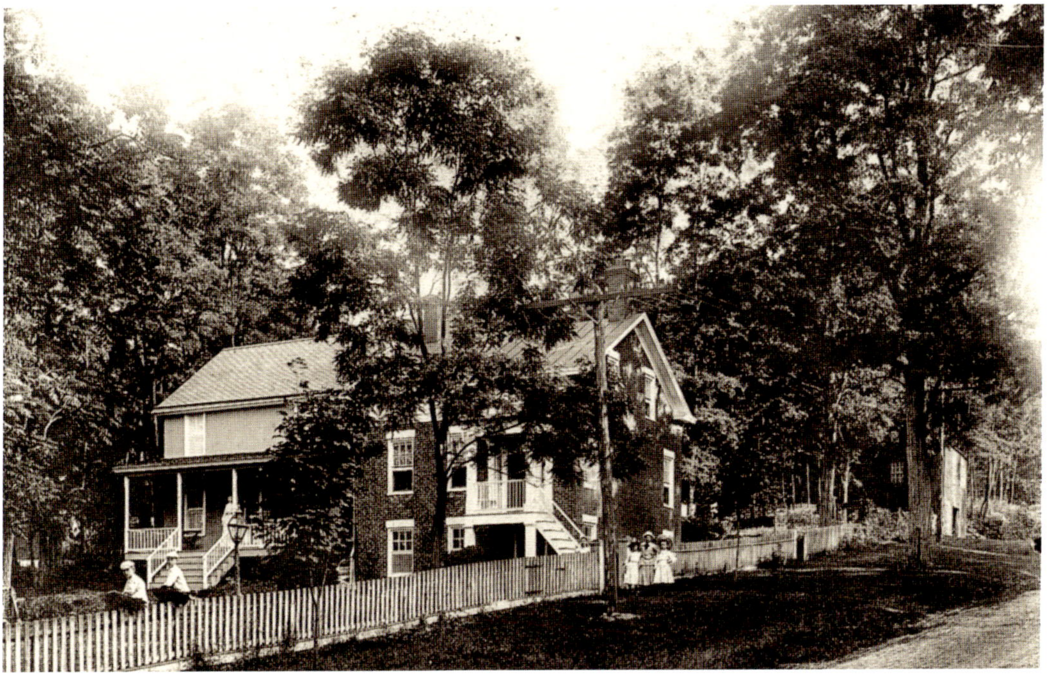

Elisha Norton house: This brick house was built about 1810, and the frame building adjacent to it was built in 1902 for Fannie T. Davis to provide rooms for her boarders. A close look at the photo shows children sitting on the fence and peering from behind the trees. The adjacent building was converted to a family home when Fannie's grandson married in 1931. The modern picture shows the two buildings relatively unchanged, trees and shrubs have changed and the fence is gone. The two homes are still owned by descendants of the Davis family in 2015.

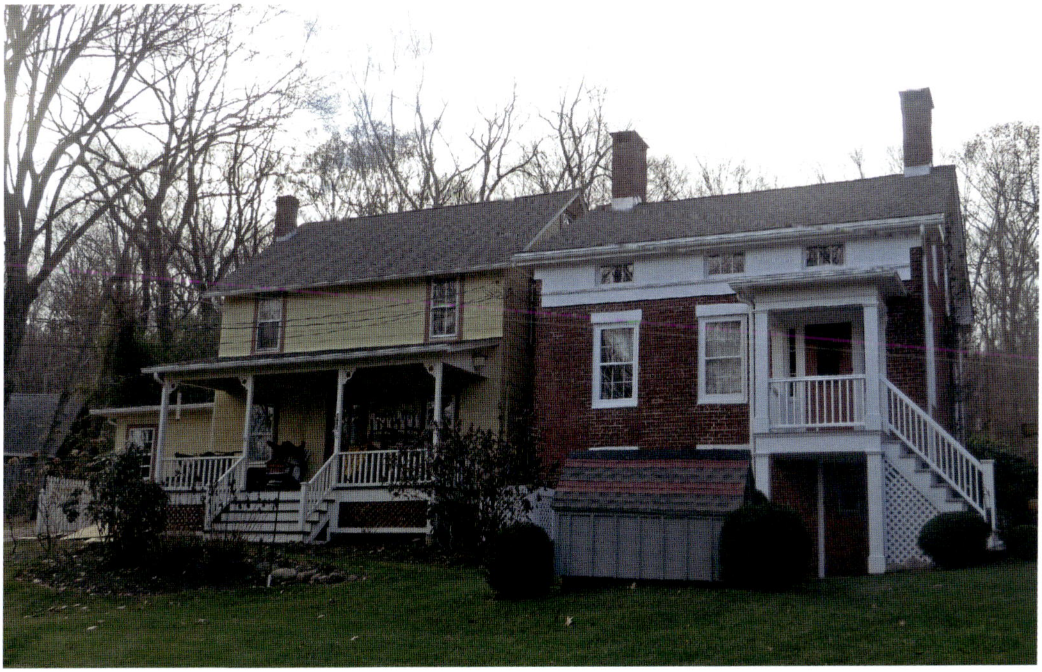

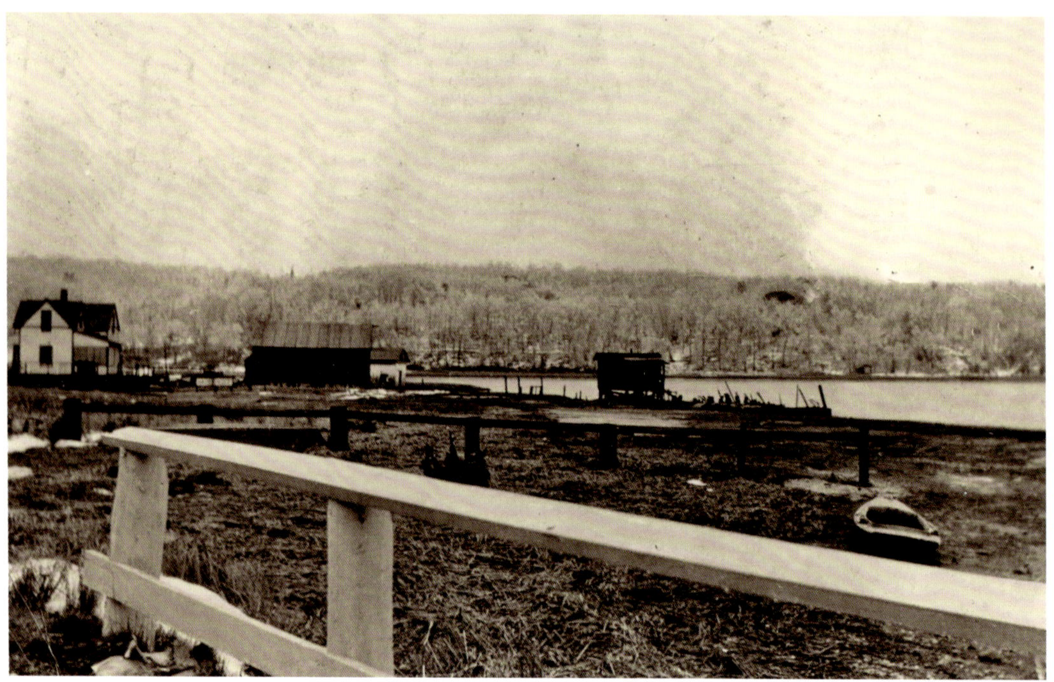

SATTERLY'S LANDING: Minor Satterly obtained a permit to build a dock on Mount Sinai harbor where he rented boats and provided bathing facilities for summer residents and the tourists staying in the various boarding houses. He was succeeded by George Platford, who maintained a boat rental and repair facility from 1930s to 1950s. In 1961 Ralph and Barbara Davenport purchased the boat yard and provided facilities for boaters until 1977 when Ralph's Fishing Station moved to the northern side of the harbor. The Town removed all the buildings and established a park, named after the first person to develop the boating facility.

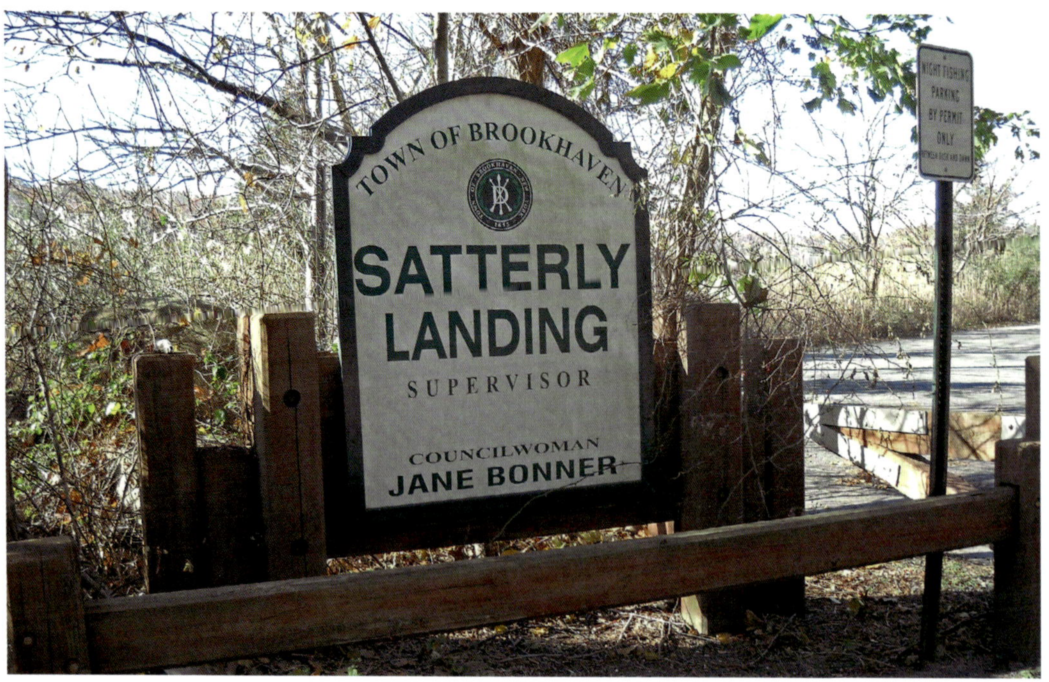

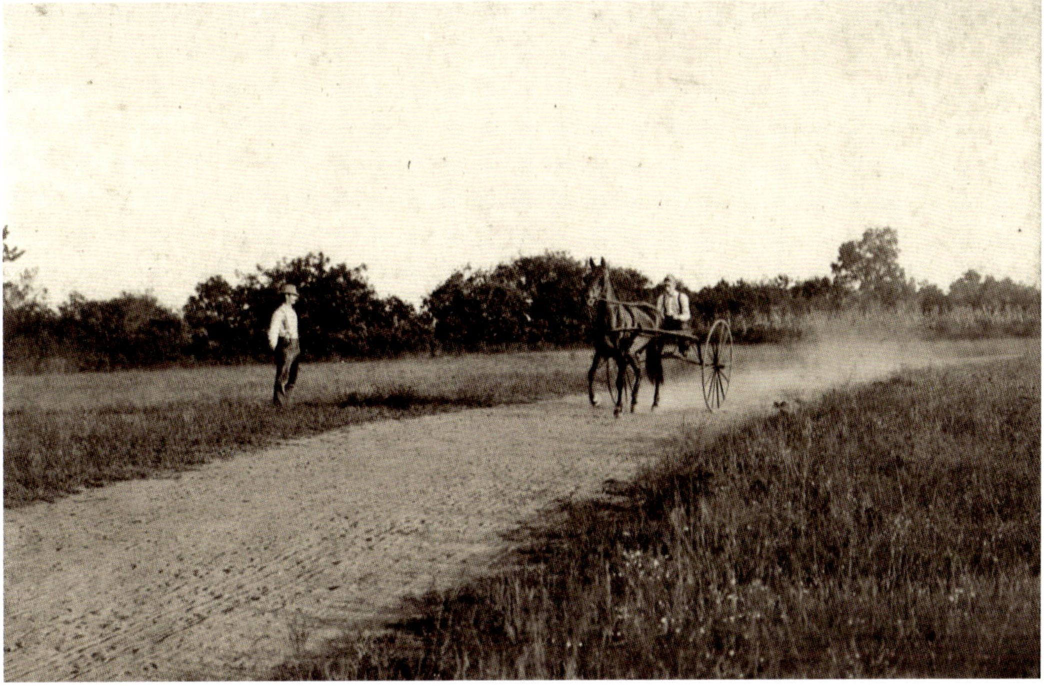

RACE TRACK: Stafford S. Rowland and his son Arthur S. Rowland were well-known trainers of trotting horses from the 1880s to 1906. Arthur improved the practice track to one-half mile on their farm south of present-day Route 25A and west of Mt. Sinai-Coram Road. The property continued as a farm, lastly as the McGovern Sod Farm. The Mount Sinai Farm and Garden farm stand stood on what was a part of the Rowland farm during the early 2000s. The Commons at Mt. Sinai replaced the Farm Stand in 2013.

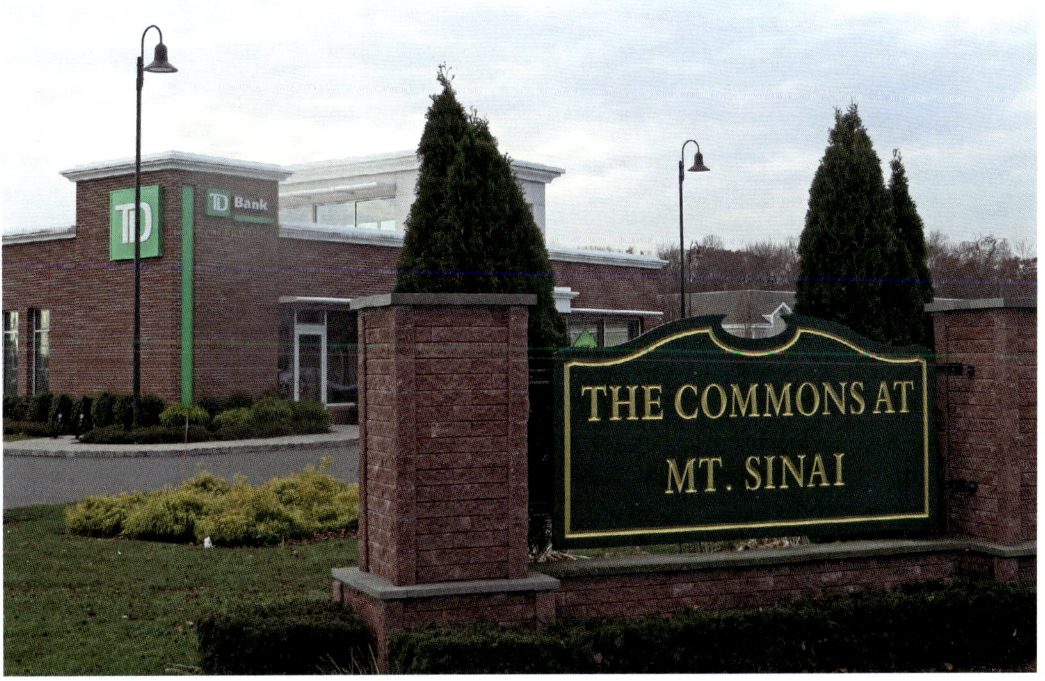

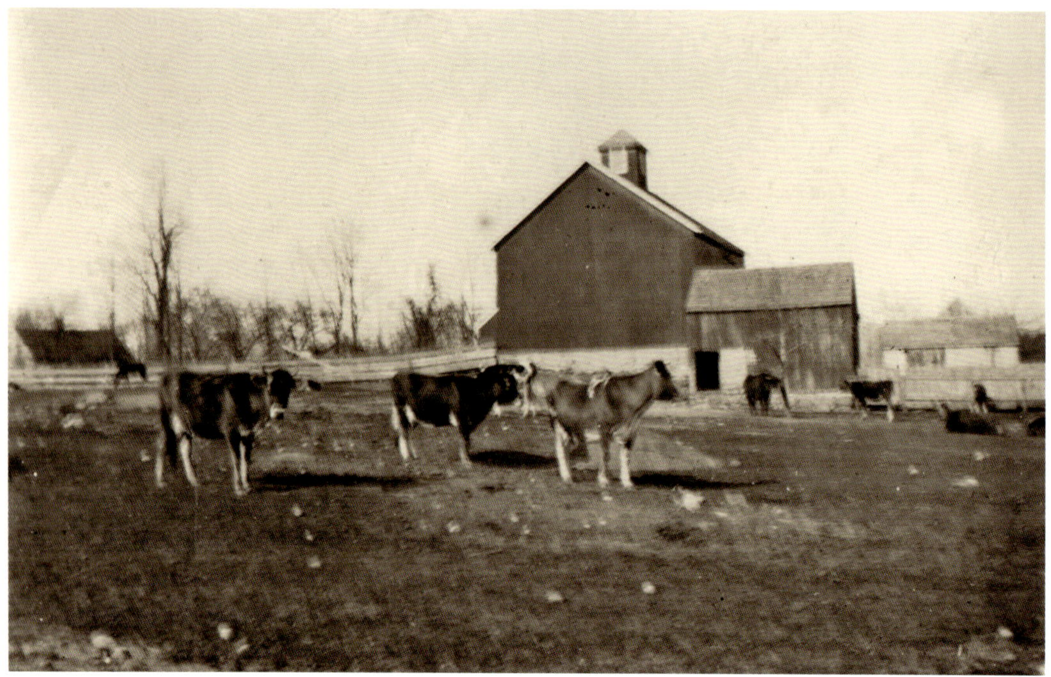

RANDALL FARMS SILO: John S. Randall purchased the Charles Phillips farm in Mount Sinai in 1884. Upon his death 1886, his sixteen-year old son Forrest took over the farm. While continuing to grow crops for city and Connecticut markets, he also started a dairy herd. At first he had crossbred cows, but started a herd of Guernsey cows in the 1930s, as their milk provided a high cream content. As the dairy expanded, the number of buildings required for the farm increased. These two photos show the farm before the first silo was built and after. The pond was a continued presence on the farm for many years.

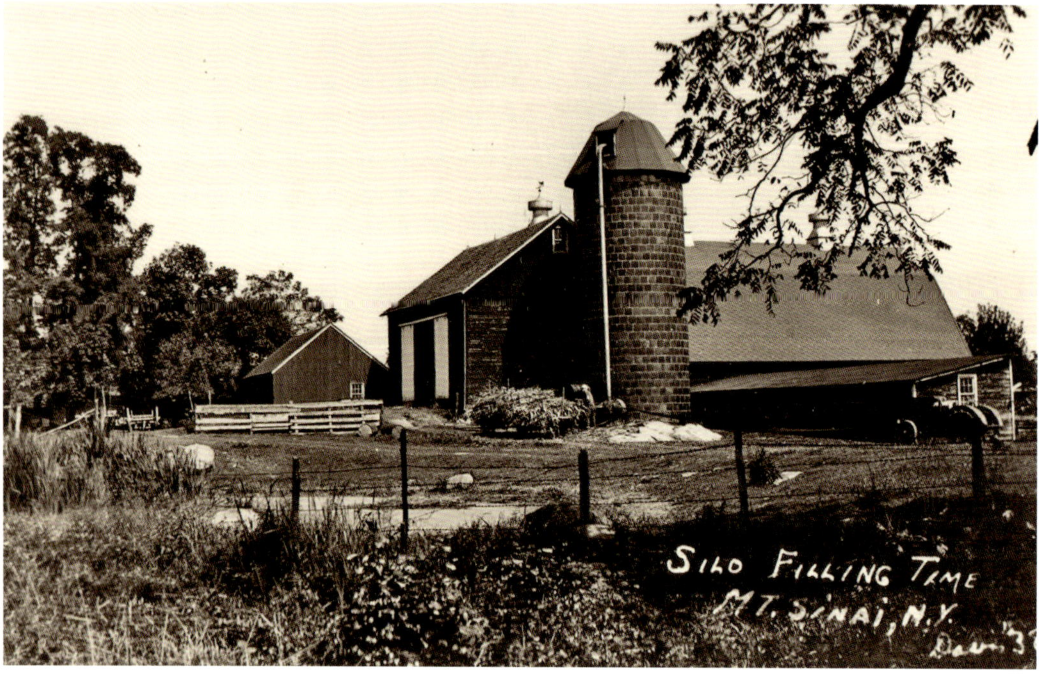

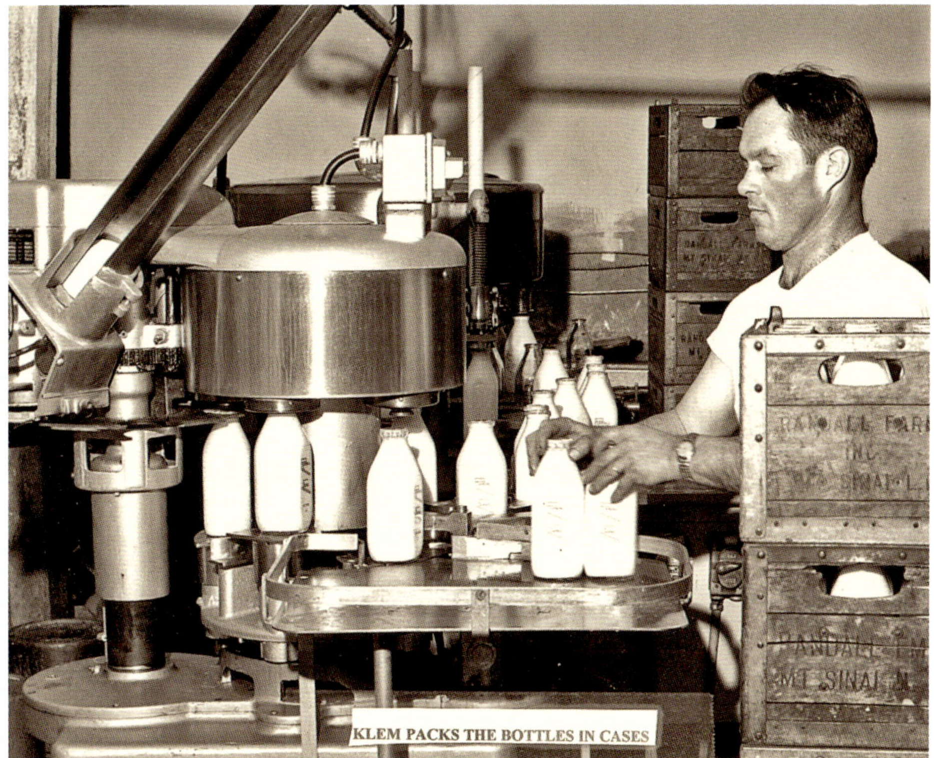

BOTTLING PLANT: This facility was built by the Randall family to process milk, and additional raw milk was purchased from other local dairy farms and sold here. Starting in the 1970s, the farm production grew smaller until 1982 when the farm was sold and a development built. The lower picture shows one of the demolished buildings in 1984.

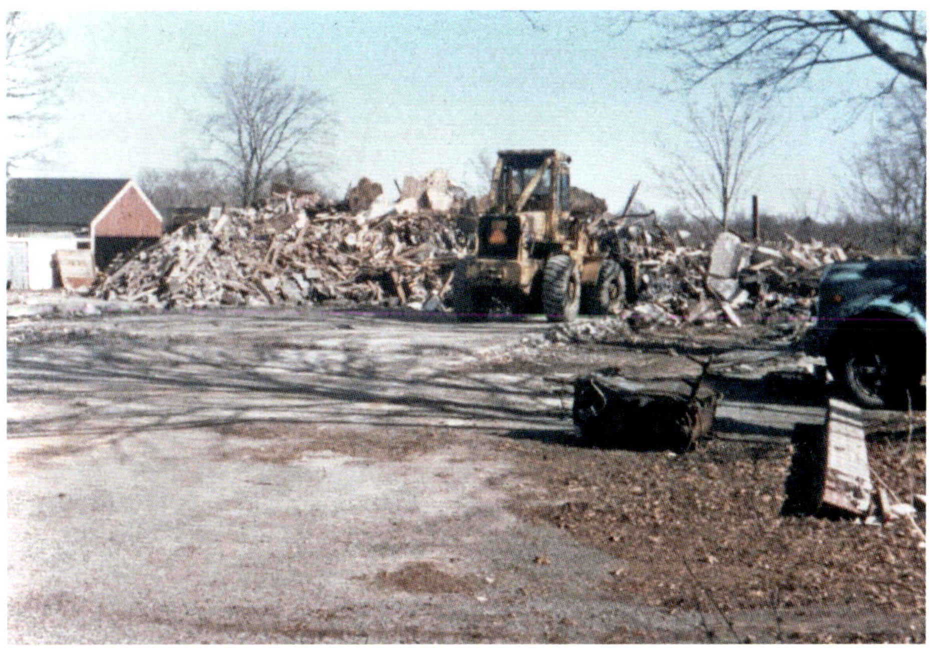

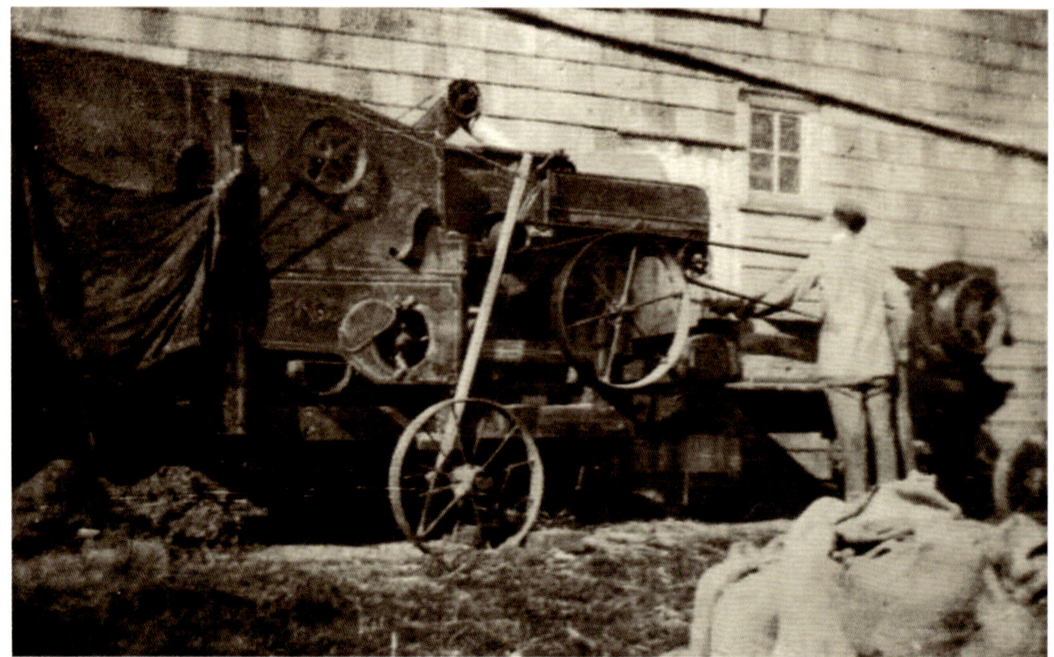

FARM MACHINERY: Farmers who bought steam-powered machines such as this thresher would hire it out to other farmers, as this equipment worked faster and allowed the farmer to work longer than horses did. Lorenzo H. Davis used this thresher at the farm of his grandfather, Lorenzo G. Davis. Steam machines were available before tractors so horses were still necessary for farm tasks such as pulling wagons and plows. Tractors and other farm machinery, when used, increased in size. Now old tractors and farm machinery have become collectors' items. Shows are held to display tractors and other steam-powered machinery, and other pieces are often displayed on lawns.

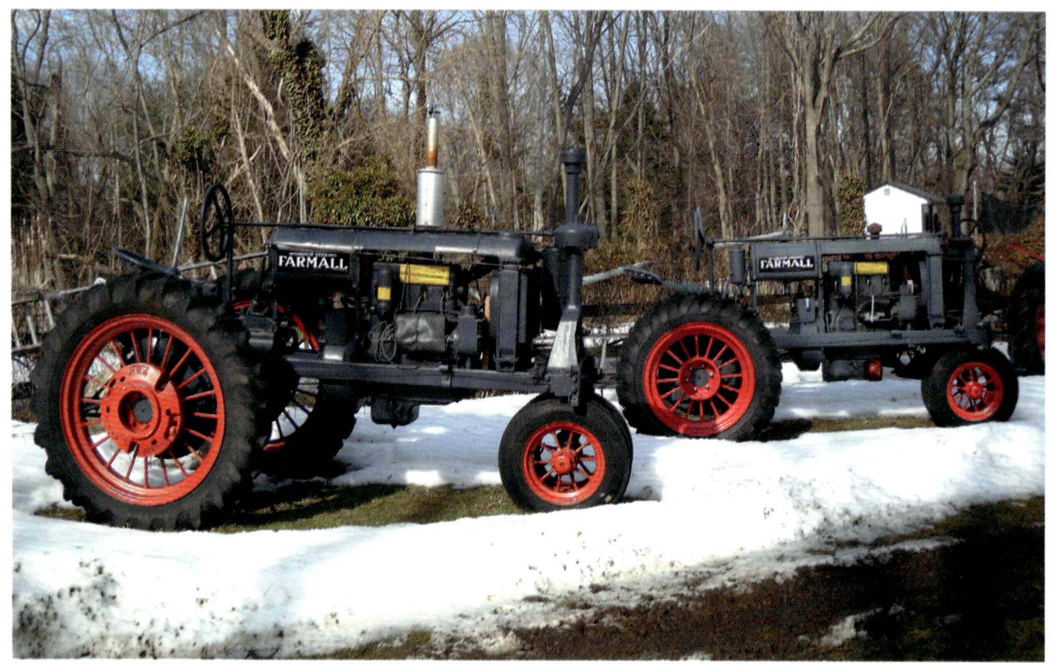

CHAPTER 2

HISTORICAL PRESERVATION

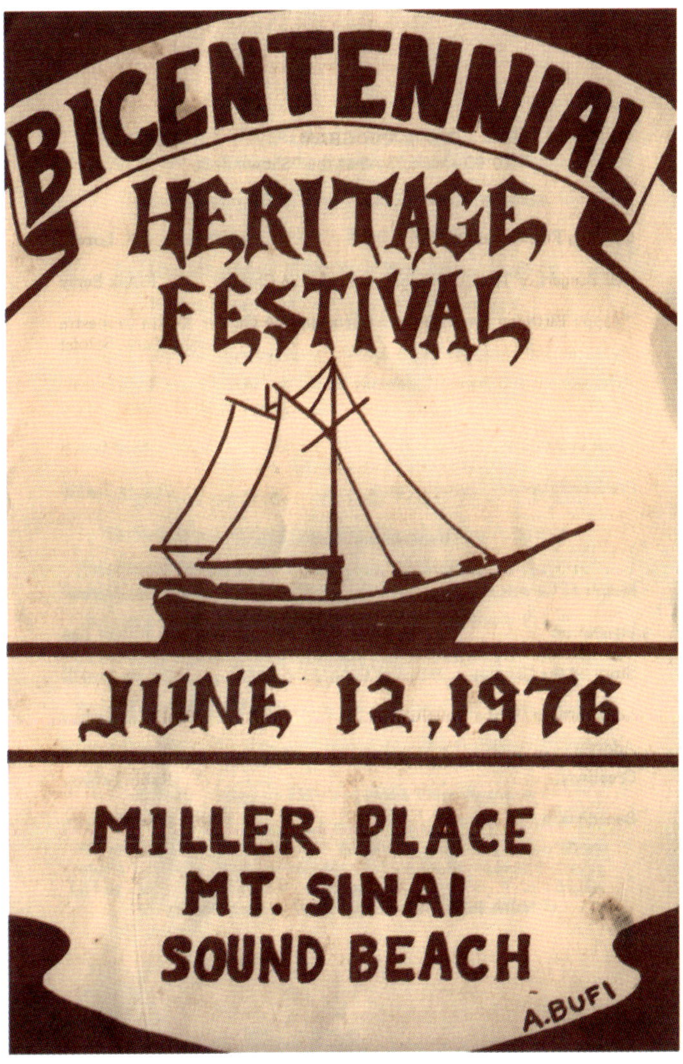

BICENTENNIAL CELEBRATION: Many organizations participated in the events of that day. This brochure listed the various events, times, and locations all of which took place along North Country Road, Miller Place.

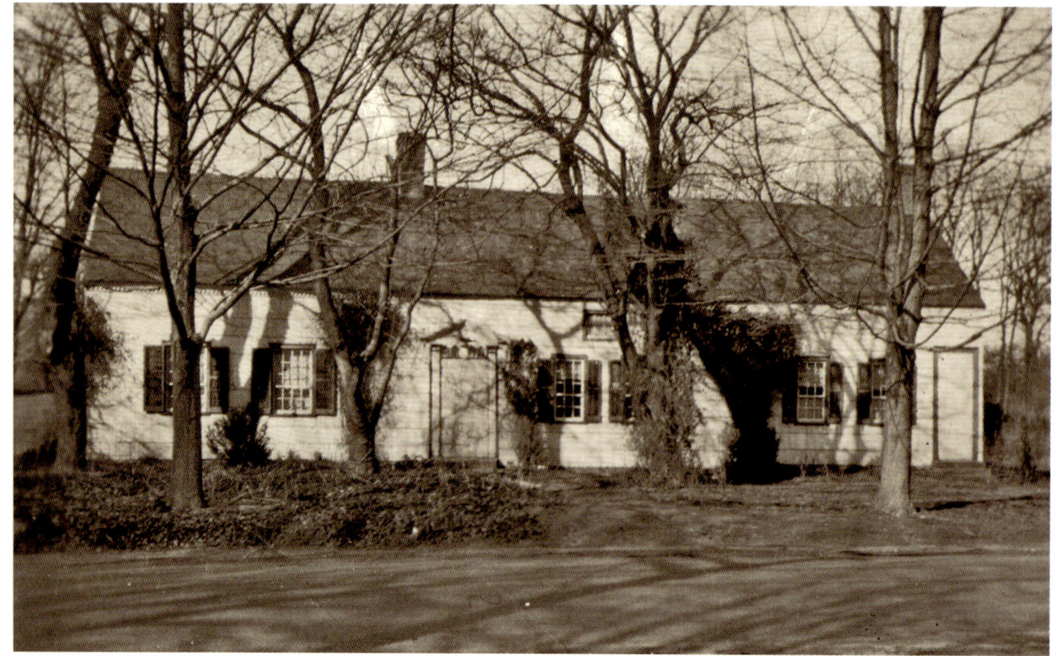

WILLIAM MILLER HOUSE: The oldest house still standing in Miller Place, owned from its initial construction in 1720 through 1978 by William Miller and his descendants. During two separate additions, previously constructed homes were moved to this site and added as wings to the original house in 1750 and in 1815. The house is depicted here in the early 1900s and in 1932. A study of both photographs shows the changes in vegetation, the replacement of older trees resulting in younger, smaller trees becoming dominant. The fence that had been present in 1894 has also been removed. North Country Road in the top photo was not paved; however by 1932 it had been paved over.

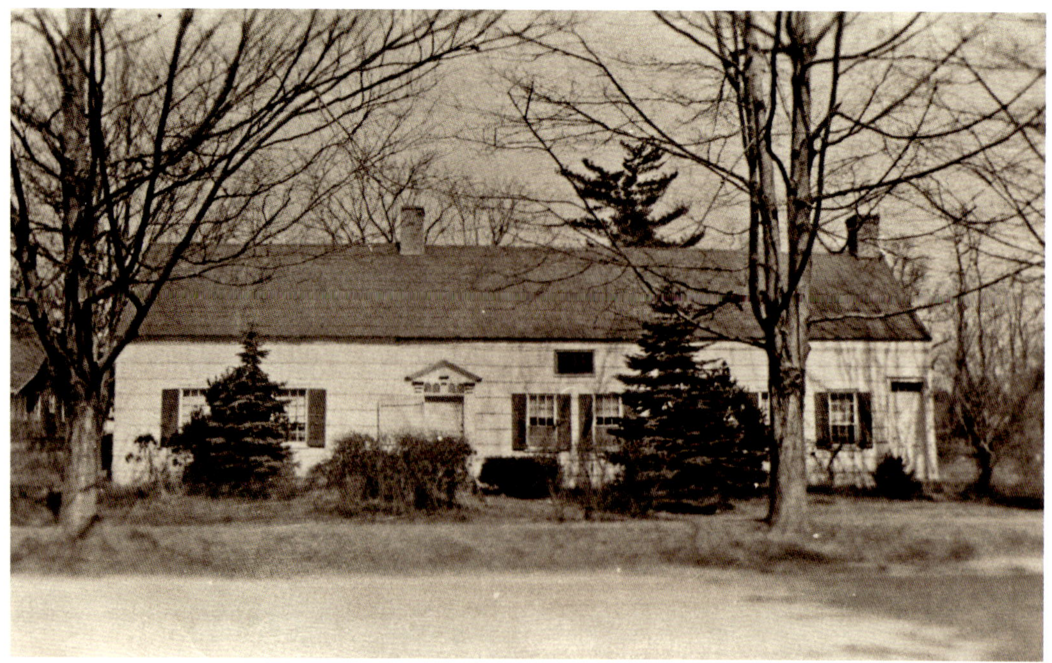

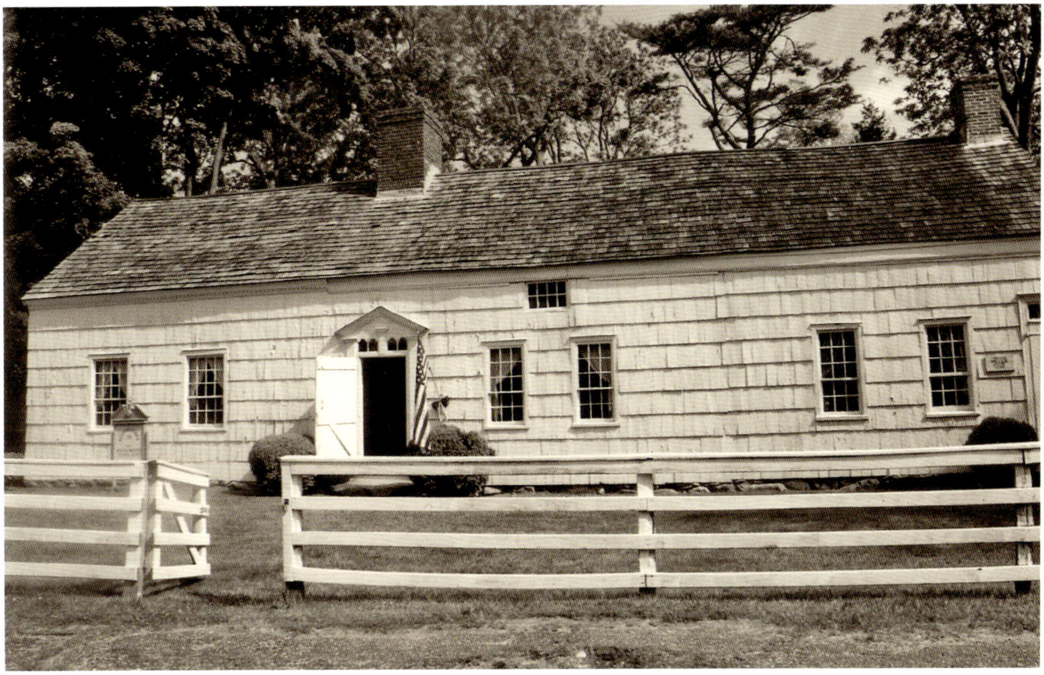

MILLER PLACE HISTORICAL SOCIETY: The William Miller house was purchased by this newly formed group from the estate of Harry Millard, the last lineal descendant of William Miller to live in the house. Serving as the headquarters of the Miller Place-Mount Sinai Historical Society, the building is open for tours in the summer and various community and historical events are conducted here. A unique building constructed of three separate houses brought together, this connection can only be seen from the rear of the building as the front has always had a unified look since the earliest photographs of the house.

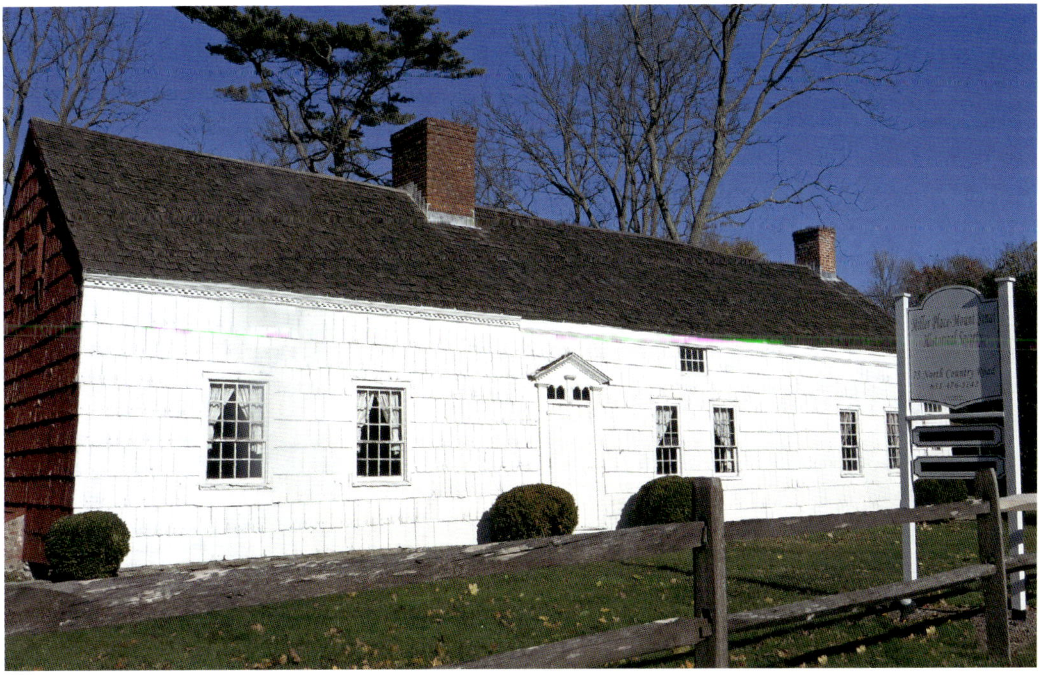

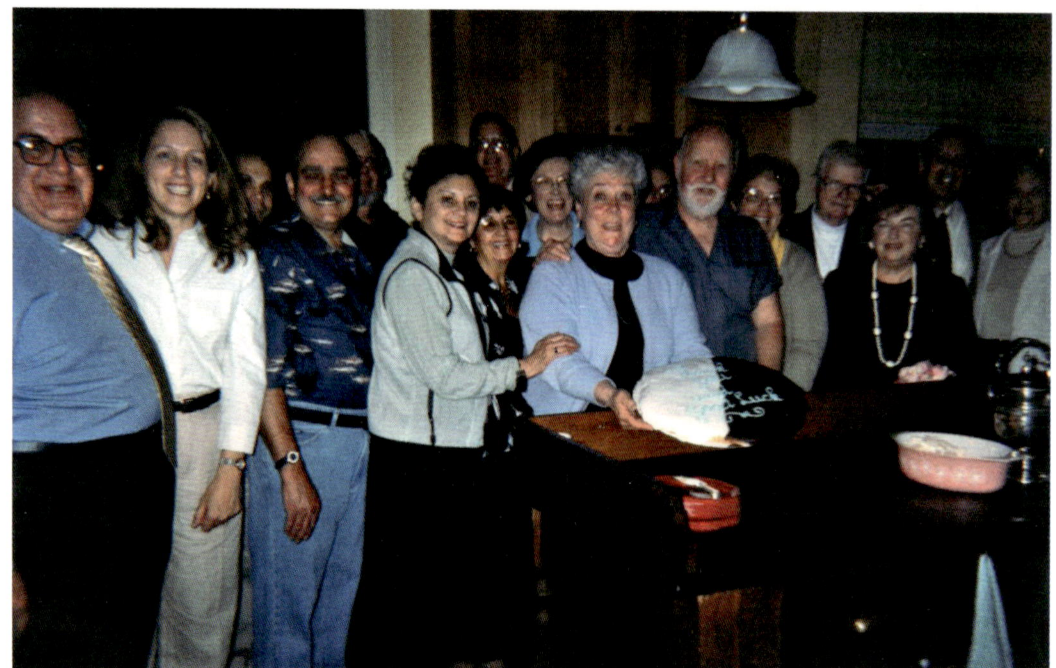

HISTORICAL SOCIETY MEMBERSHIP: The Historical Society holds events at members' homes for a variety of purposes. In 2004 a farewell party was given for the retiring president of the Society, Ken Goss. Held at the home of J. Kirkland Grant, also known as Davis Island, the party was well attended. Other events were the annual Christmas celebration fundraiser at Point Place, Miller Place in the 1980s and early 1990s, followed by Twelfth Night in the 1990s and early 2000s. The Board of Trustees meets monthly, with the 2014-2015 Board pictured here.

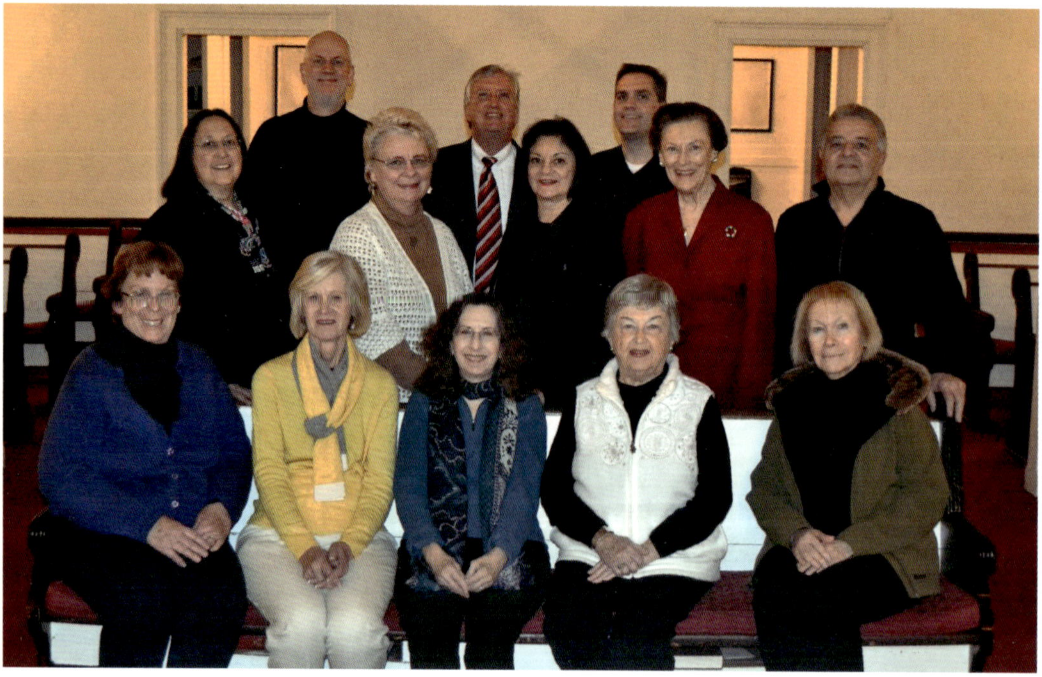

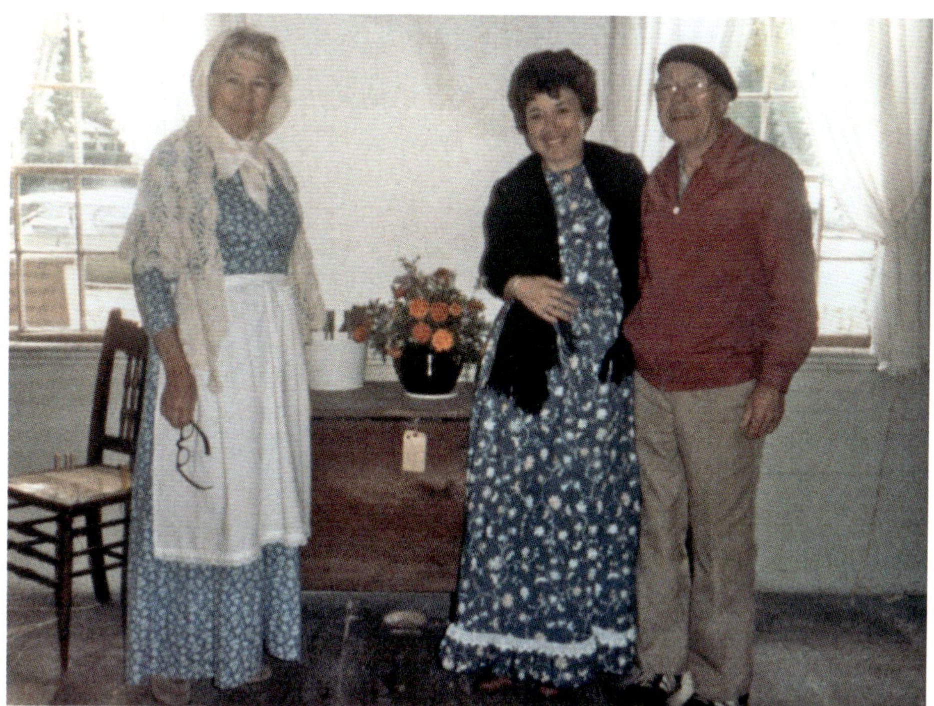

VOLUNTEERS: Charlotte and Bob McDowell flank Elena Cameraro in 1984 in the East Room of the William Miller house, ready to provide tours during the Country Fair. In the early 2000s a picnic was held on the grounds of the William Miller house to honor the many volunteers of the Society. The Miller Place Historical Society was founded in 1974; Mount Sinai was added to the name in 1984.

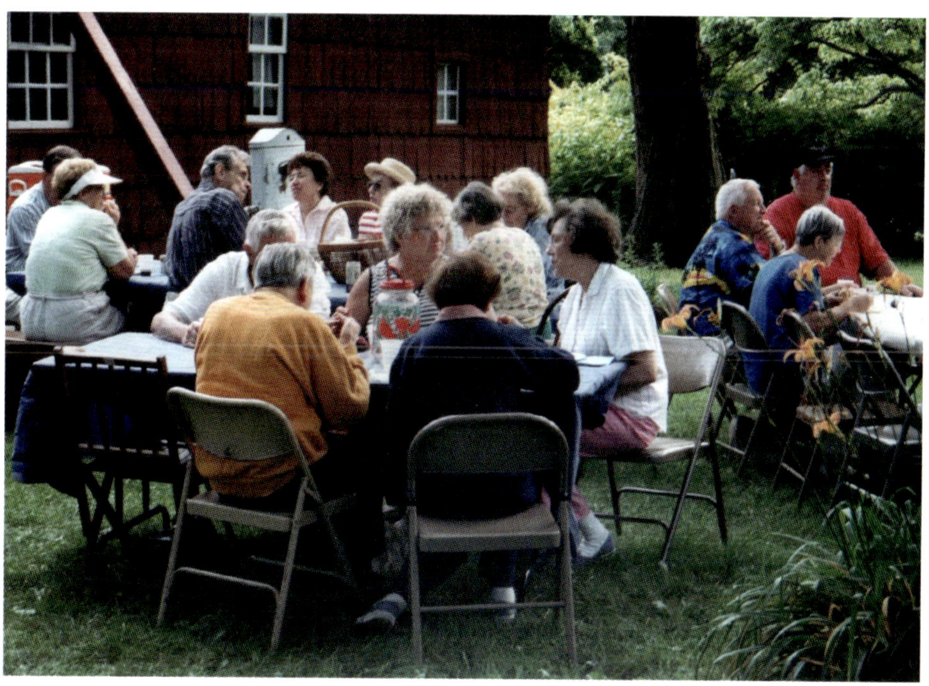

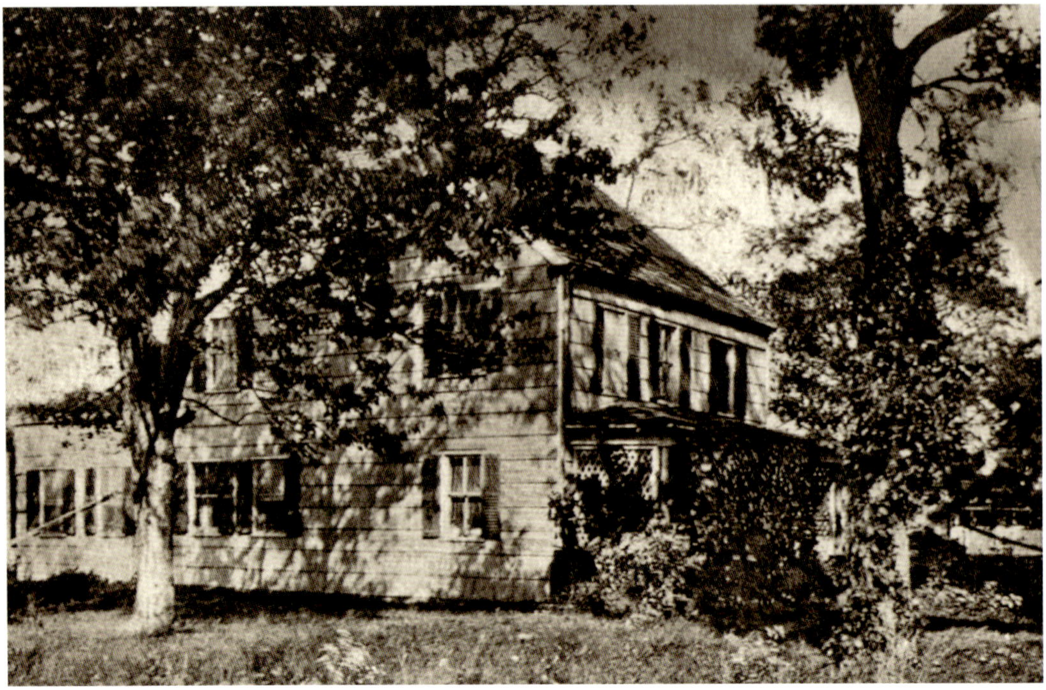

DANIEL HAWKINS HOUSE: Originally the home of Daniel and Bethia Hawkins *circa* 1810, located at 111 North Country Road this home passed to one of their grandsons, and was donated to the Historical Society in 1995 through the generosity of Arthur and Linda Calace. Belle J. E. Rowell rented the house in the early 1900s, and created this postcard. A widow, she used her camera skills to take many photographs in Miller Place, selling the postcards she made to help support her children.

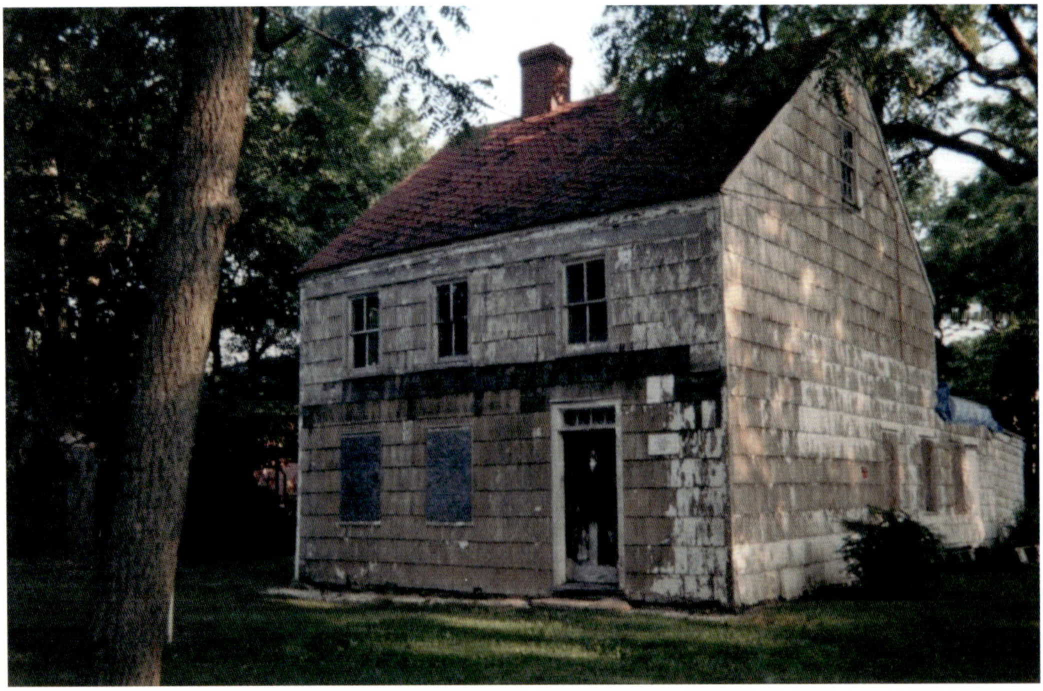

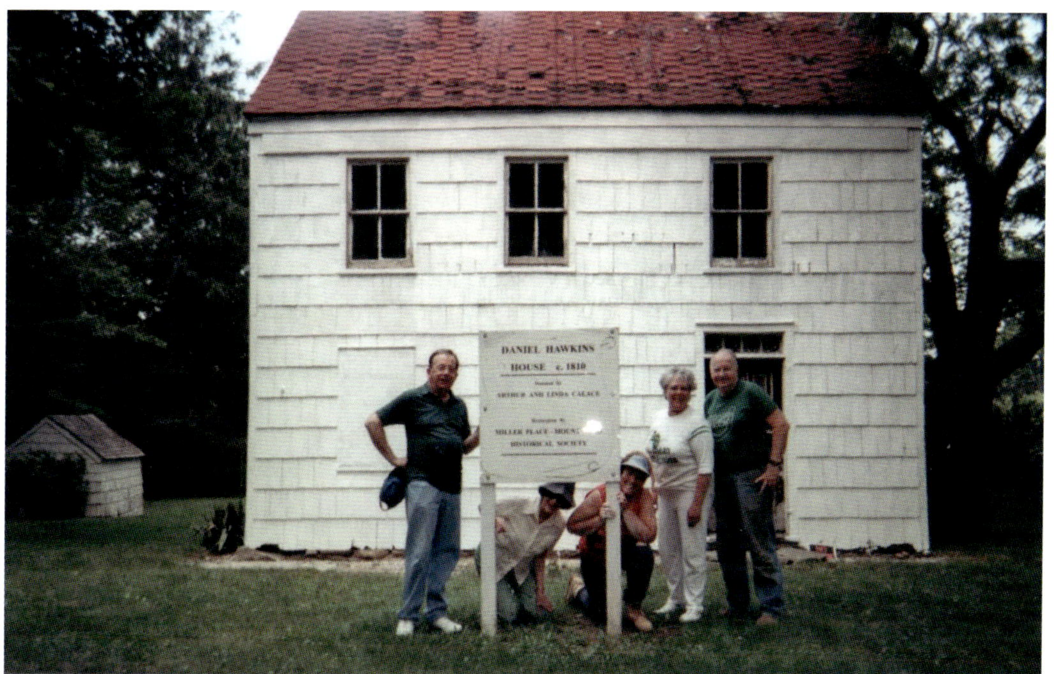

HAWKINS HOUSE RENOVATION: Five Historical Society volunteers put a layer of primer on the front wall of the Daniel Hawkins house. Funds were raised several years after the acquisition, and the three exterior shingle walls were painted and the roof replaced. In 2013 two Eagle Scout projects were completed by Kevin Palmer, who constructed a new stoop and walkway and by John Clancy, who installed a new sign and plantings. Once completed, the Hawkins House will provide broader access to historical activities, artifacts and information for local community members.

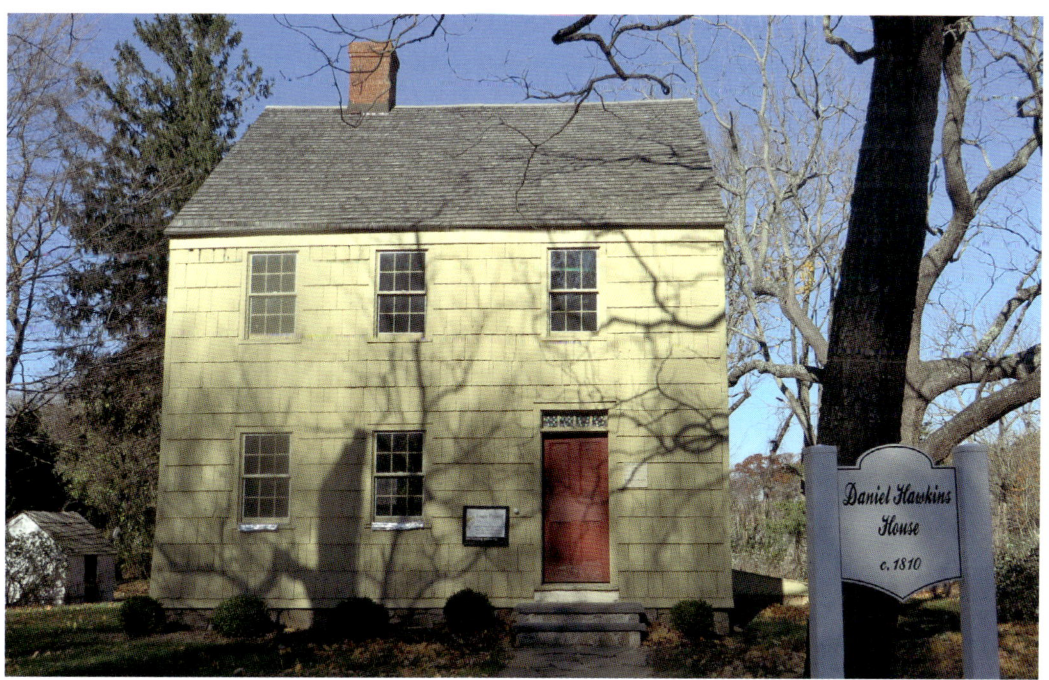

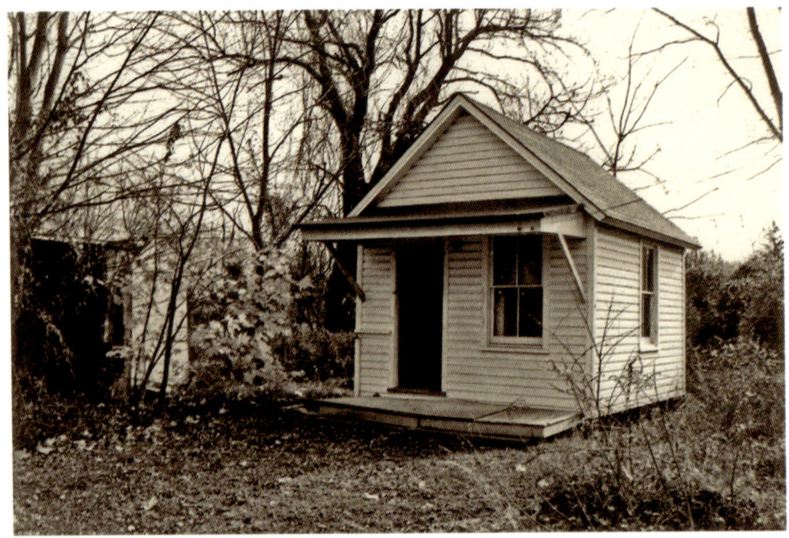

MILLER PLACE POST OFFICE: This little building originally stood on the corner of Sylvan Avenue and North Country Road when Samuel H. Miller was postmaster from 1901 to 1914. In 1981 the building was donated to the Historical Society and moved to the William Miller house property on North Country Road. The building is now the locus of the annual event known as "Postman Pete." Children bring their letters addressed to Santa to the post office where "Postman Pete" stamps the letter for delivery to Santa at the North Pole. Robert and Mary Fitton are pictured here with Peter "Postman Pete" Mott, having just delivered their letters.

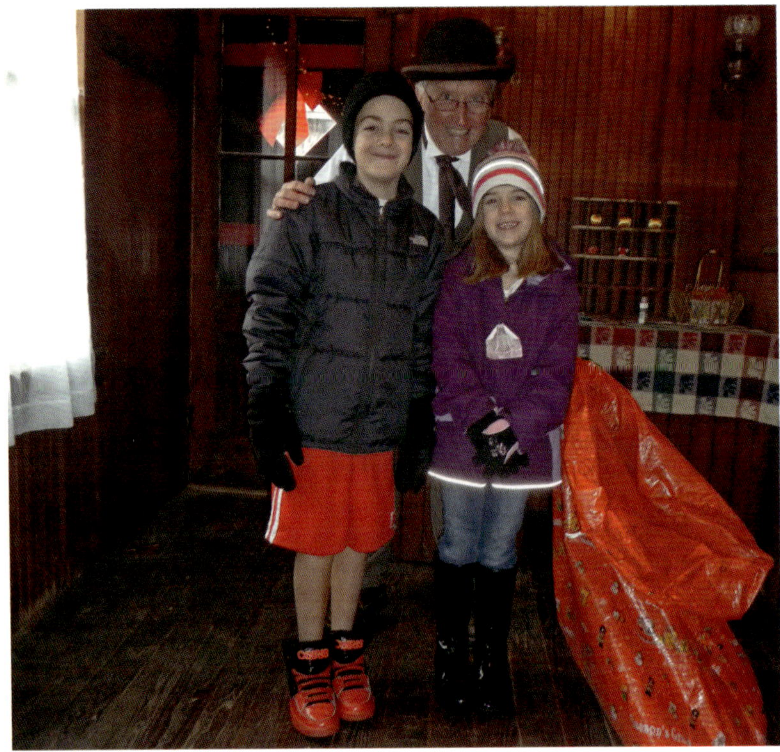

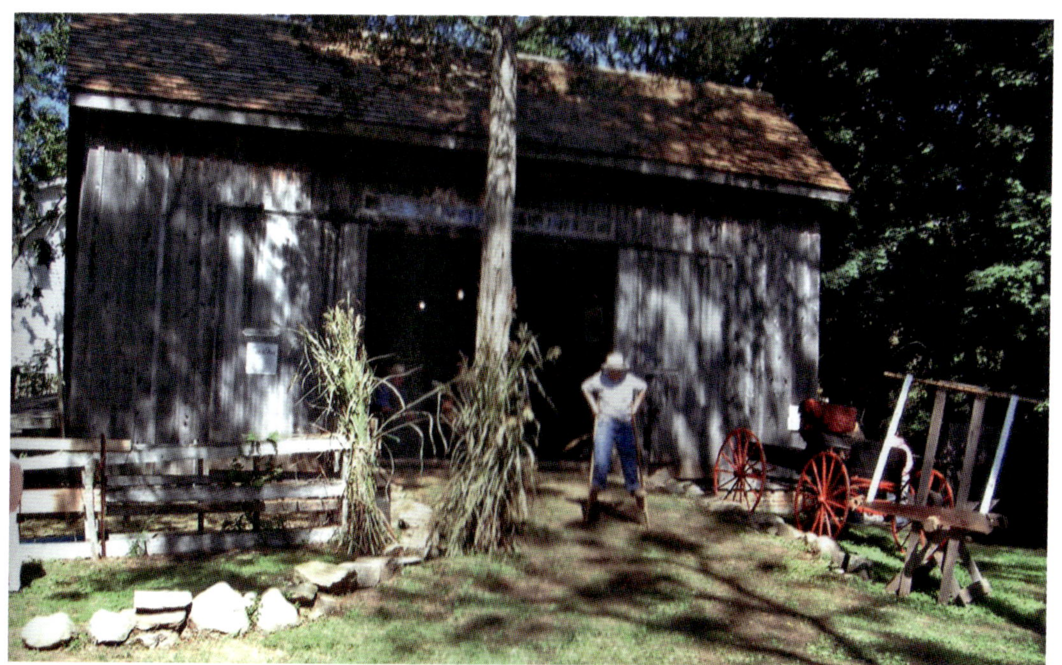

NATHANIEL GASS: A member of the Historical Society from a young age, Nate walks on his first pair of stilts at the annual Country Fair. As part of his performance activity, he also taught fair visitors how to use them, and came back each year with taller stilts. His 2014 Eagle Scout Project was to complete the renovation of the one-hundred year old Bergold Corn Crib on the Historical Society grounds, which included building brick pylons and placing the building on them, re-painting to the original color, and placing the large stone in front of the building. Below he is shown making a donation and receiving a certificate of appreciation from Gerard Mannarino, president of the Historical Society.

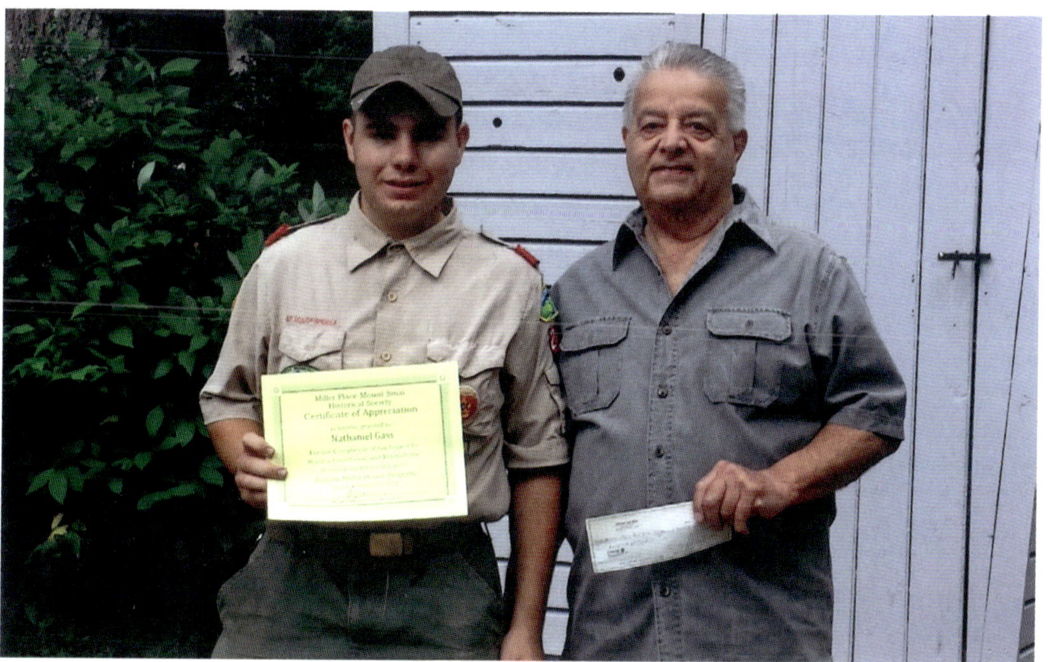

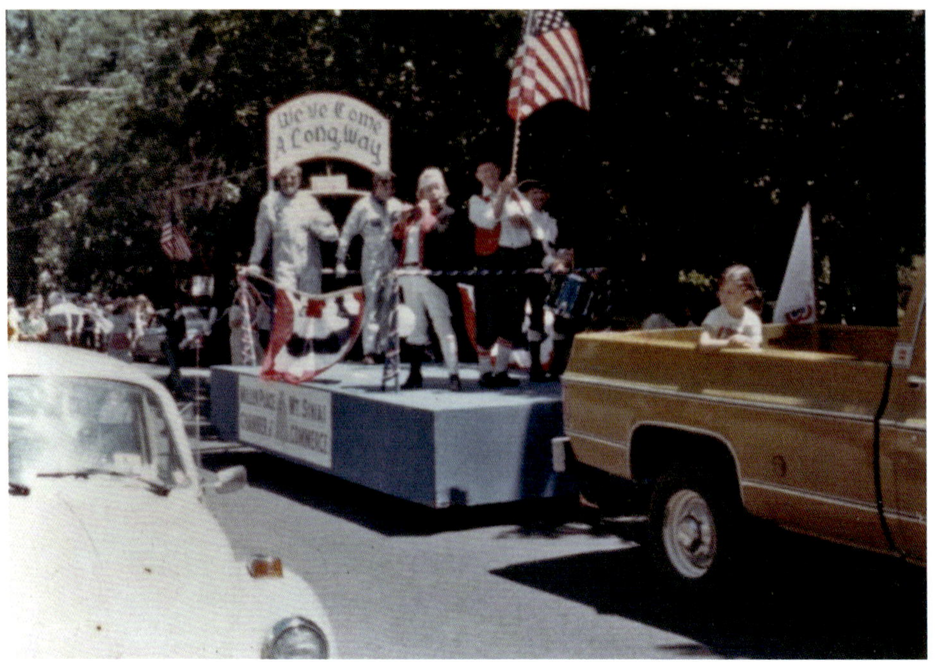

BICENTENNIAL PARADE: Many groups and individuals participated in this, the first major event of the Society, in 1976. Rupert W. Hopkins drove a horse and carriage with members of his family as passengers. The Chamber of Commerce had a float reenacting the painting "The Spirit of 76."

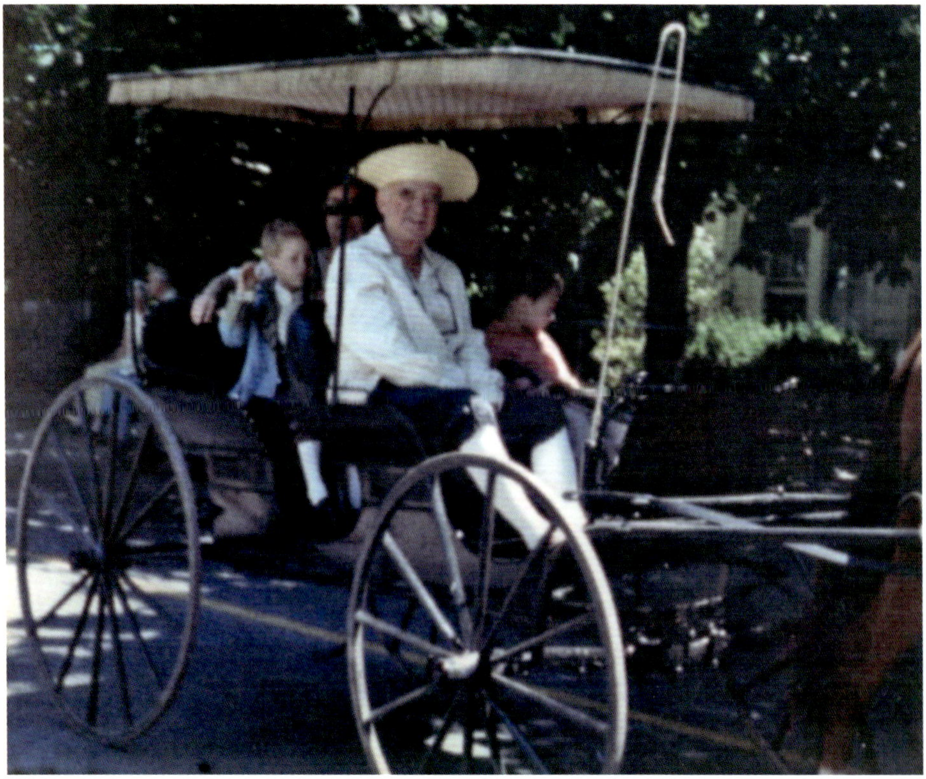

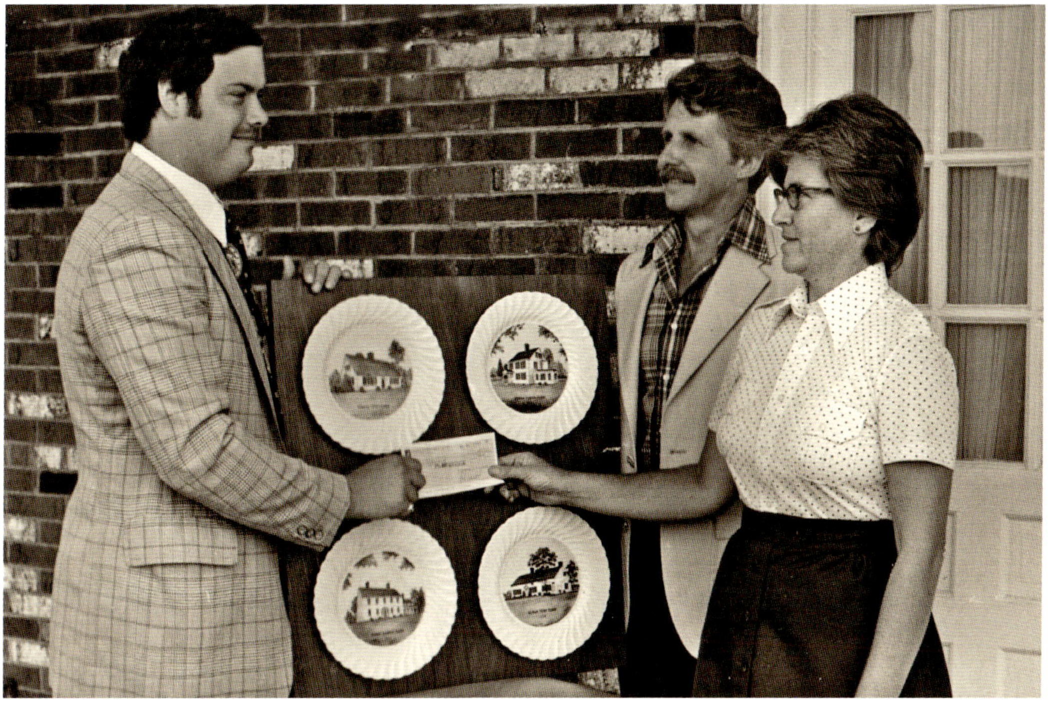

COMMUNITY SUPPORT: The Suffolk County Federal Savings and Loan Association provided support to the Historical Society in 1978 by donating funds raised through the sale of plates depicting four historic Miller Place homes. Helen Samuels and Robert Arnold are shown accepting a check from John S. Arnold Jr., of the Miller Place branch of the bank. As part of the Bicentennial a group of women designed and made this quilt. Each block represents a place or scene in Miller Place. The Liberty Bell, Eagle, and Bicentennial symbol, as well as the seals of the Town of Brookhaven, Suffolk County, and the State of New York, are also included.

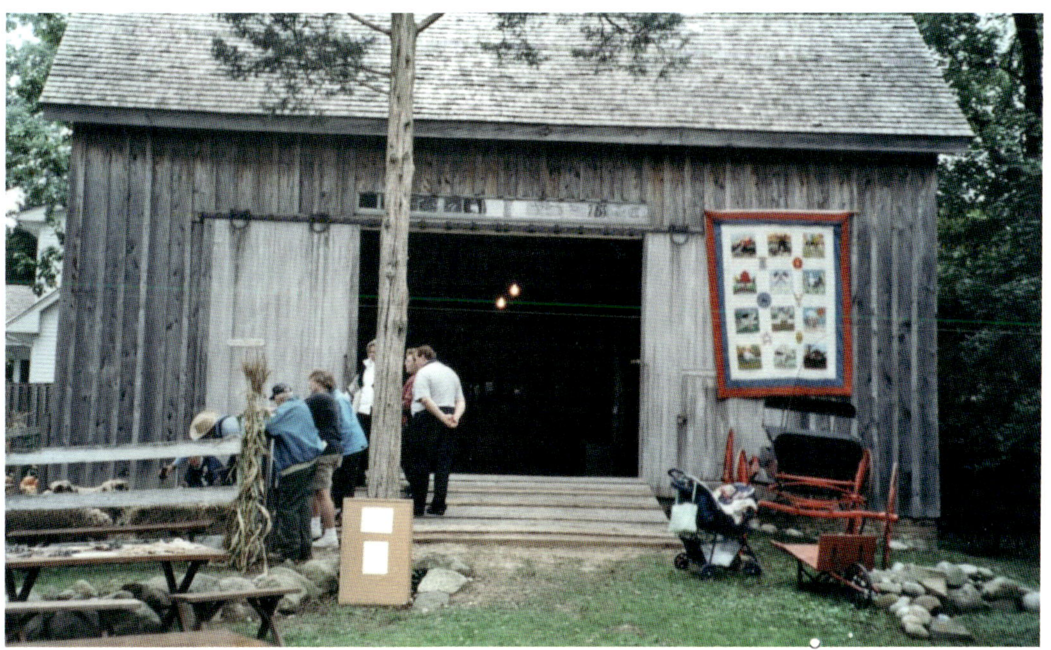

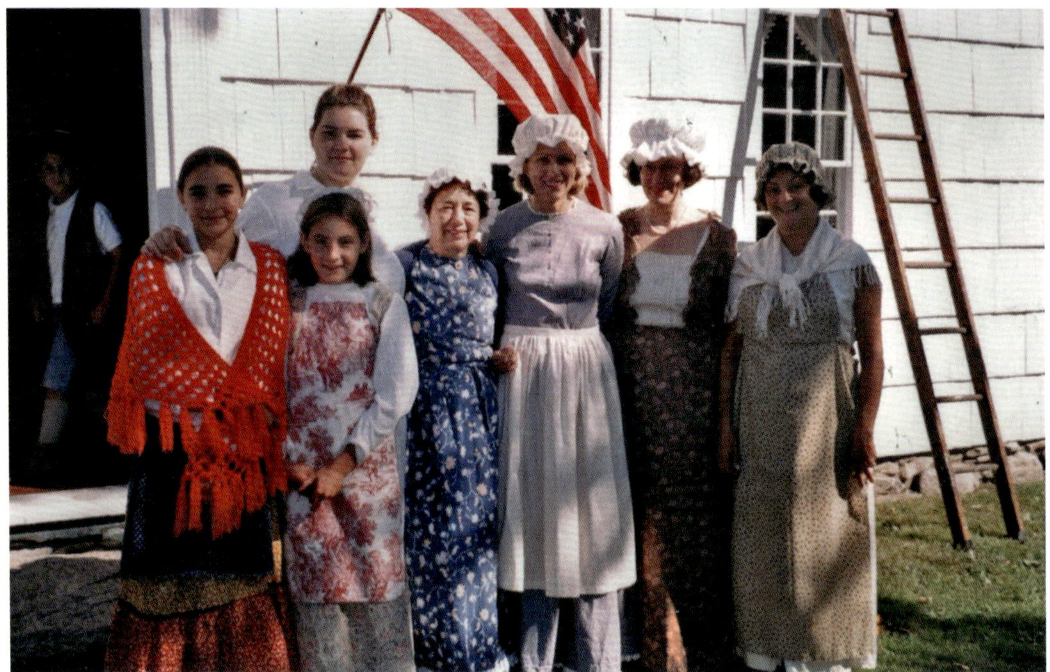

VOLUNTEER SUPPORT: The Country Fair has been a long-time tradition of the Historical Society, both as a fundraising event, and to raise community awareness, and would not be possible without the support of many volunteers, who have been the backbone of the Society since its creation. This group photo was taken in the 1990s. Bea Davis demonstrated her skill at tatting (knotted lace made by hand) in 1983. She enjoyed talking to people and demonstrating the intricacies of this art form. Here she sits next to a large doily she made to be raffled for the benefit of the Society.

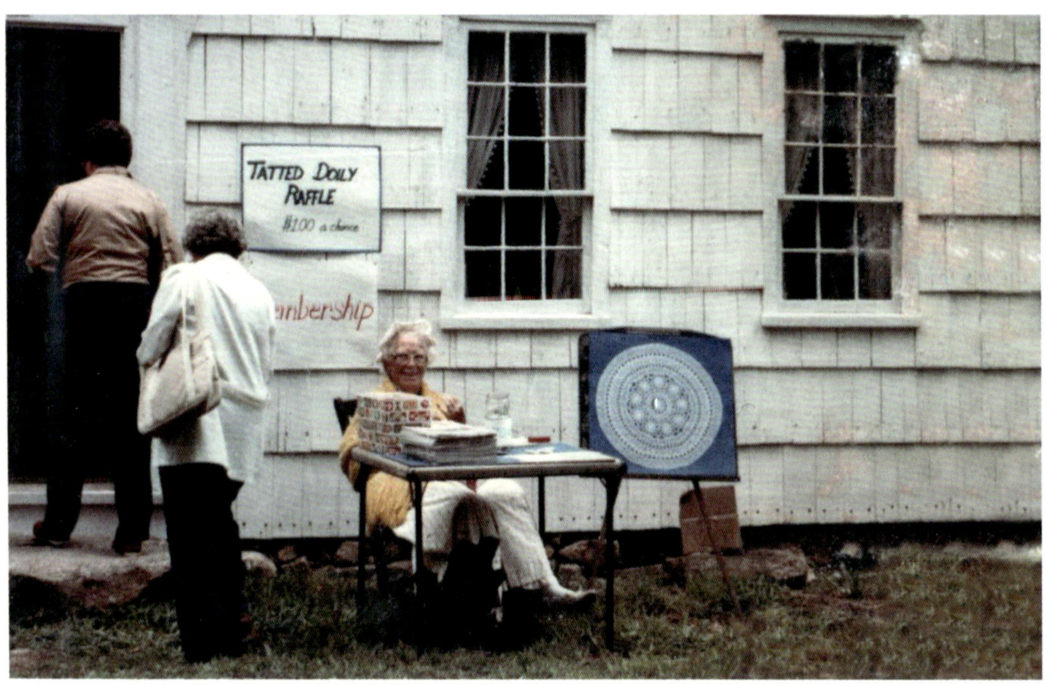

Cherub Barn: Local resident Harry Randall, a long-time volunteer and supporter of the Historical Society, has participated in the fair for many years, and frequently brought his sheep, chickens, and pony for people to see, and demonstrated sheep shearing. Harry filled this barn with farm tools from both his family farm, as well as those of other farmers in the area, and demonstrated how tools worked, described farm life in Mount Sinai, and answered the many questions visitors posed. The barn is always the most popular building for children and adults.

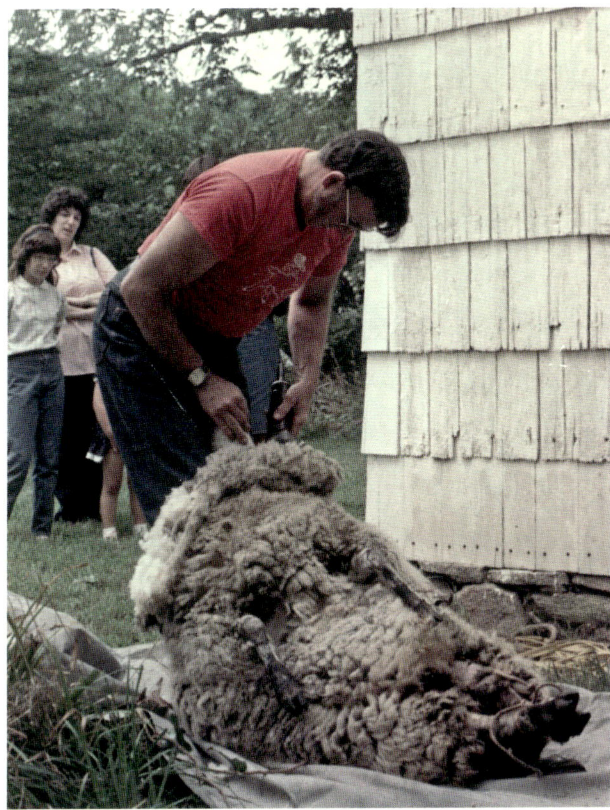

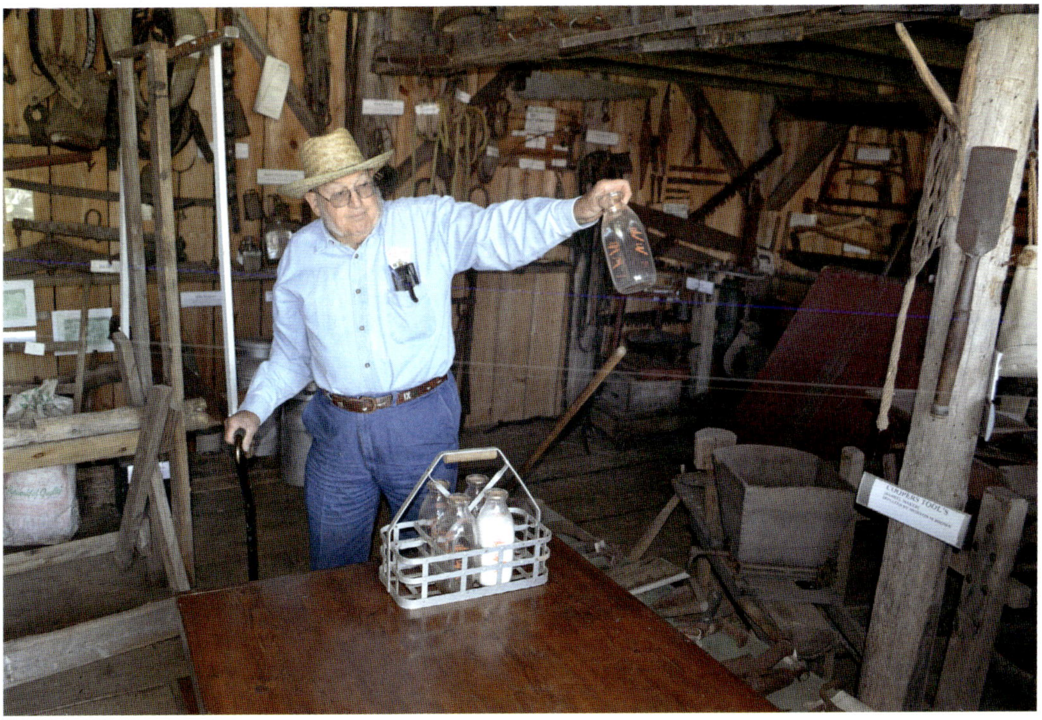

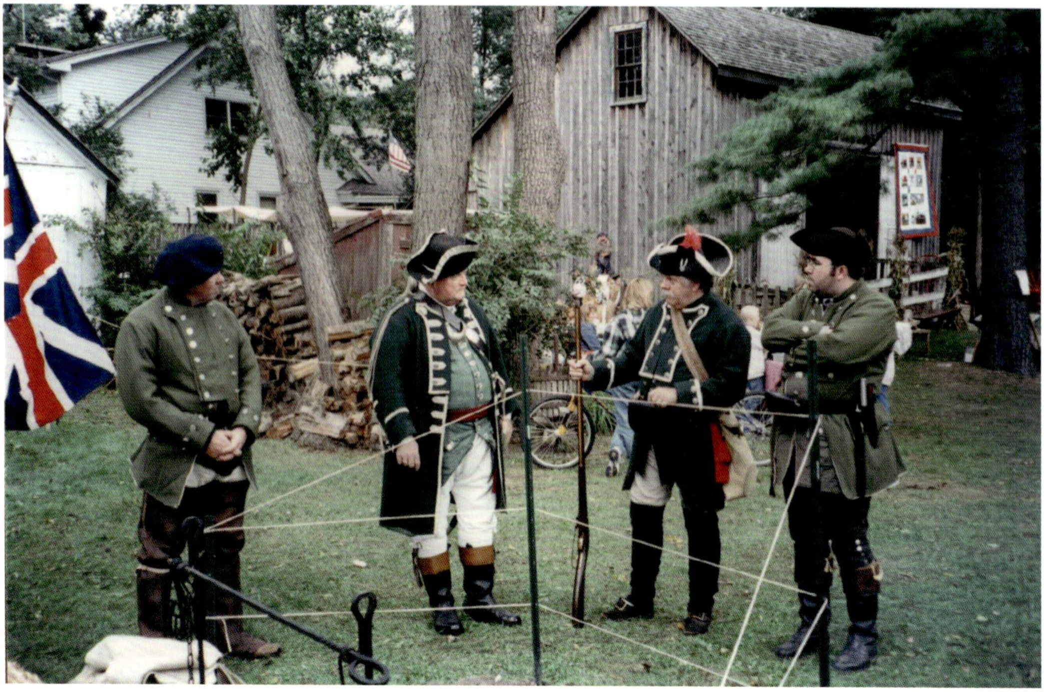

REENACTORS: Captain Thomas Terry's Suffolk County Militia, depicting soldiers from the French and Indian War era, had regularly set up camp at the Fair in the 1990s. The original Captain Terry's group actually stayed at the William Miller house in 1759, enlisting men to serve in upstate colonial New York. Here Captain Terry (James Downey) is shown speaking with some of his men. In the 2000s, the 30th Virginia Company of the Civil War began camping and demonstrating during the Country Fair.

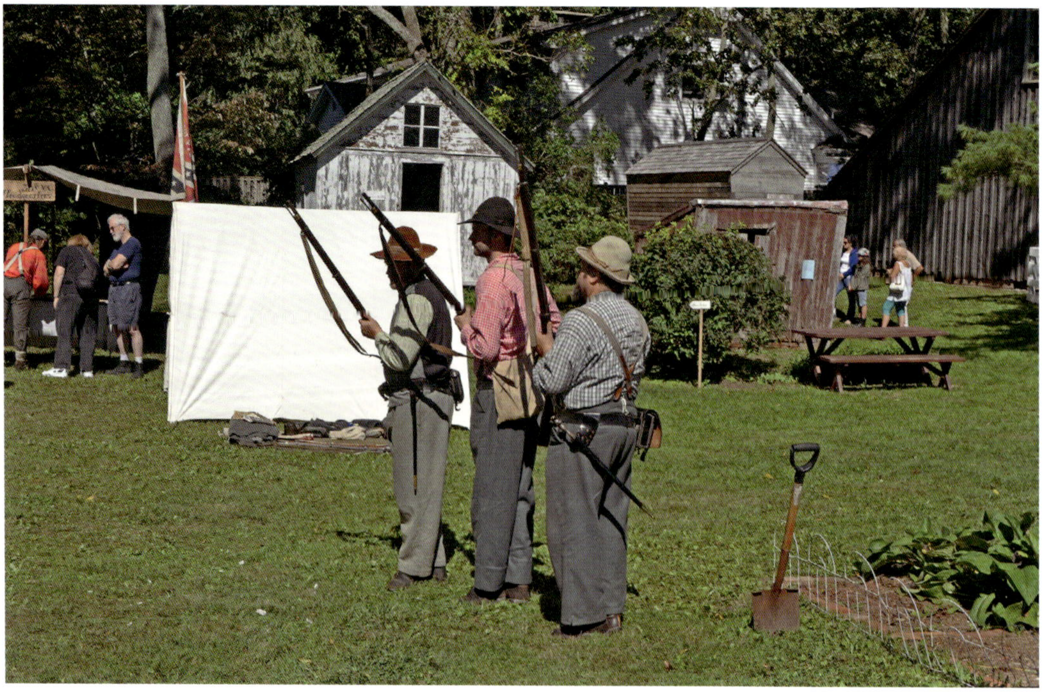

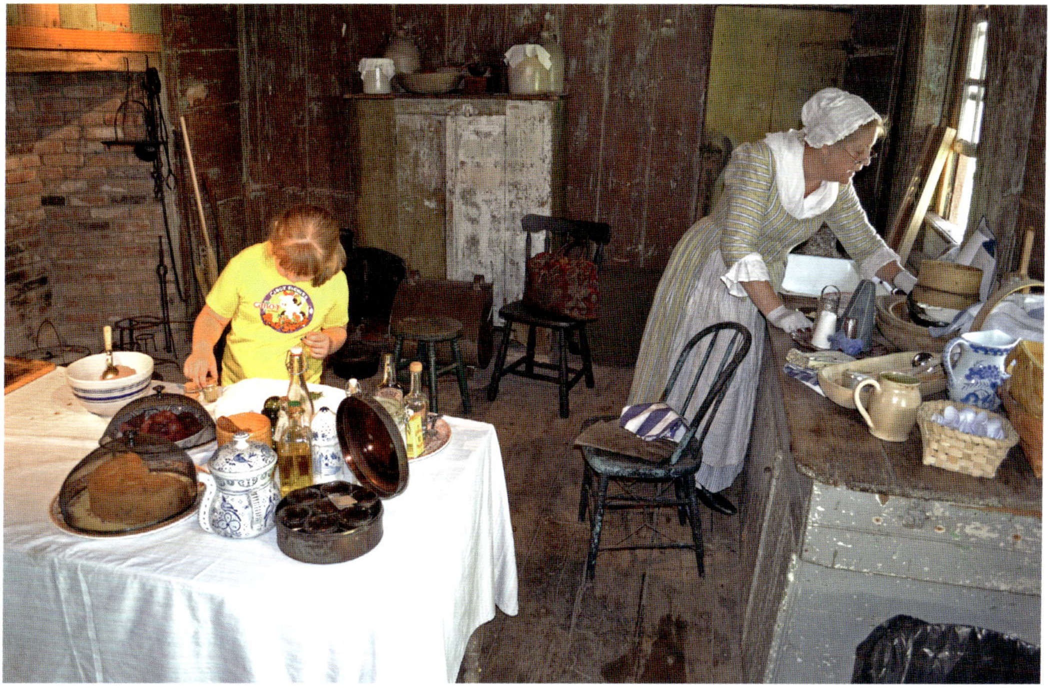

PERIOD DEMONSTRATIONS: Bringing their specialties to the Fair, costumed interpreters are popular with both children and adults. Diane Fish demonstrates open hearth cooking, and provides the history of food and cooking methods during the colonial era. The kitchen is always crowded. The blacksmith shows how he was a vital part of every community. Children are allowed to don gloves and apron and, using the hammer, make an S-hook. Other demonstrators demonstrate pottery and wampum making.

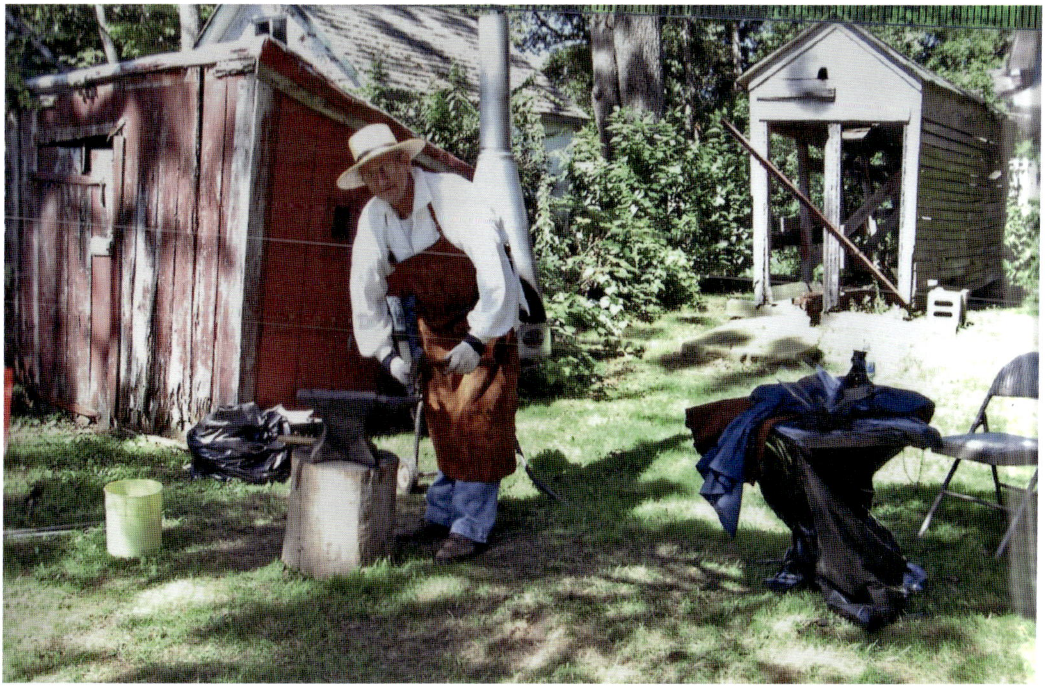

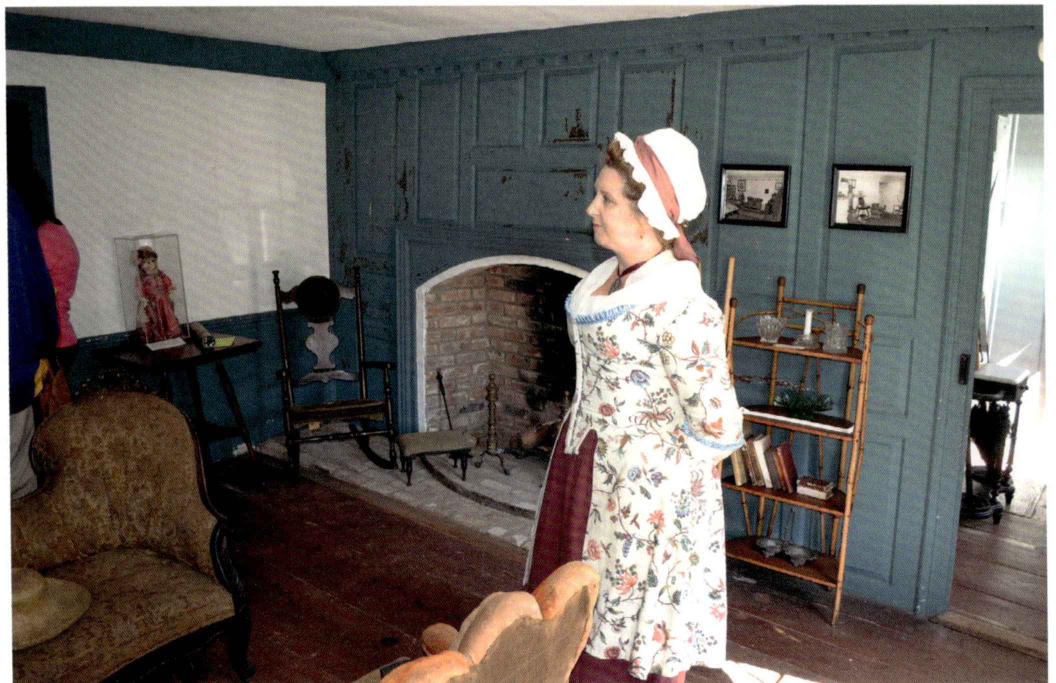

DOCENTS: Guided tours of the William Miller house began in the early 1980s. The house is open Saturdays during the summer for general visits. Group tours are provided to many organizations including Scouts, library groups, and school groups. Tours are provided during events held at the house such as the Country Fair and Car Show. Donna Rodman is giving a tour during the Country Fair in 2012. Peter Mott is giving a tour to one of the groups of seventh graders from the North Country Road School, Miller Place in 2014.

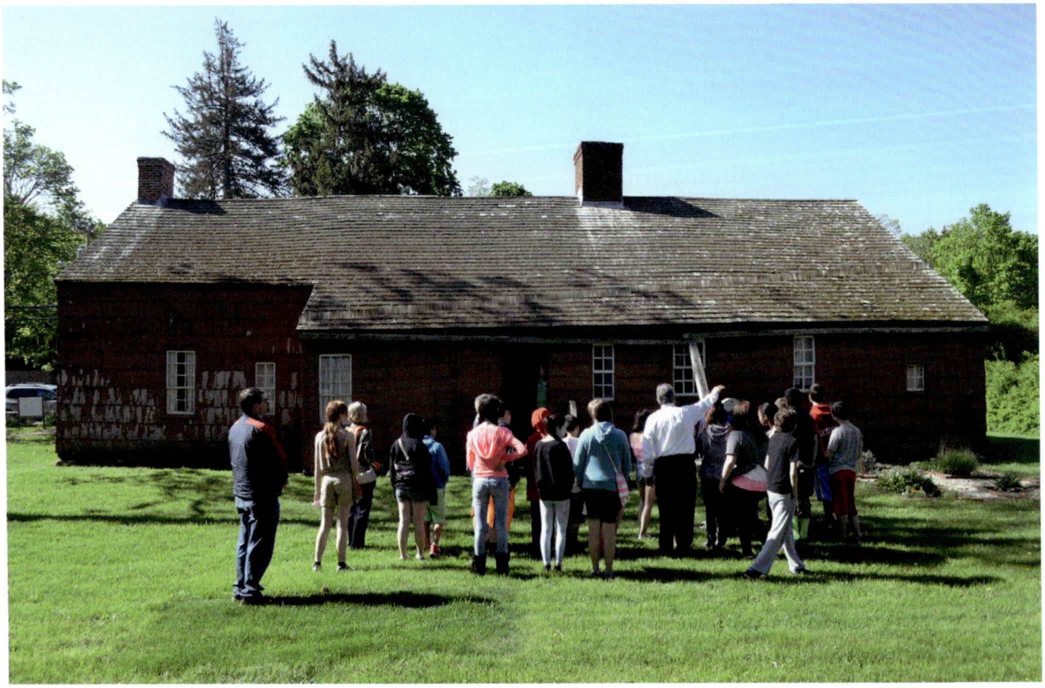

Chapter 3

Communities Grow and Change

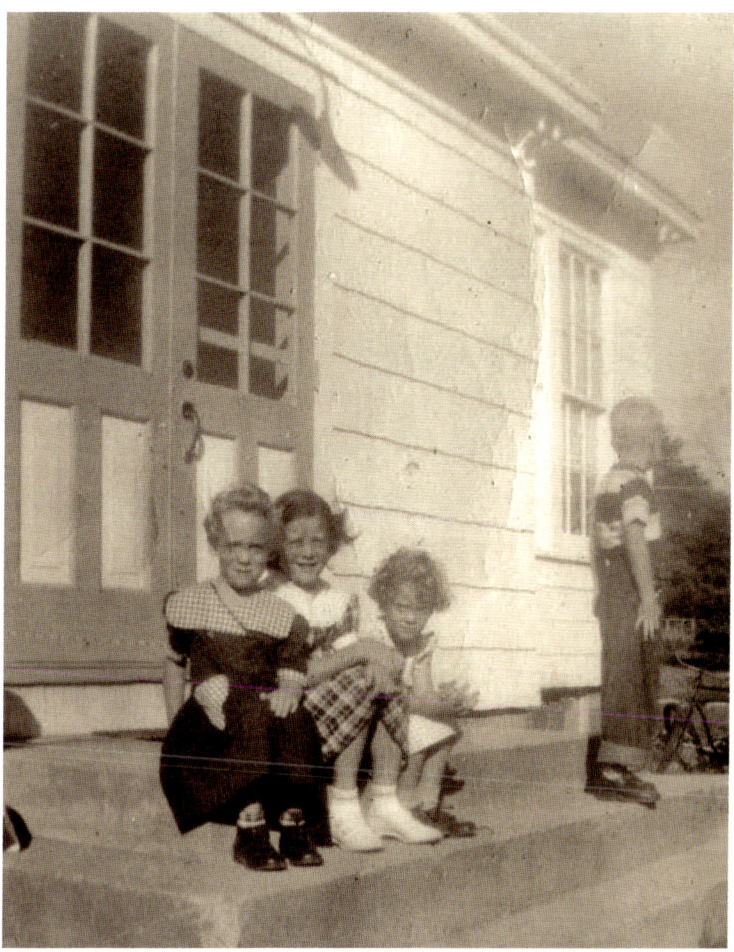

First Day of School: Edna Davis, Arlene Maier, and Linda Davis are pictured sitting on the steps of the two-room school house in Mount Sinai in 1951. It was Edna's first day and she walked with her mother, sister, and Arlene to school. For the rest of the school year, Edna, in first grade, and Arlene, in third grade, walked to school by themselves from Shore Road.

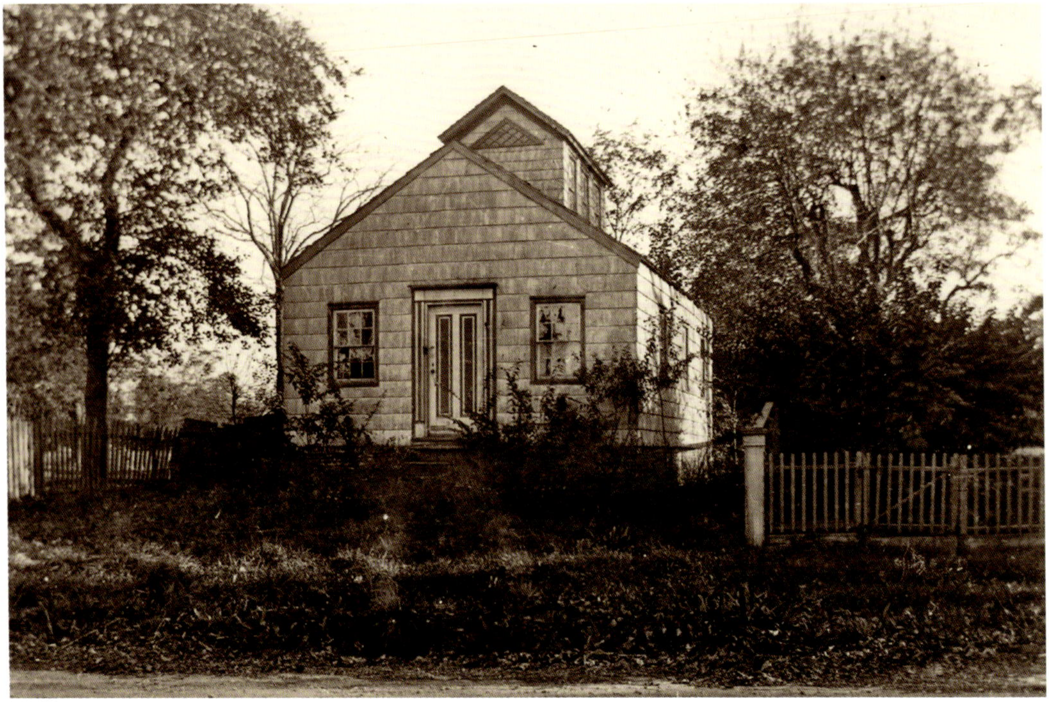

Miller Place schools: Located between what is now 170 and 172 North Country Road, this one-room schoolhouse operated until the late 1890s. When it was finally closed, the school district used the Academy as the local public school until 1937 when a new four-room school was opened on Lower Rocky Point and North Country Roads.

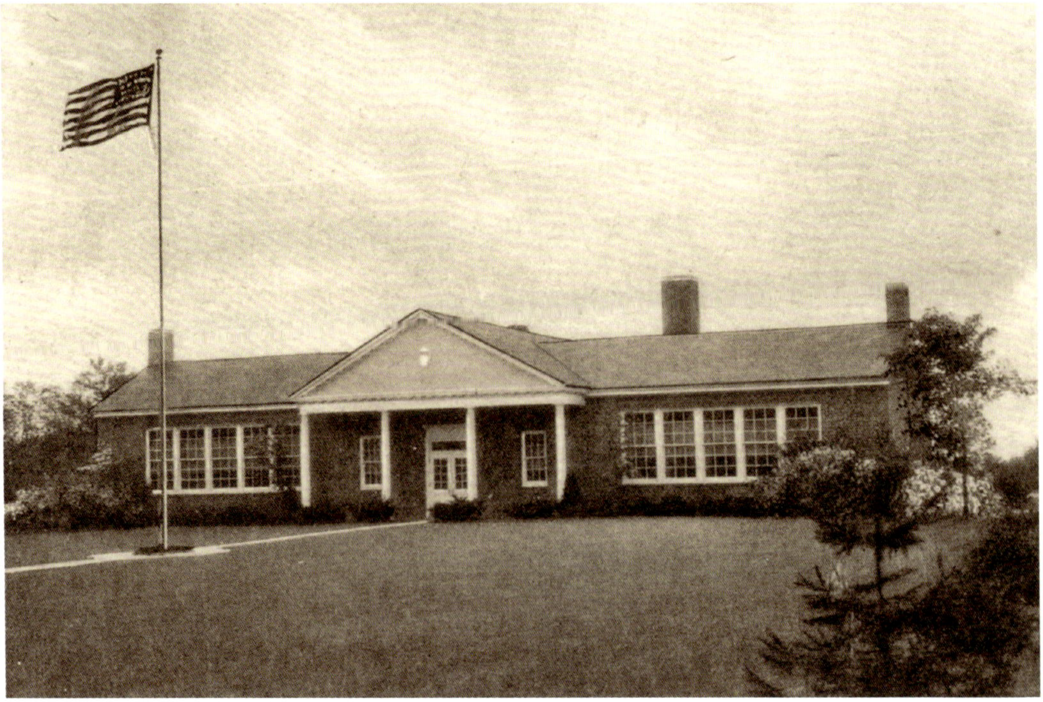

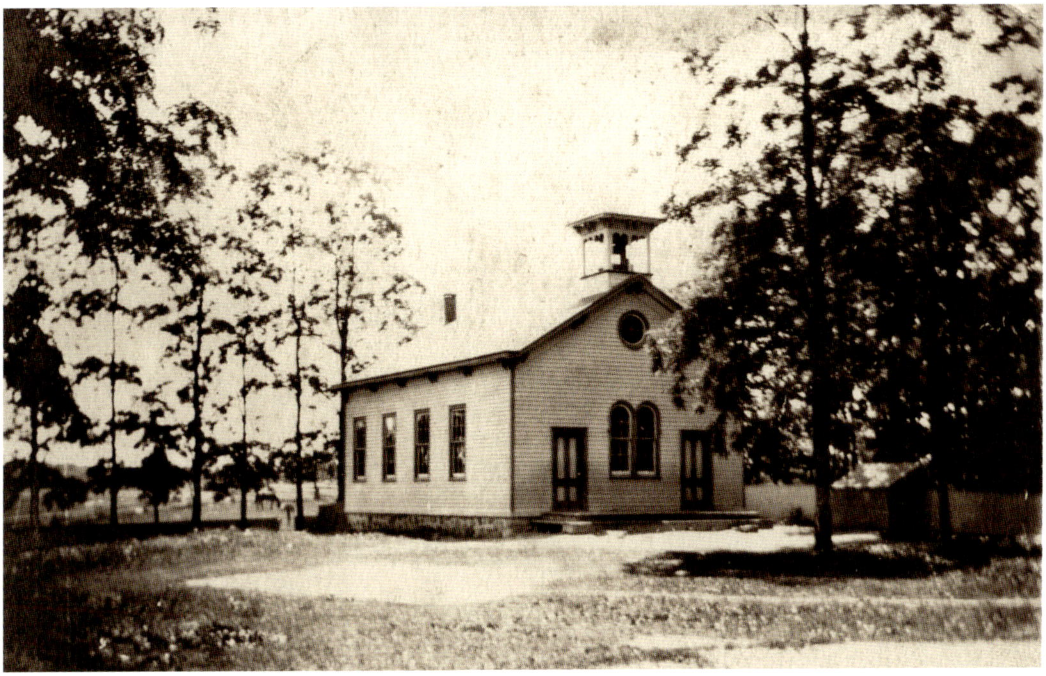

MOUNT SINAI SCHOOLS: In 1870 the hamlet built a new one-room school to replace the original building (location and date of original building unknown), and in 1908 a second room was added. Initially, grades one through eight were housed in the school, but by the 1950s only one through five were there. The school was used until it closed in 1958. High school education for local students was available, at first in Huntington. Beginning in 1894, students attended Port Jefferson high school, which had served as a regional high school for area students.

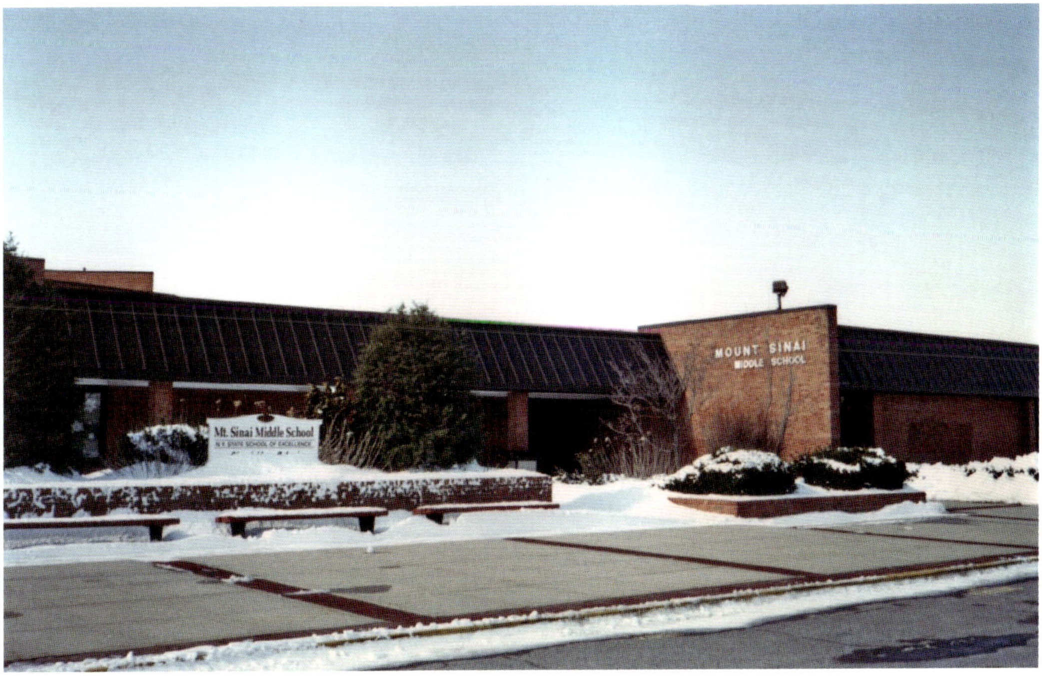

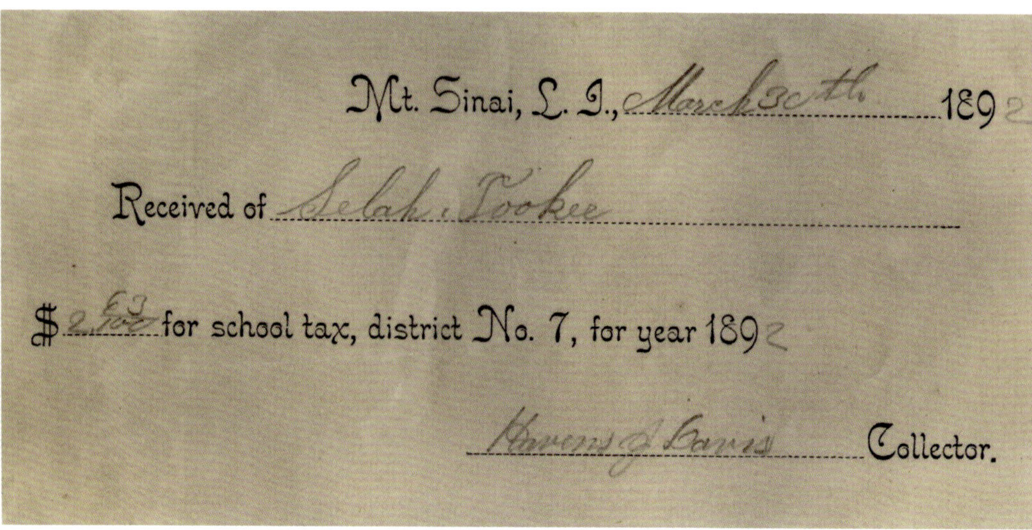
Mt. Sinai, L. I., March 30th 1892

Received of Selah Tooker

$2 63/100 for school tax, district No. 7, for year 1892

Havens J. Davis Collector.

SCHOOL TAXES: There were only four school board positons in each school district during the early years: president, secretary, librarian and tax collector. Generally, the same members of the community were re-elected to the same positon annually until that person finally said "no more." At times the tax collector would place a notice in the local paper that he would be at the general store on a specific date and time so that the public could come and pay the taxes.

Levy Description	District Taxable Value	District Tax Amount	Prior Year % Change	Exempt Code	Taxable Value Adjusted by Exemption	Tax Rate Per $100	Tax Amount
SCHOOL TAX		72.63 %	of total bill		School Tax Amount		8,532.21
SCHOOL DIST - MOUNT SINAI UFSD	15,392,716	32,803,774.37	0.20		3,325	245.226	8,153.76
LIBRARY DIST - MOUNT SINAI UFSD	15,392,716	1,751,999.23	2.60		3,325	11.382	378.45
COUNTY TAX		10.95 %	of total bill		County Tax Amount		1,286.81
COUNTY OF SUFFOLK	458,048,923	12,165,773.67	0.00		3,325	2.656	88.31
COUNTY OF SUFFOLK - POLICE	458,048,923	165,103,866.29	2.40		3,325	36.045	1,198.50
TOWN TAX		5.84 %	of total bill		Town Tax Amount		686.45
TOWN GENERAL - TOWN WIDE FUND	458,089,070	21,200,381.47	25.20		3,325	4.628	153.88
HIGHWAY - TOWN WIDE FUND	458,089,070	8,492,987.91	-33.50		3,325	1.854	61.65
TOWN GENERAL - PART TOWN FUND	391,911,858	7,947,990.36	18.80		3,325	2.028	67.43
HIGHWAY - PART TOWN FUND	391,911,858	47,558,616.87	1.70		3,325	12.135	403.49
OTHER TAX		10.58 %	of total bill		Other Tax Amount		1,242.45
SNOW RECOVERY TAXES	391,911,858	7,003,487.25	92.90		3,325	1.787	59.43
NEW YORK STATE MTA TAX	458,048,923	607,517.76	2.60		3,313	0.155	5.15
2004 $100M BOND ACT & OPEN SPACE	458,089,070	8,309,732.23	13.70		3,325	1.814	60.32
BROOKHAVEN REFUSE RECYCLING IMP 1 FAMI	282,685,732	37,733,120.30	-1.30		0	0.000	359.86
FIRE DIST - MT SINAI	15,470,435	1,503,109.22	1.60		3,325	9.716	323.06
BROOKHAVEN LIGHTING DISTRICT	416,852,592	4,918,941.52	-5.00		3,325	1.180	39.24
AMBULANCE DIST - MOUNT SINAI	15,467,192	756,348.41	-18.80		3,325	4.890	162.59
REAL PROPERTY TAX LAW	458,048,923	29,516,692.28	25.80		3,325	6.444	214.26
OUT OF COUNTY TUITION TAX	458,048,923	2,555,951.19	0.00		3,325	0.558	18.55

First Half Tax	5,873.96	Second Half Tax	5,873.96	Total Tax	11,747.92
Due December 1, 2014. Payable without penalty to January 10, 2015. See reverse side for penalty schedule.		Due December 1, 2014. Payable without penalty to May 31, 2015. See reverse side for penalty schedule and County Treasurer's Notice.		This total tax may be paid in one or two installments.	

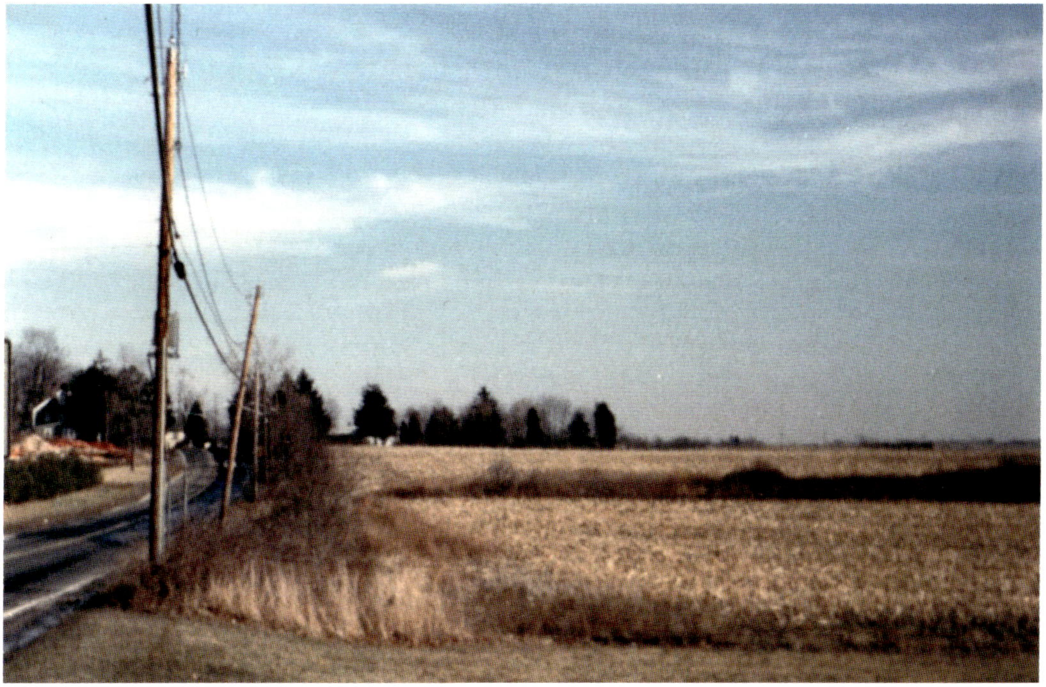

MOUNT SINAI SCHOOL PROPERTY: In 1973 part of the estate of William V. P. Davis was sold to the Mount Sinai School District for the construction of new schools, facilitating the return of Mount Sinai students from Port Jefferson. The photo above shows the field before the construction of the middle school in 1980, and the high school in 1991. The aerial view of the school complex, with the high school under construction, and athletic fields on what was once a farm field that had grown a variety of crops since the 1700s.

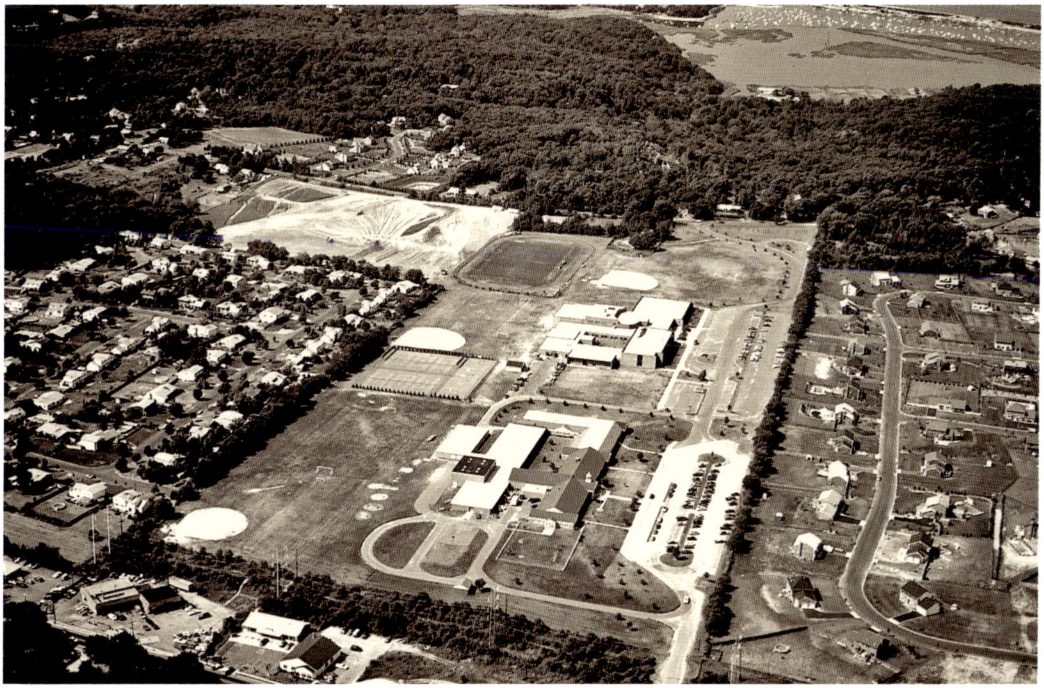

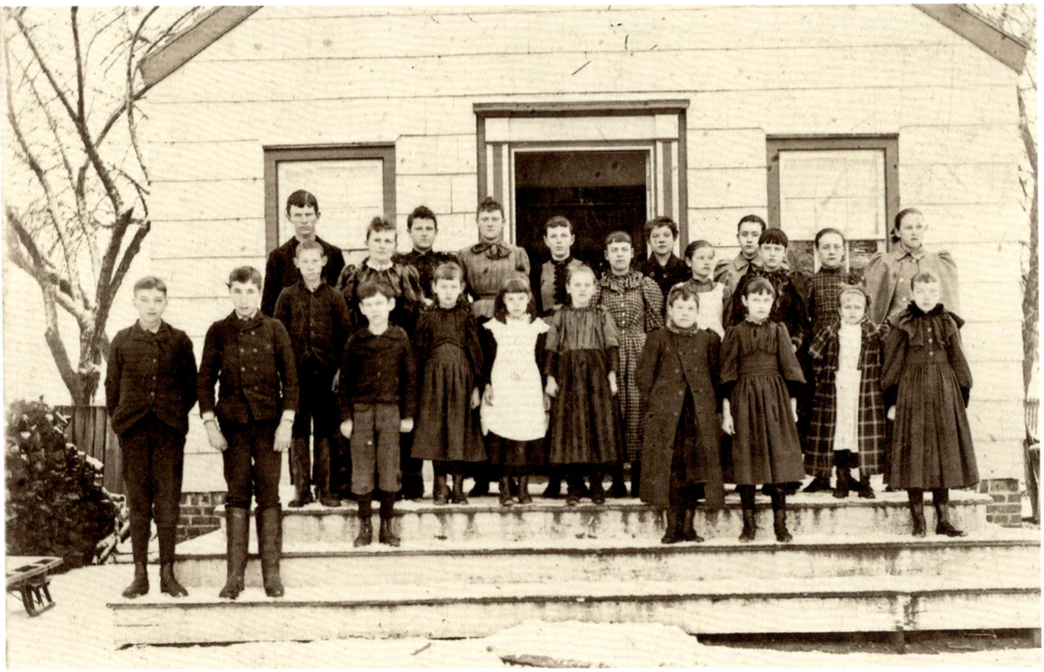

SCHOOL PHOTOS: School pictures were usually taken outside during the late 1800s and early 1900s. In the Miller Place photo taken in 1895, the twenty-two students stood out in the cold. A close look at the photo shows snow on the ground, a sled and the wood pile to the students' right. Mount Sinai waited for warmer weather for the annual school picture. This was taken in 1906, before the second room was added to the one-room school. Miss Guiletta Hutchinson, the teacher, attended the one-room school as a child, she also taught at Miller Place. When she retired in 1907 she moved to the orange groves of Auburn, California.

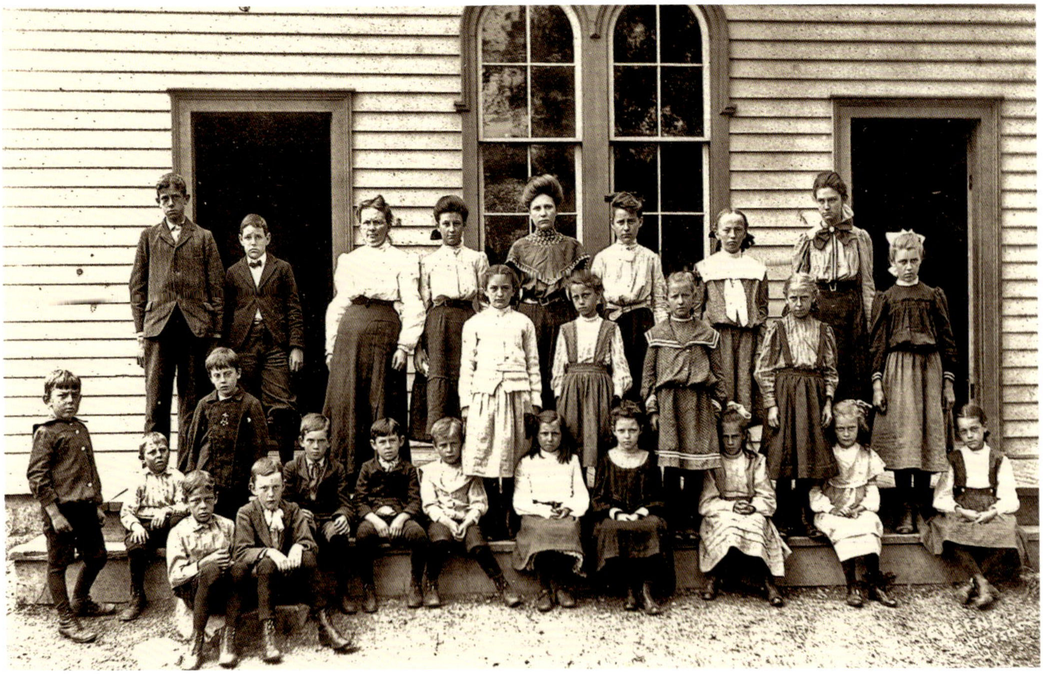

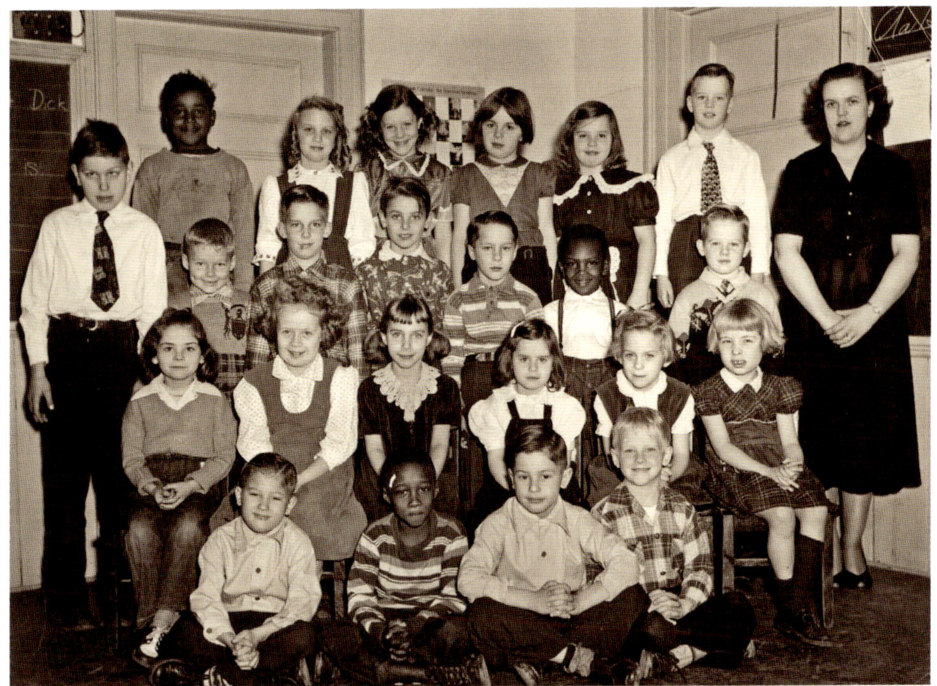

MID-CENTURY PHOTOS: In 1958 the Miller Place eighth grade had twenty-eight students. They had their photo taken with their teacher Mr. Peter. In the spring of 1952 Mrs. Kempster had her photo taken with her students in the first, second, and third grades in the old room of the Mount Sinai school, pictured here, while the fourth and fifth grades had their picture taken with their teacher Mrs. Van Nostrand in the other room.

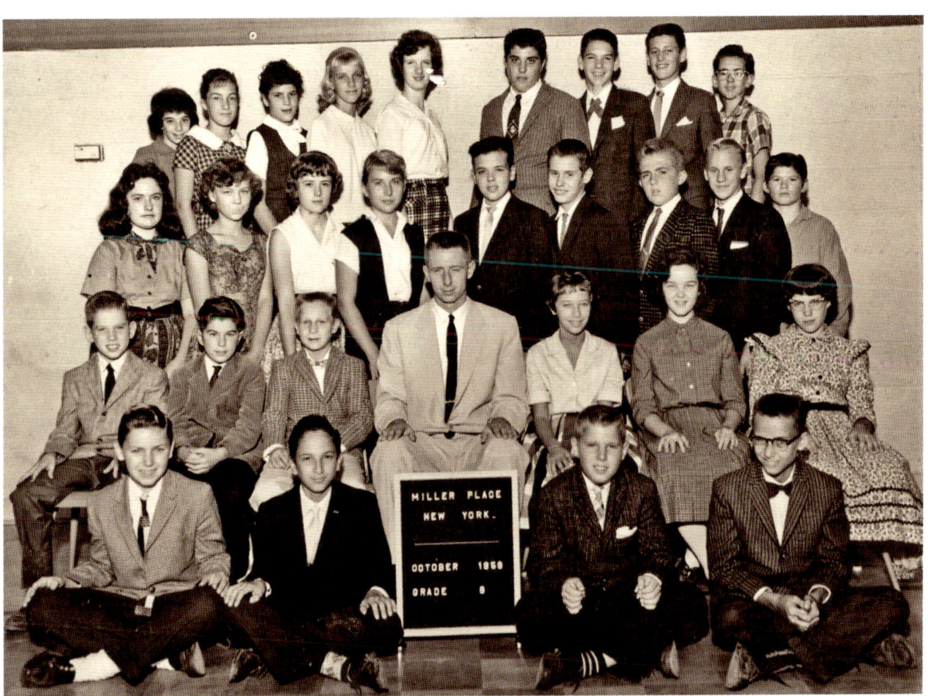

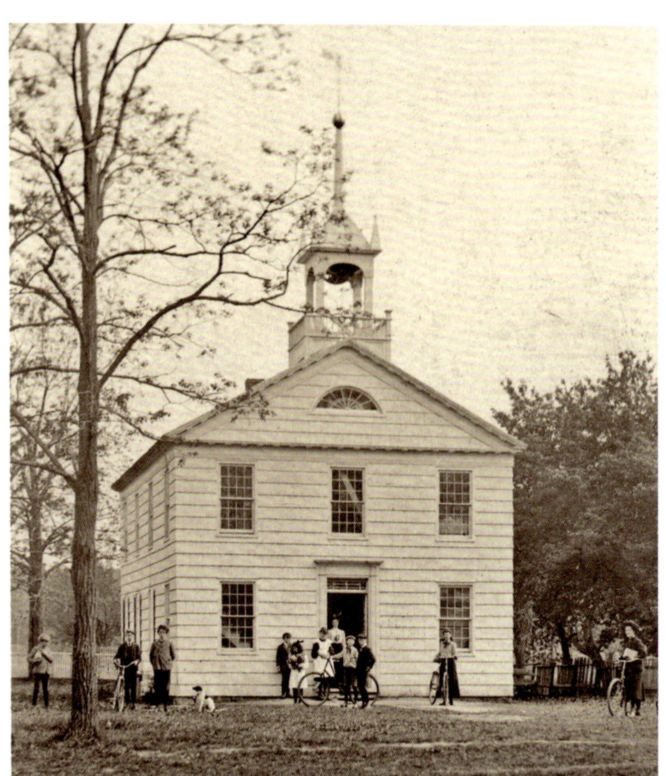

MILLER PLACE ACADEMY: This private school was built in 1834 and remained open until 1868. The building served as the local public school from the early 1900s until 1937, and has served as a community library since 1938. Above, the Academy is shown as a public school with students posing outside. The lower picture is from October 2014, showing seventh grade students from the North Country Road school walking to the Academy as part of a new local history designed by members of the Historical Society, School, the North Country Road Alumni Association, and Academy volunteers.

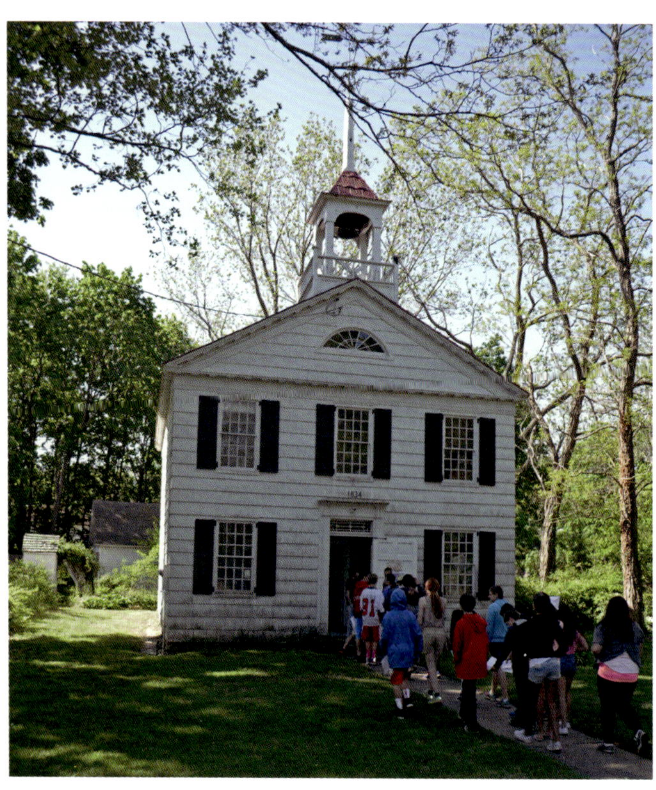

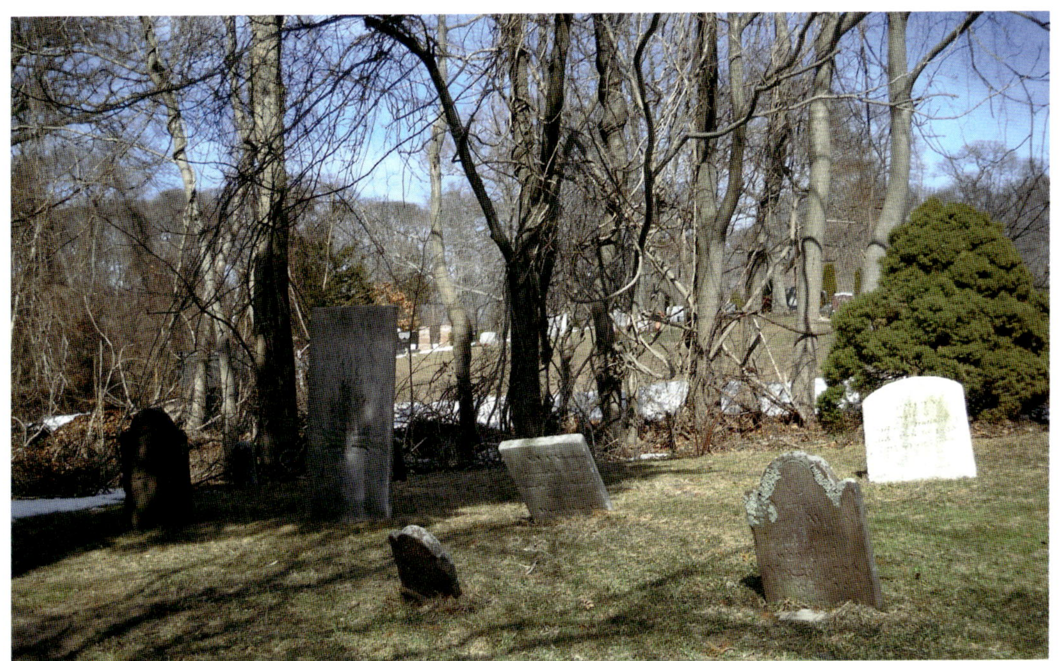

FAMILY BURIAL GROUNDS: Private cemeteries served as the final resting place for the communities of Mount Sinai and Miller Place during the 17th and 18th centuries. In 1841 the Congregational Church opened a cemetery for members of the parish. In 1890 the Burial Ground was separated from the church and became known as the Sea View Cemetery, named as the farmland surrounding the cemetery was clear-cut so that Long Island Sound and Mount Sinai harbor could be seen. Joseph Davis had a burial ground behind his barn, and in 1839 Samuel Hopkins gave a Quit Claim to the descendants of those buried here after he had bought the farm.

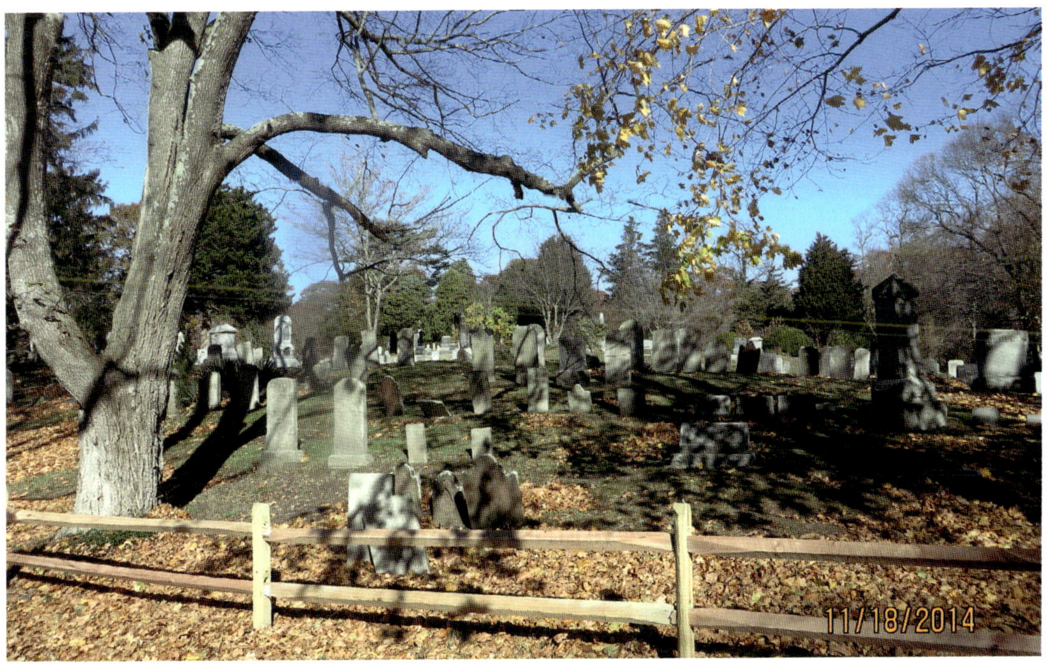

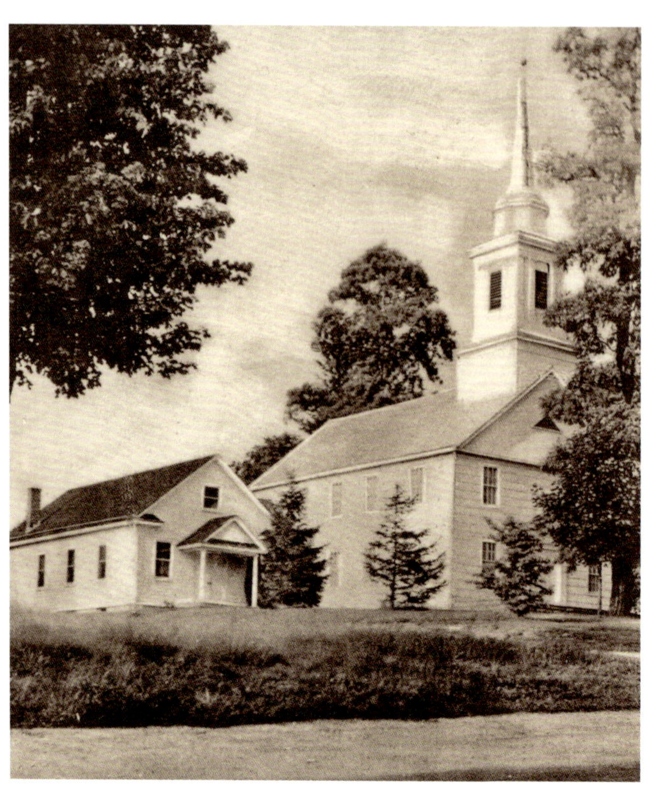

MOUNT SINAI CONGREGATIONAL CHURCH: Established in 1789 as the Strict Congregational Church of Old Man's, Miller's Place, and Rocky Point, the present building was erected in 1807, with the steeple and narthex added in 1850, and the parish house in 1927. The above photograph shows the church and parish house soon after this addition. Although several additions have been made to both buildings only those to the parish house are visible.

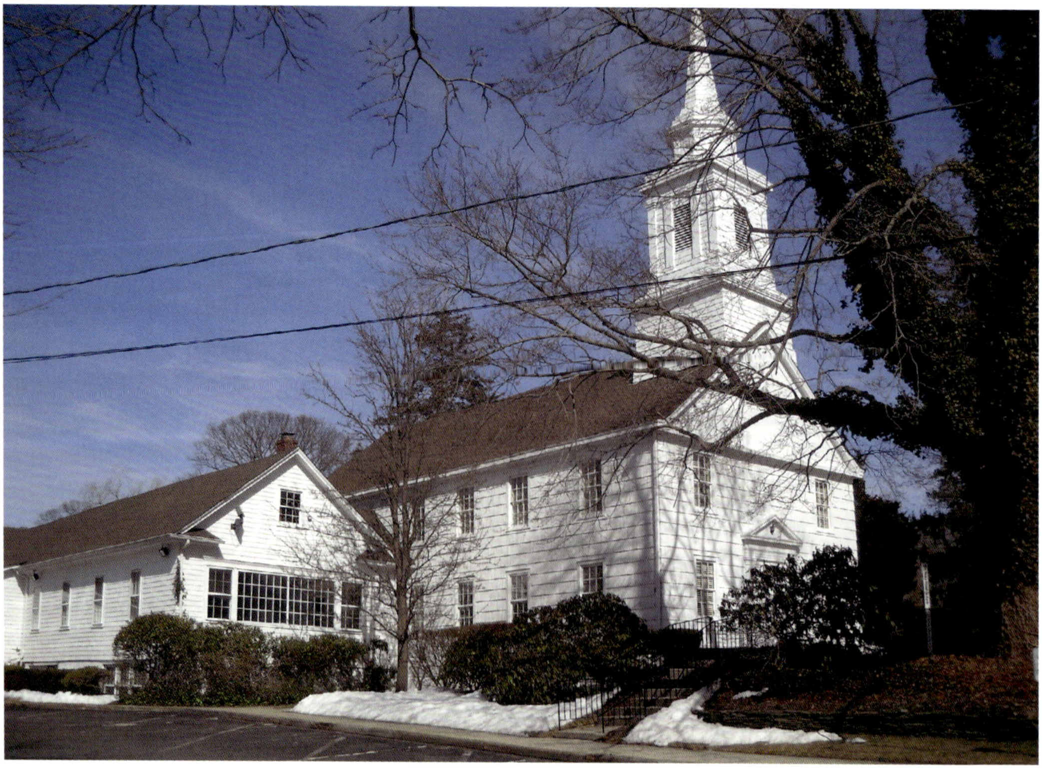

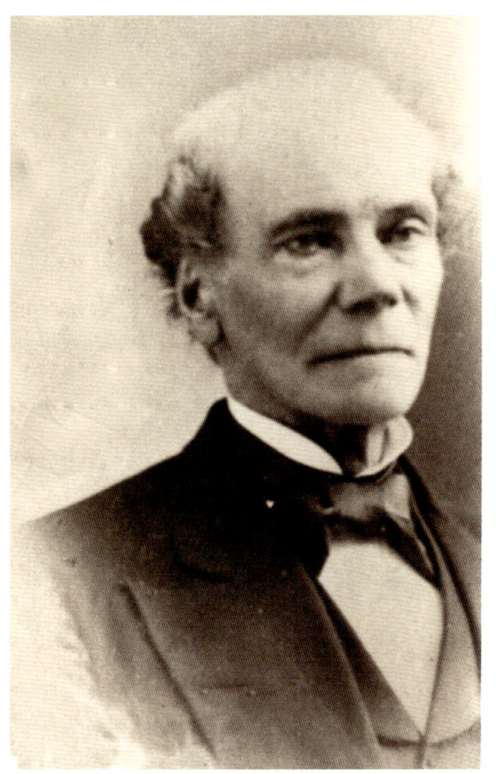

CONGREGATIONAL MINISTERS: There have been twenty-six ministers of the Congregational Church, the first being Noah Hallock Jr., who served a congregation of twelve from 1790 until 1818. The earliest photo of a minister is that of the Rev. Aaron Snow. He was a well-respected and cherished minister. Upon his death a special memorial plaque was made for him and hung in the church until a renovation. The plaque is now in the history cabinet in the parish house. Reverend Diane (Samuels) Cangelosi is the first woman and twenty-sixth minister of the church. She attended the church since childhood, served in several ministerial capacities and became senior minister in 2002.

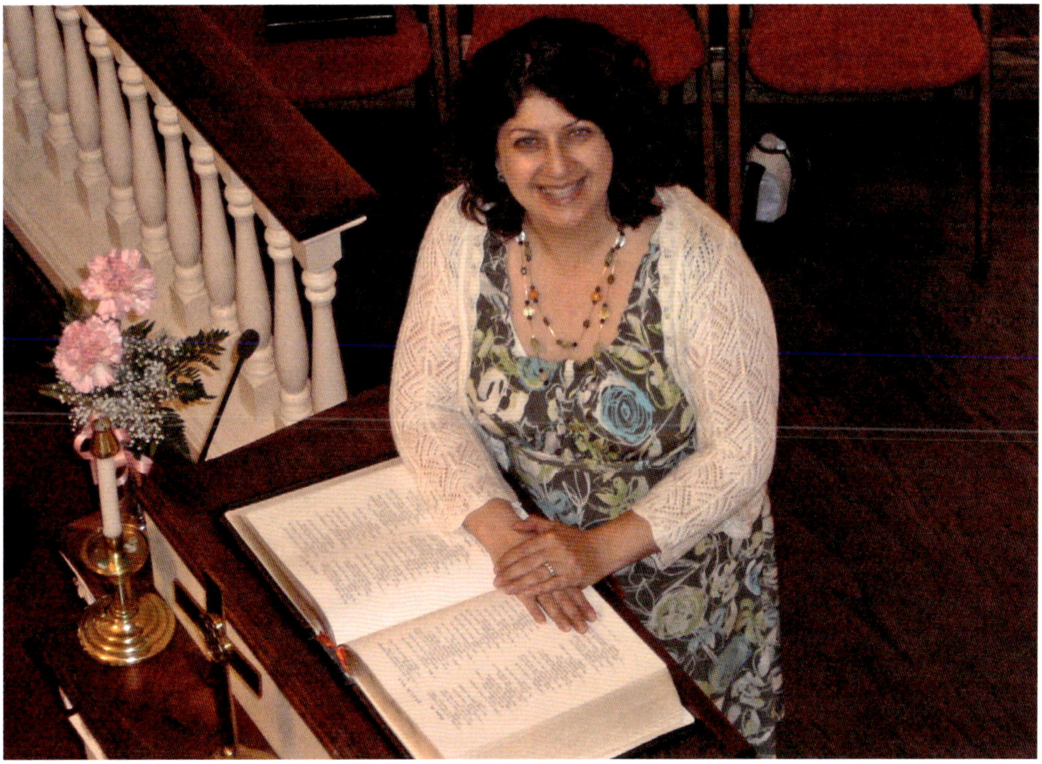

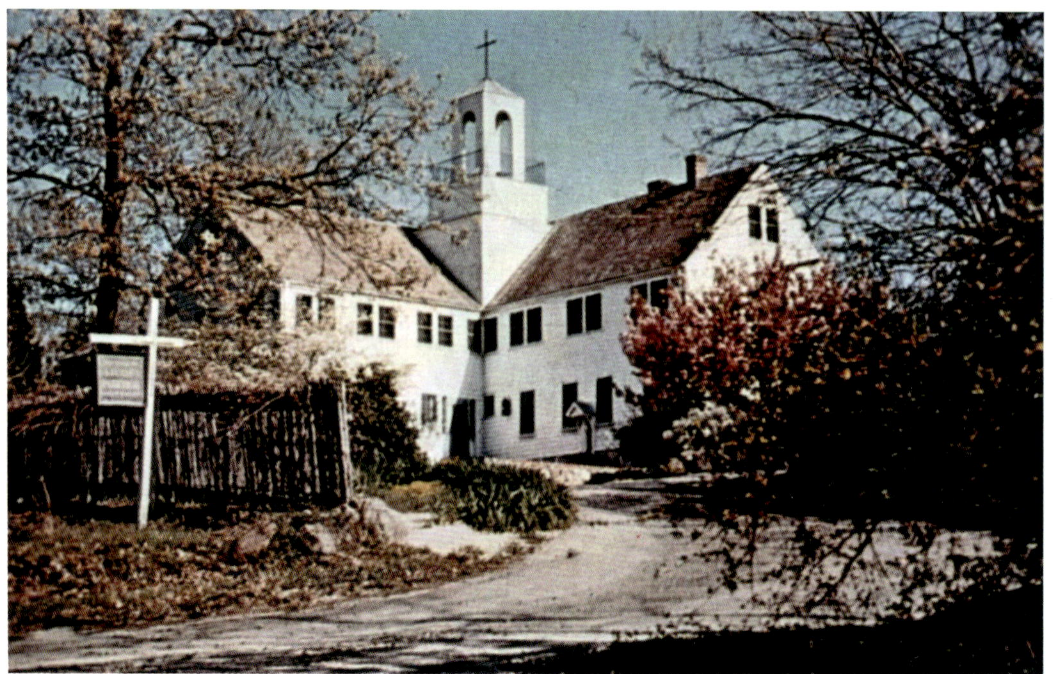

Little Portion Friary of St. Francis: This Episcopal Church entity was established in 1928 with a gift of land from Charles Metcalfe Simms. During the 1940s, '50s, and '60s the community of Friars was large, but began to decline beginning in 1970s. In 2013, Suffolk County bought forty-four acres of undeveloped land from the Friary in an effort to preserve its viability; however the Friary announced its closing in 2014. The two pictures show that the exterior of the buildings facing the road have not changed, although fifty years separate the photos.

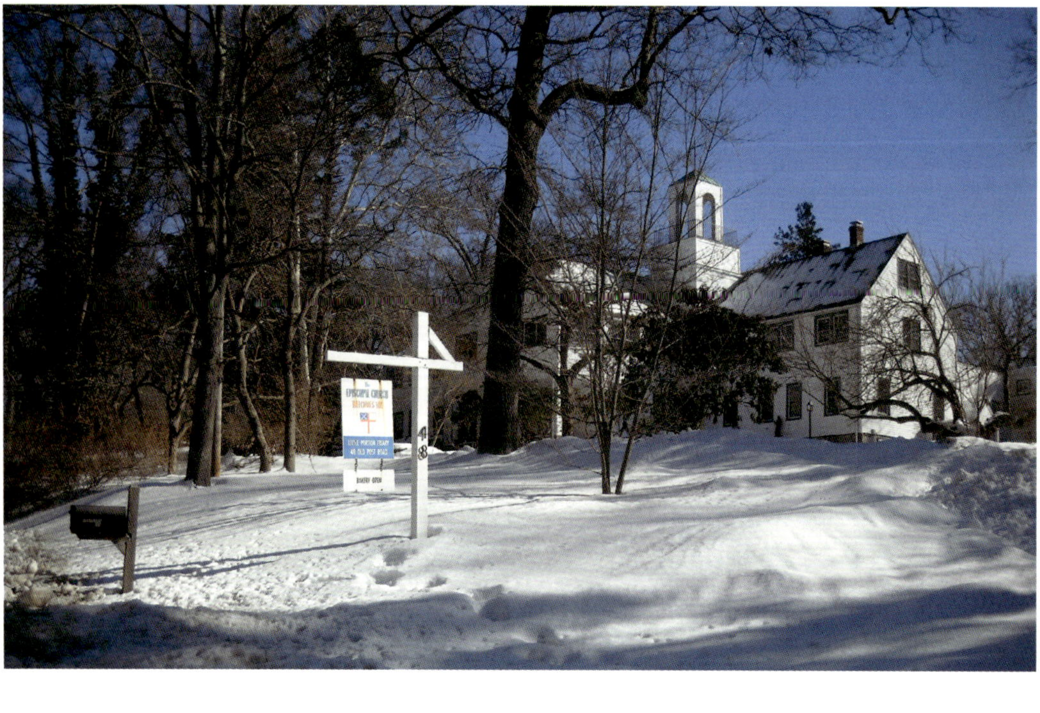

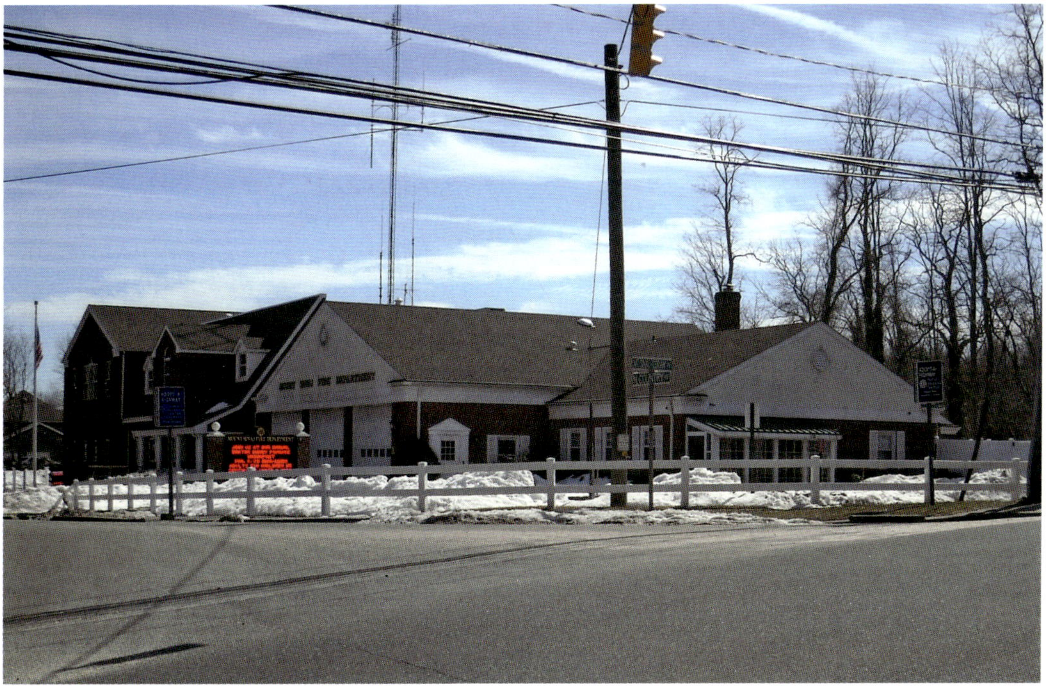

FIREHOUSES: The Miller Place Fire House is on its original location of 1954, whereas the Mount Sinai Fire House moved to the old school property on the corner of Mt. Sinai-Coram and North Country roads in 1963. Both Departments have enlarged and added to their firehouses as the size of trucks and the equipment requirements have increased, and have constructed substations south of Route 25A to accommodate the population increase over time.

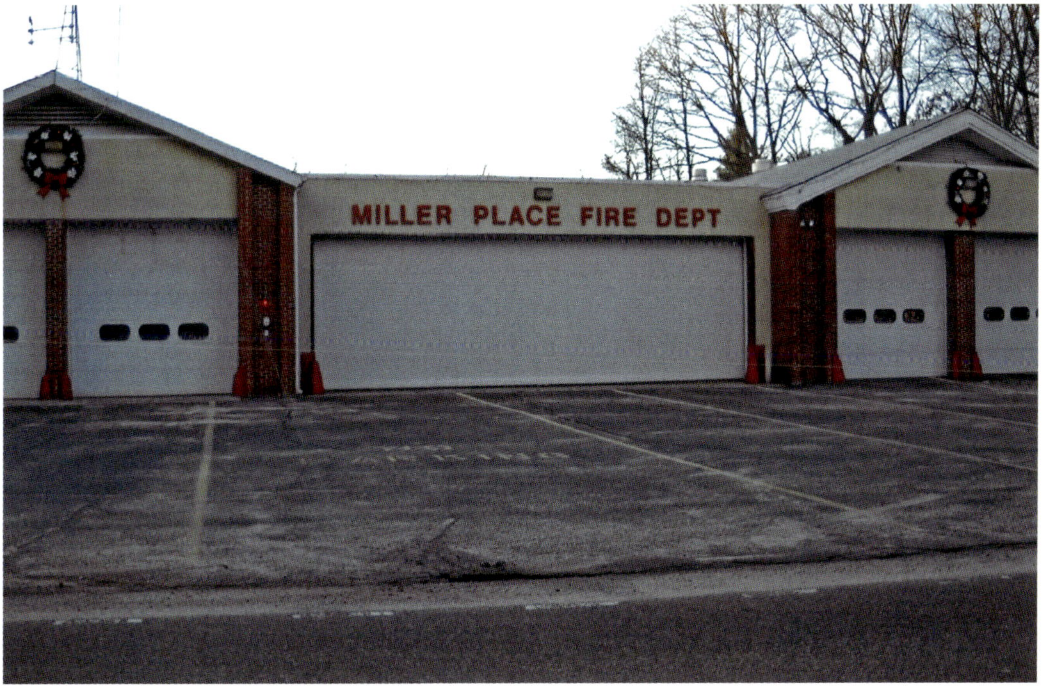

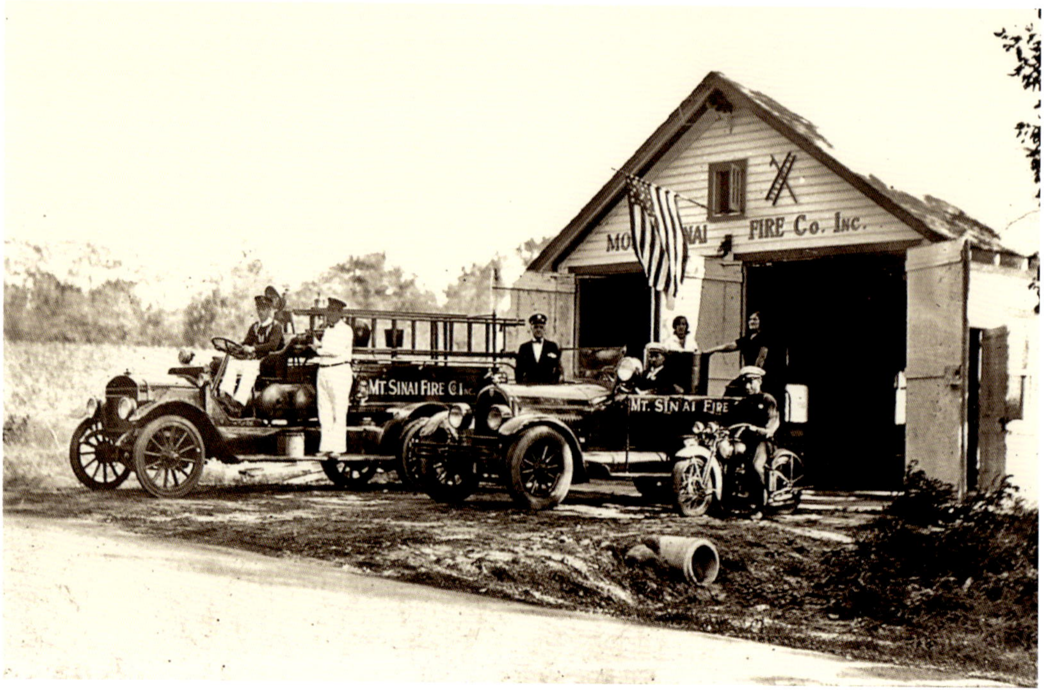

MOUNT SINAI FIRE DEPARTMENT: Established in 1930, five volunteers are assembled with the fire trucks in front of the original firehouse located on the south side of North Country Road. Interest in the early history of the department led to the restoration of a truck originally purchased in 1942. The restored "Brush Truck" has become a show piece, and driven in events such as the July 4th parade in Port Jefferson and car show at Heritage Park.

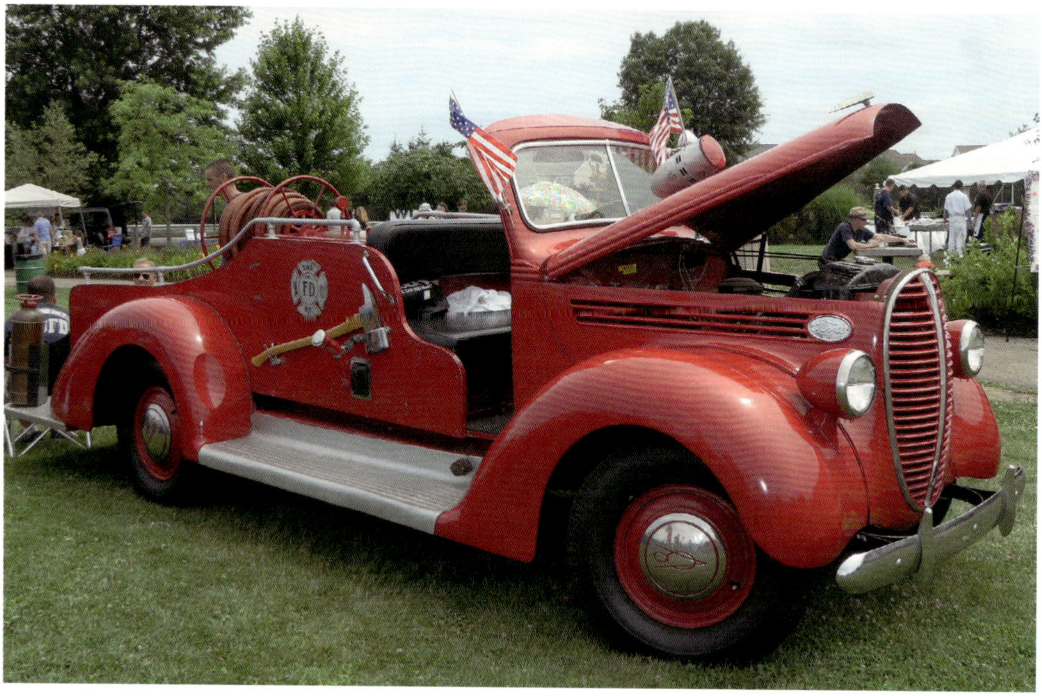

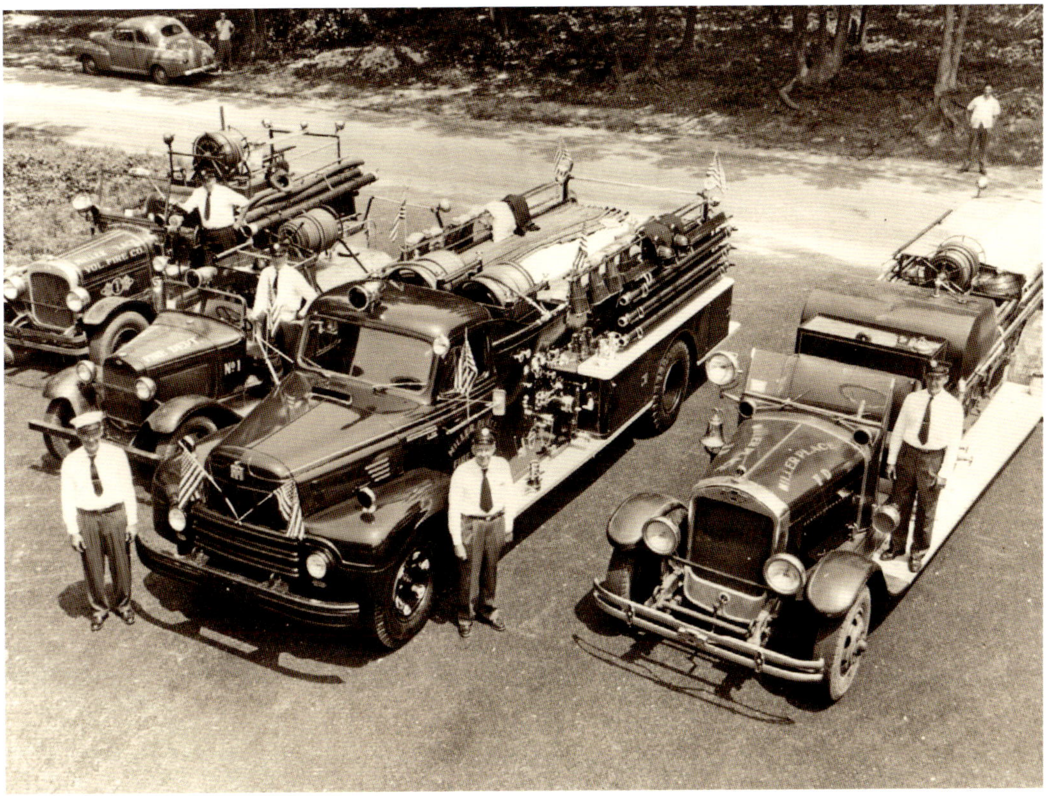

MILLER PLACE FIRE DEPARTMENT: Established in 1952, prior to this date, the Mount Sinai and Sound Beach Fire Departments protected the Miller Place community. In the 1950s the department had these four trucks, but by 2000 the number, size, and function of the department's vehicles had increased as a result of population growth and new technologies.

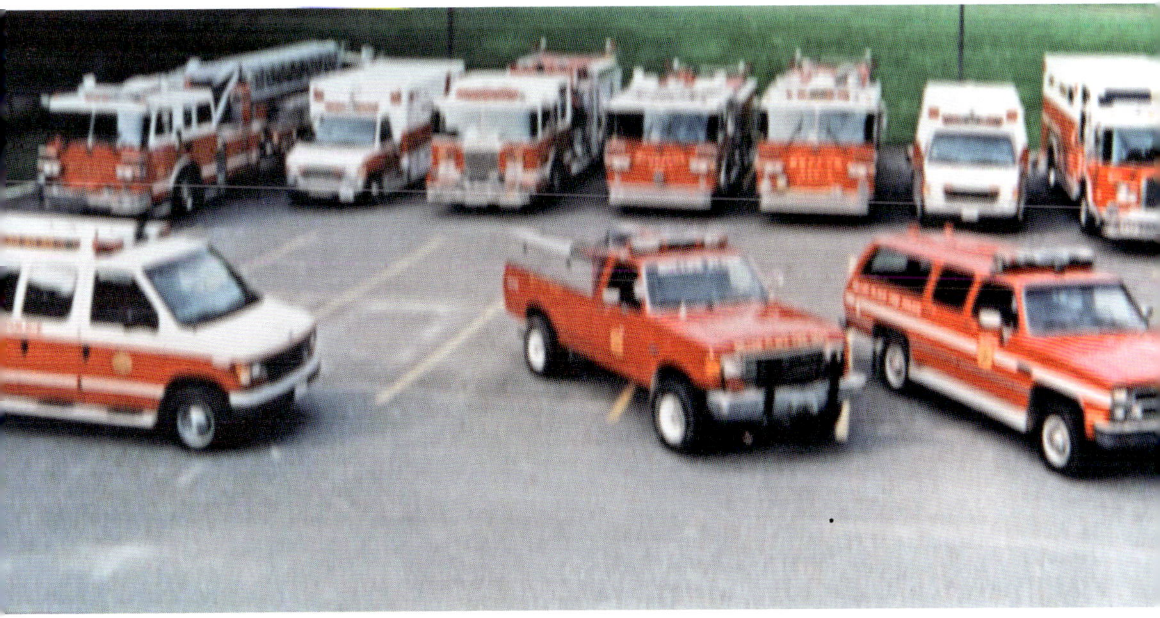

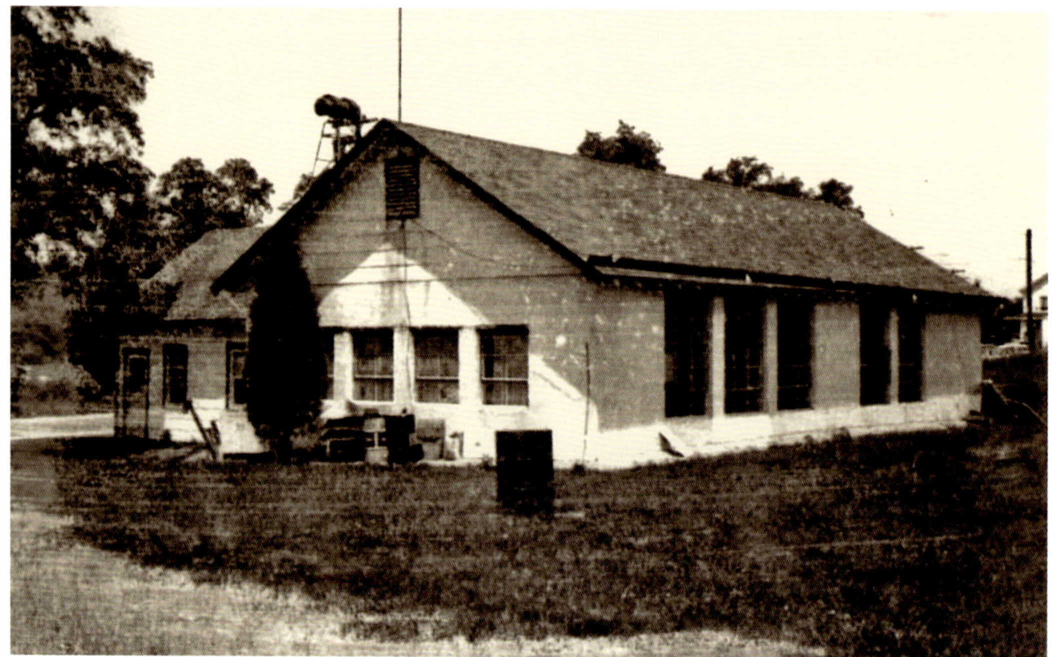

THE ANNEX: The Mt. Sinai Fire Department added a meeting room onto the firehouse in 1948. The firemen used the room for meetings, dinners, dances, entertainments, and card parties. Other organizations, including the Farm Bureau, Home Bureau, and Girl Scouts, have also met here. When the fire department relocated from its original building, the firehouse was removed, and the meeting room was taken over by the Town of Brookhaven. Senior citizens groups met in the building until moving to a new building on Route 25A. In February 2015 Town Supervisor Ed Romaine announced that the building has been leased to the Ancient Order of Hibernians, Division 9, formerly of Port Jefferson.

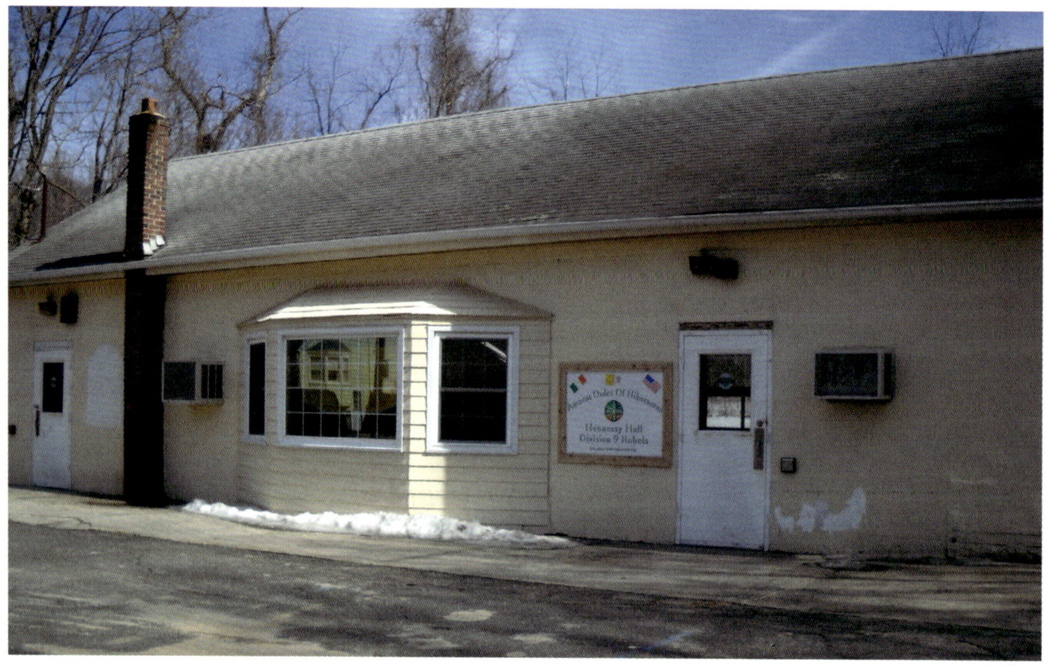

Chapter 4

Recreation across the Years

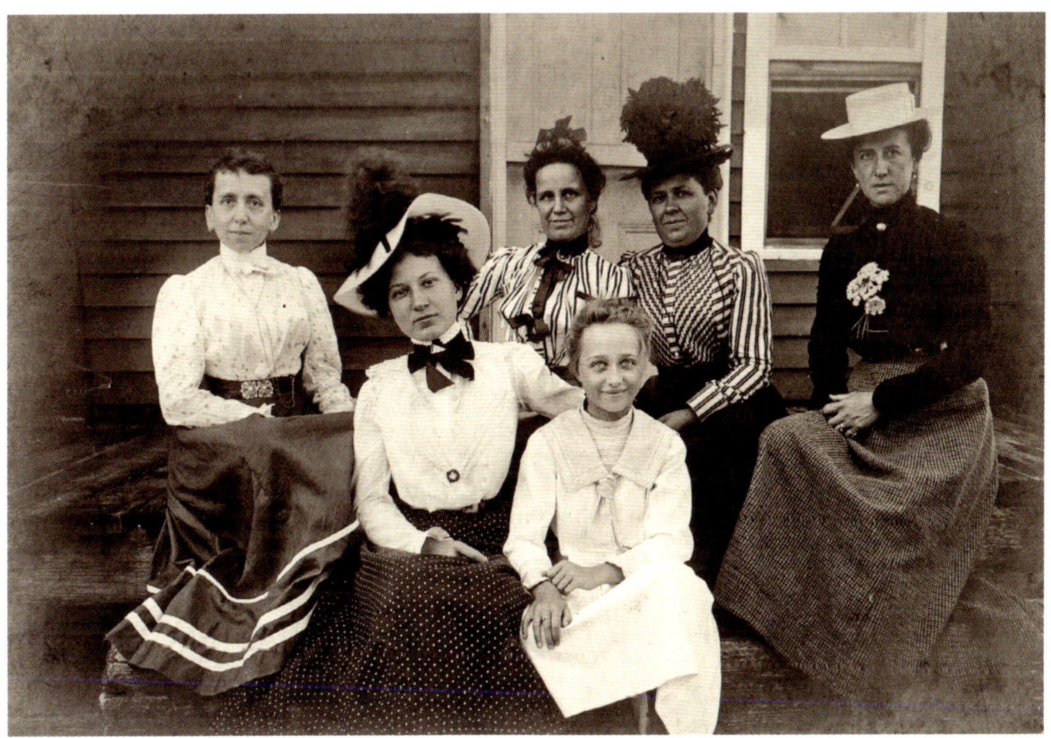

BRUNJES TRIBE: Brothers Gustave and Robert Brunjes purchased a house on Old Post Rd., Mt. Sinai, calling it Lone Pine Cottage. During their many summers here they often had relatives and friends stay with them. Mrs. Gustav Brunjes, in the dark hat, poses with some of her relatives or friends who are unidentified. The young girl in the front is probably her niece, Anna Schiffer, who often spent the summer with her aunt and uncle in Mt. Sinai.

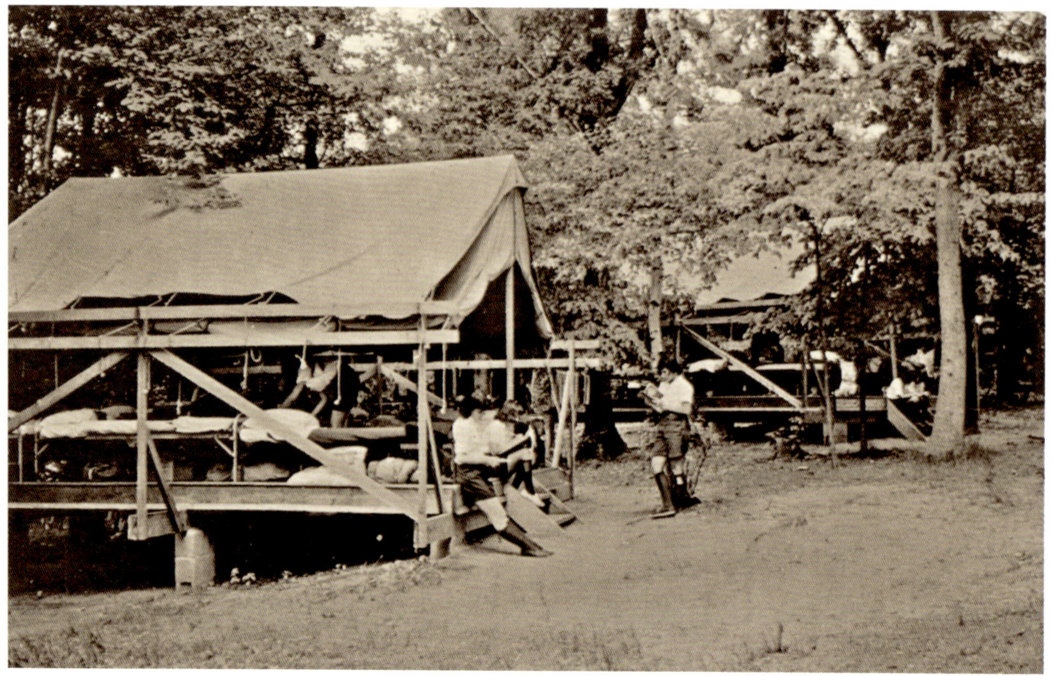

CORDWOOD LANDING PARK: The Nassau County Girl Scout Council purchased property in Miller Place to provide camping and beach facilities for its troops. Camp Francois Barstow was active from the 1950s to the 1980s, and provided tent platforms for campers. When the Council decided to sell the property, Suffolk County purchased it in 1986, when the park was created. The name commemorates an industry which flourished during the 19th and early 20th century when men loaded wood onto schooners to be sold in New York City and points north along the Hudson River.

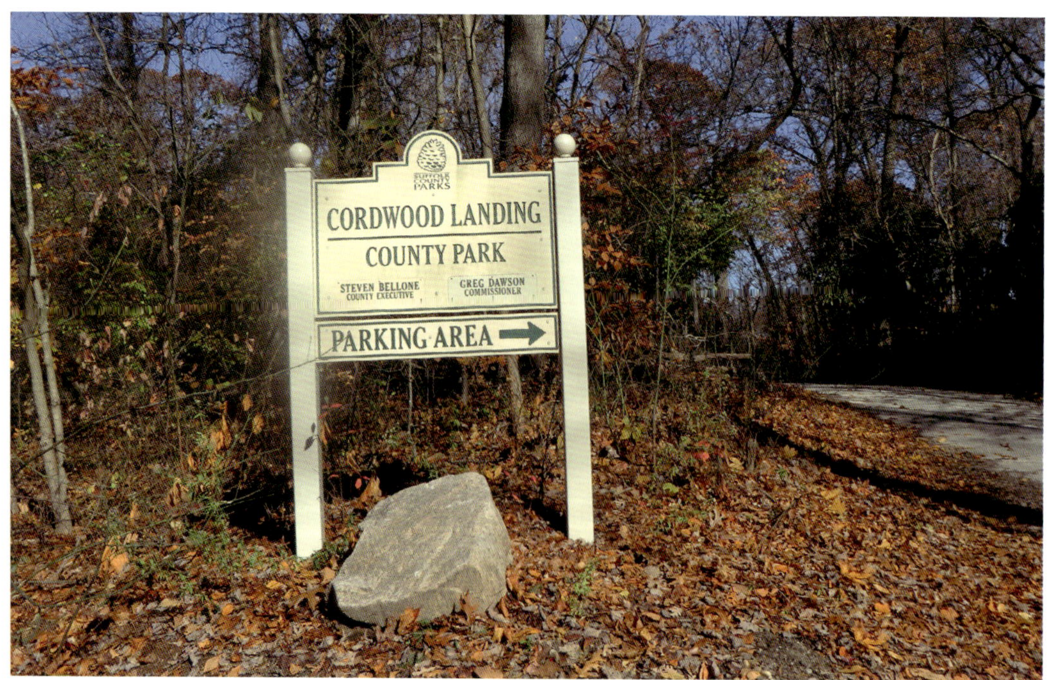

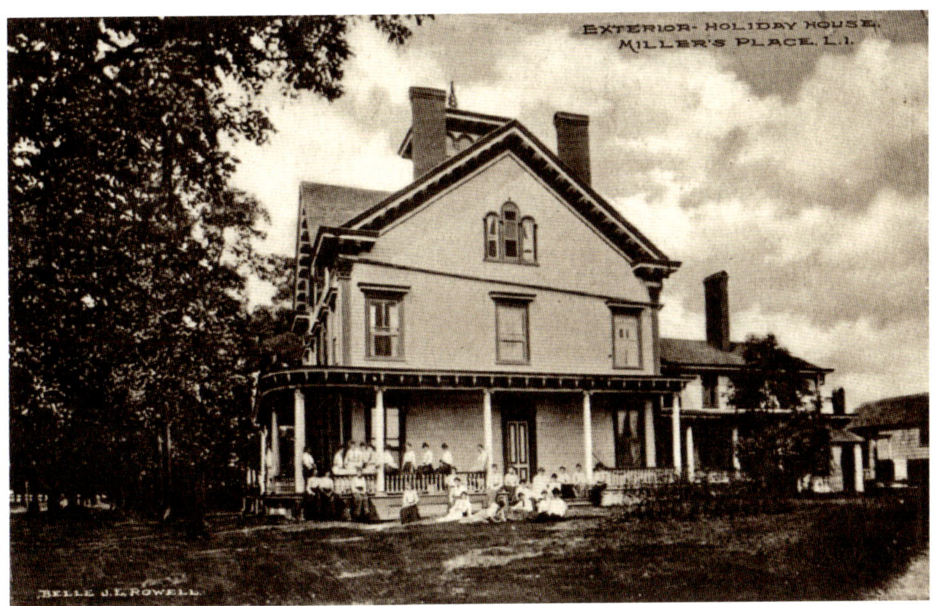

HOLIDAY HOUSE: A converted 19th century home used by the Auxillary Society of the Association of Working Girls Societies of New York as a vacation destination for young New York City women. The property ran from North Country Road to the Sound, and had beach access. Popular during the beginning of the 20th century, the resort provided a variety of recreational activities including tennis, swimming, badminton, volley ball, horseback riding, golf, beach parties, and dances. By the late 1950s Holiday House had been abandoned. Vandals and the weather took their toll, and in 1970 it was torn down, located just east of 155 North Country Road, and is a part of Cordwood Landing Park.

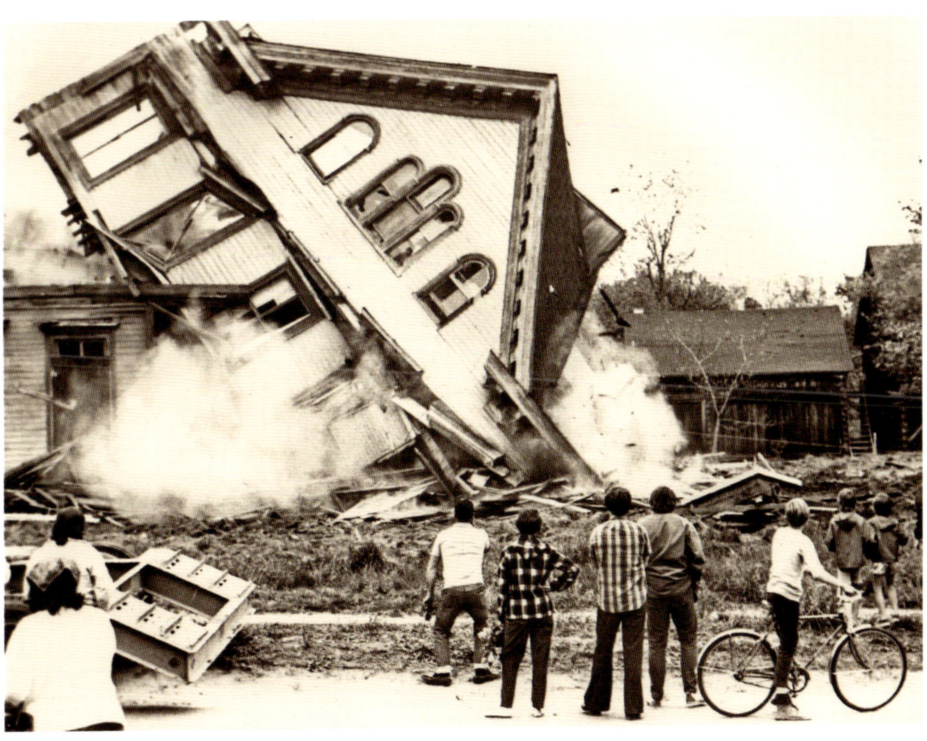

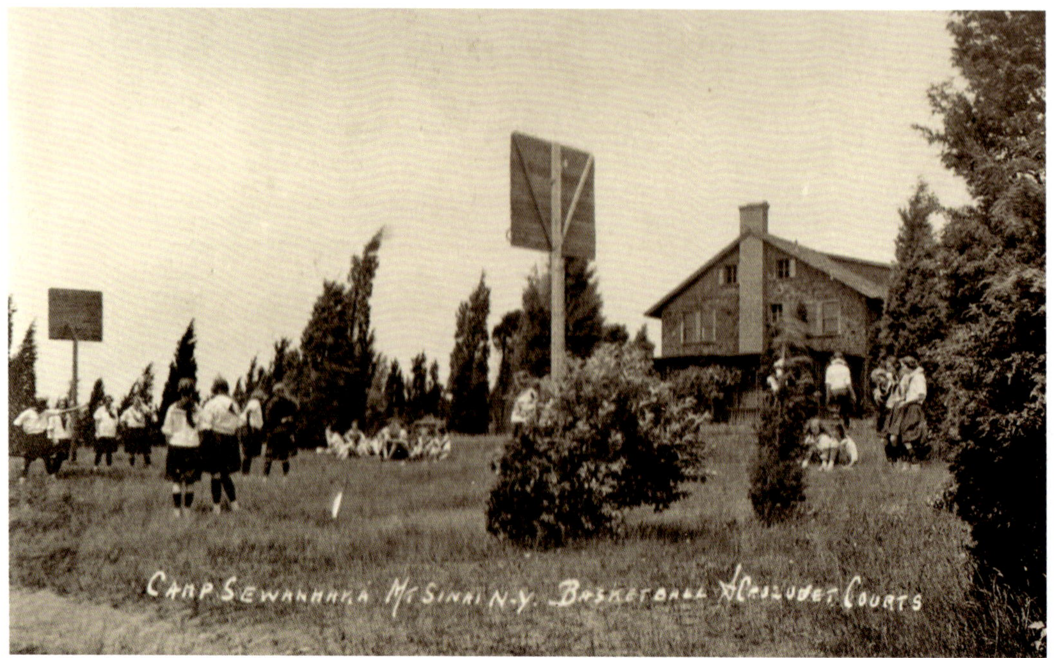

Chandler County Park: Camp Sewanhaka was one of several facilities located on a portion of land adjacent to Mount Sinai Harbor, and was a summer camp for girls offering folk and social dancing, arts and crafts, and tutoring. This upscale camp offered electricity and running water, as well as a full dining hall. Other camps continuously occupied the site well into the 1950s. The property also contained cottages built throughout the property for rental to families and groups. By the 1990s the camps were gone and the cottages were no longer being rented. In 2000 Suffolk County purchased the property as a passive park.

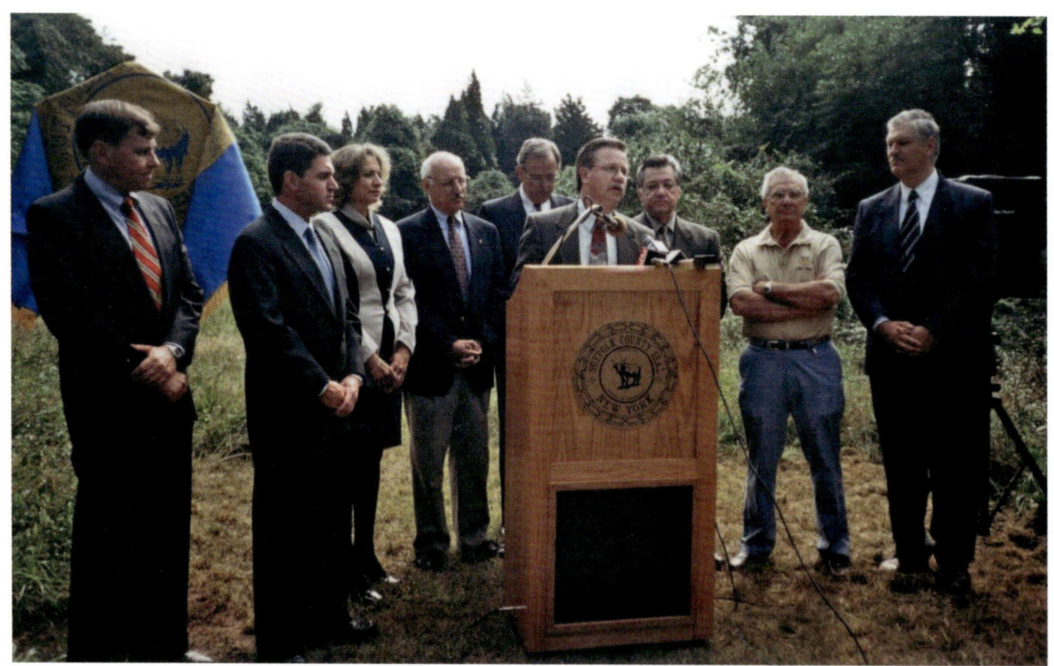

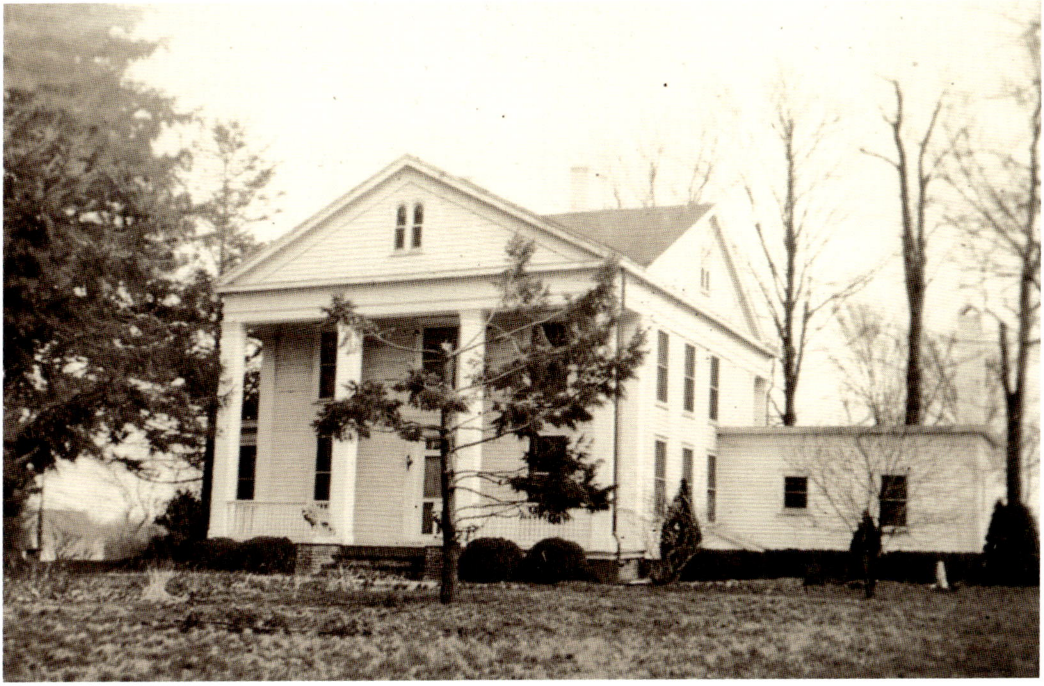

VASSILAROS PROPERTY: Reverend Ezra King, a Presbyterian minister, had this house built in 1841 when he married Eliza Helme of Miller's Place. The property bordered North Country and Woodhull Landing Roads. In 1943 John Vassilaros purchased the property for a summer house. He and his family maintained the apple orchard and woodland. In 2010 the Vassilaros family sold the property to the Town for Brookhaven to be preserved as open space.

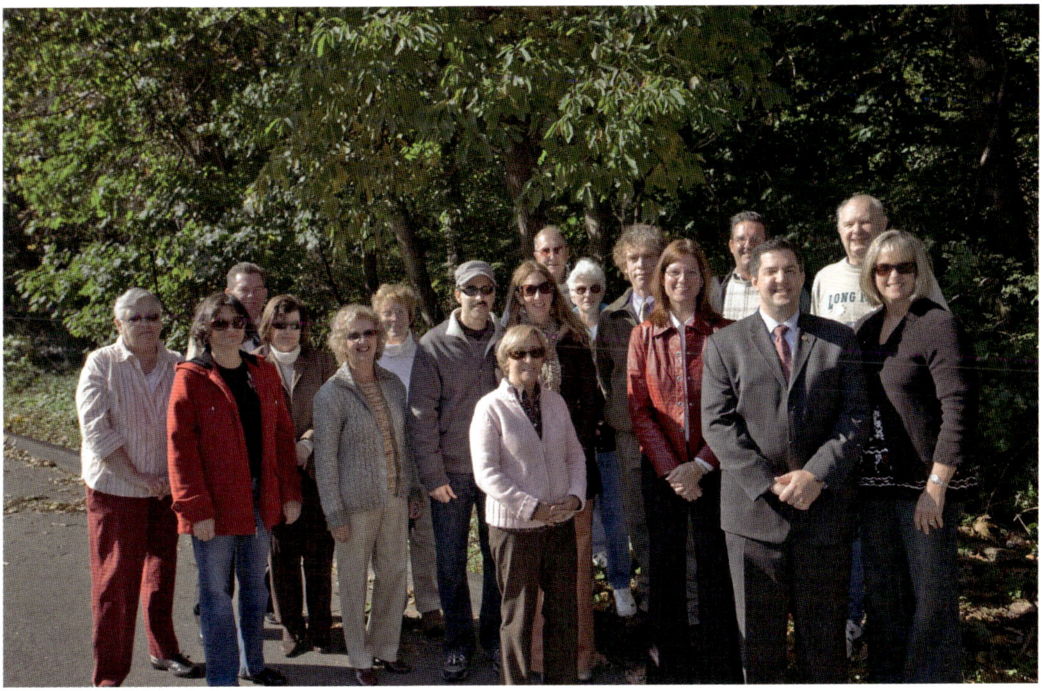

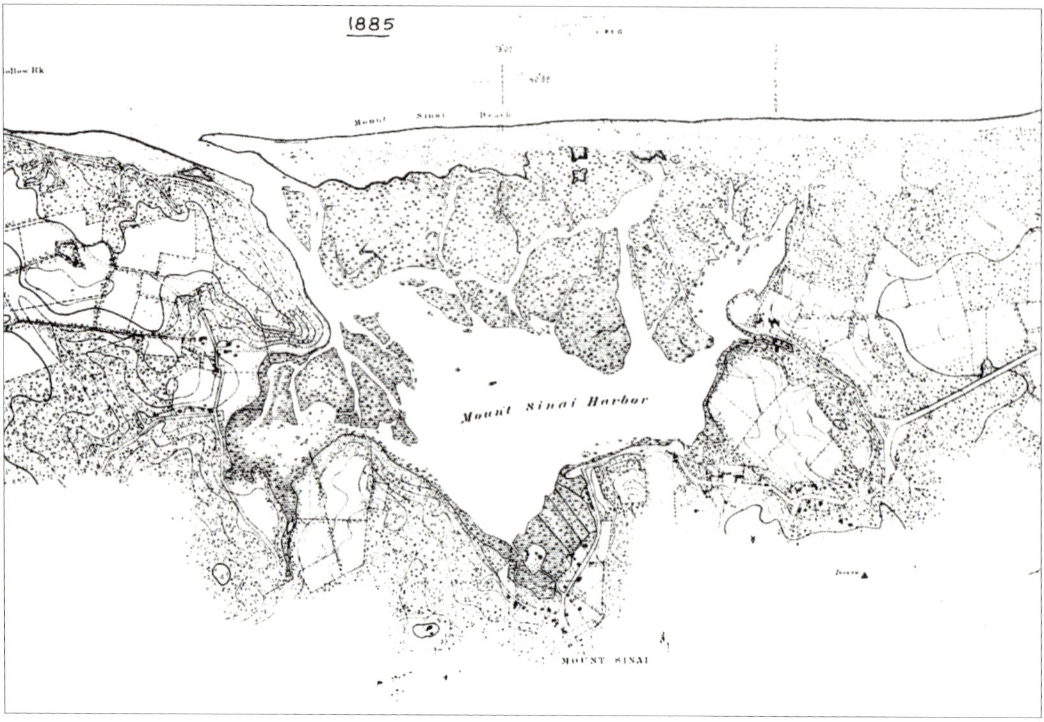

1885

Mount Sinai Harbor

MOUNT SINAI

HARBOR BEACH ROAD: The area along the road was once a spit of land separating the harbor from the Long Island Sound, continuing past Pipe Stave Hollow Road. The geodetic map of 1885 shows the beach area before development. On the harbor side were salt meadows and flats exposed at low tide, and on the Sound side stretches of sand and gravel, with areas covered by cedar trees, bayberry and beach plum shrubs. The meadows and beaches were subdivided in the 1600s and often stayed in the possession of the same families until the early 1900s when development began.

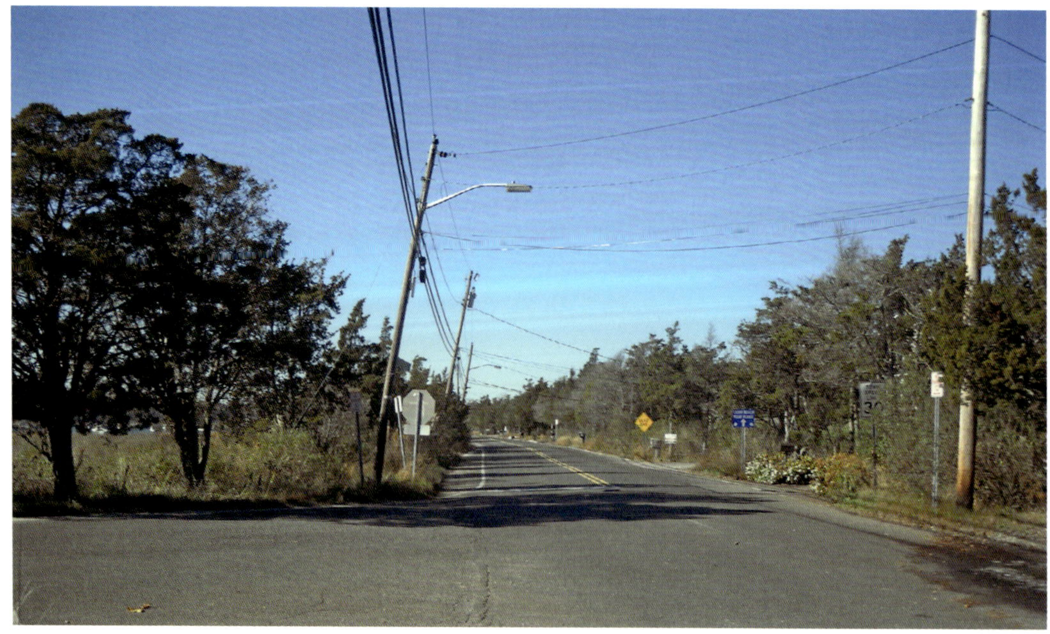

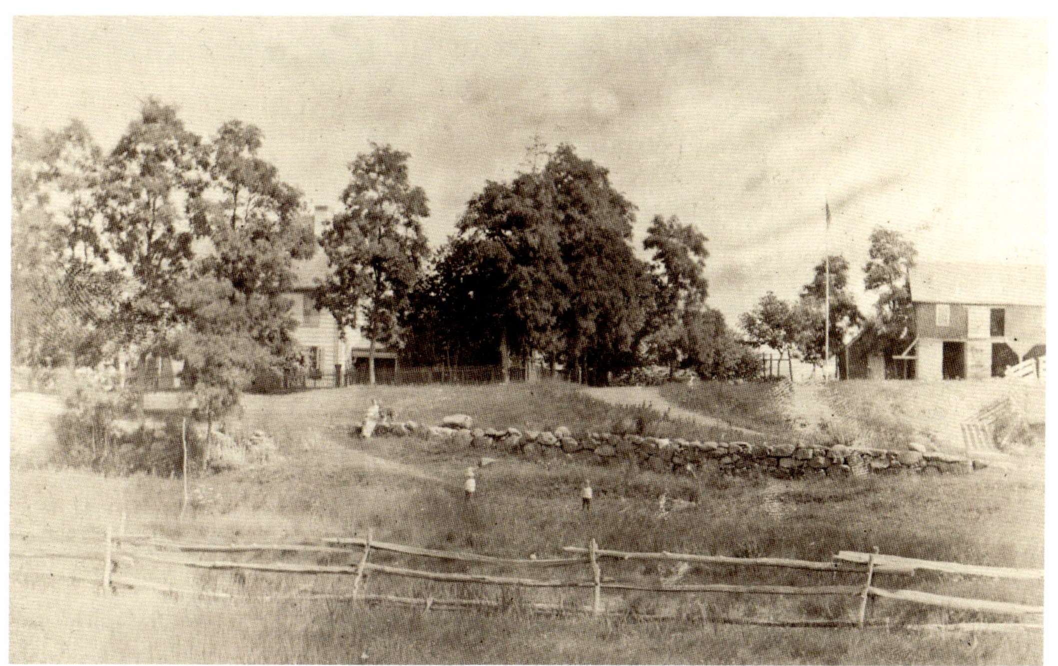

TALLMADGE RAID: Revolutionary War Major Benjamin Tallmadge landed with troops at an isolated area of Old Man's (now Mount Sinai) Harbor to conduct raids on the British Fort at the Manor of St. George and stored hay at Coram in November of 1781. Tallmadge would have seen this view – mostly empty space, the house in view replaced one there during the Revolutionary War, and an existing barn now hidden by trees. The Town of Brookhaven erected a sign about the raid on Harbor Beach Road, just west of Pipe Stave Hollow Road, and the Historical Society added a bow to commemorate the anniversary of the raid in 2014.

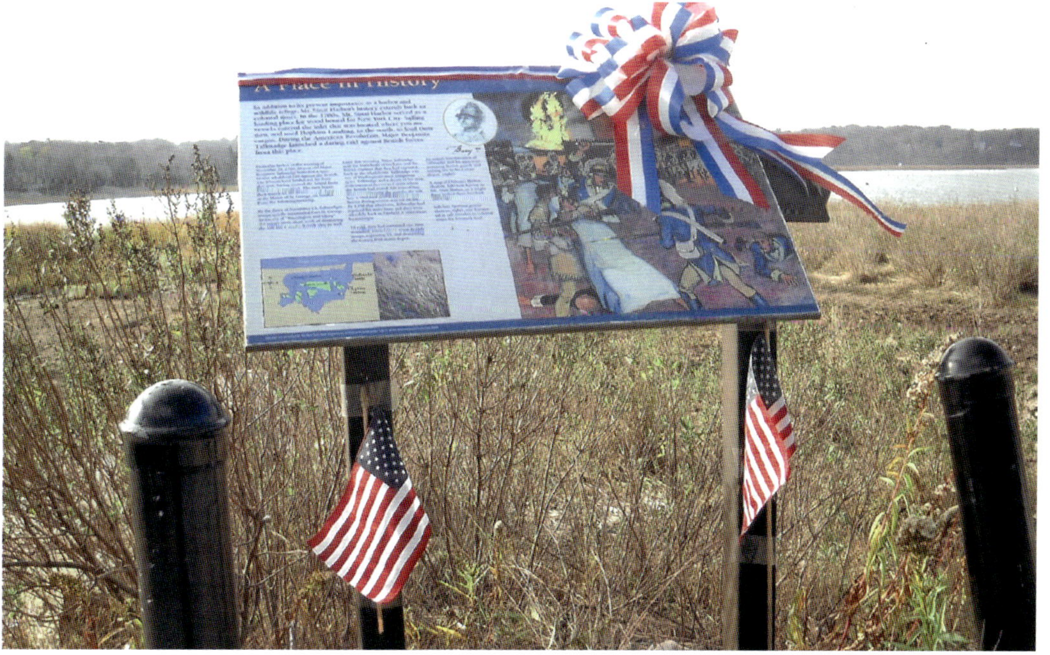

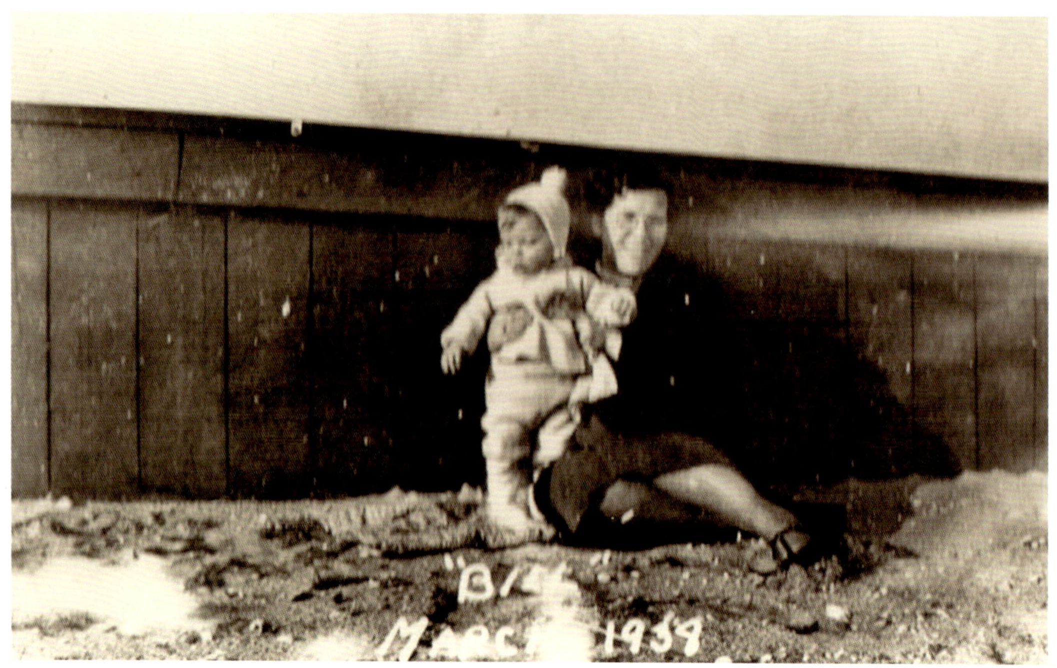

CEDAR BEACH: Established by the Town of Brookhaven to provide beach access to the residents of the Town, many changes have occurred over the years to stabilize and enlarge the beach as well as repair storm damage. In 1938 Bea Davis held her one-year old son William in front of the bulkhead at the beach. In 2014 the sand and gravel beach is at the top of the bulkhead and the parking lot is elevated.

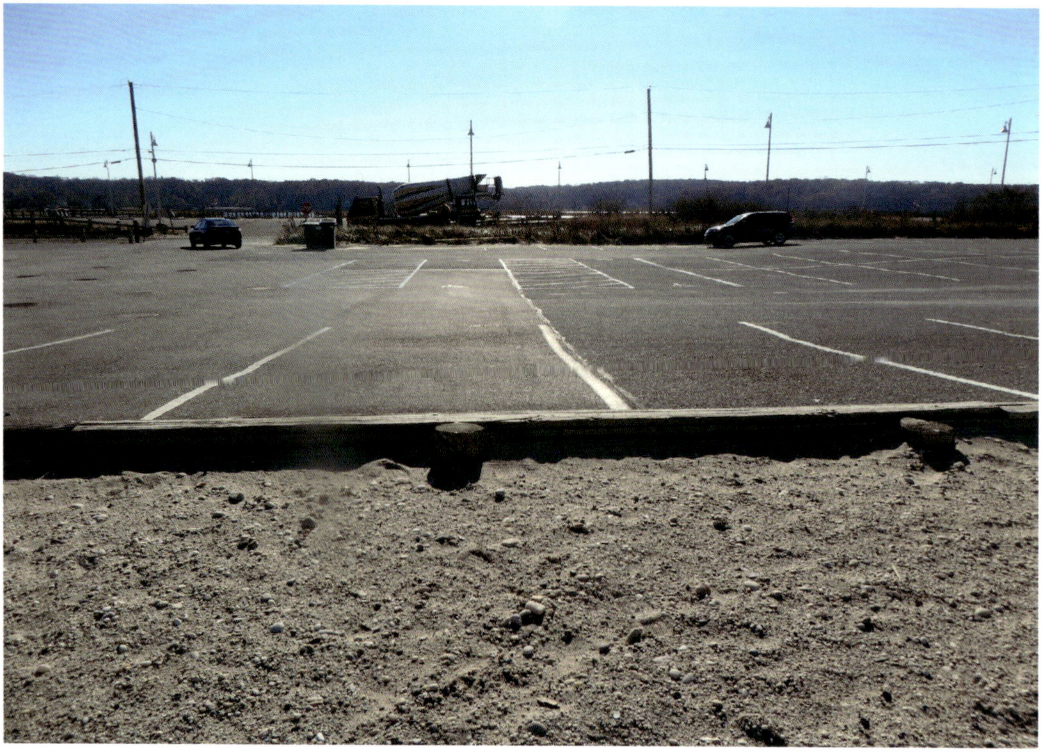

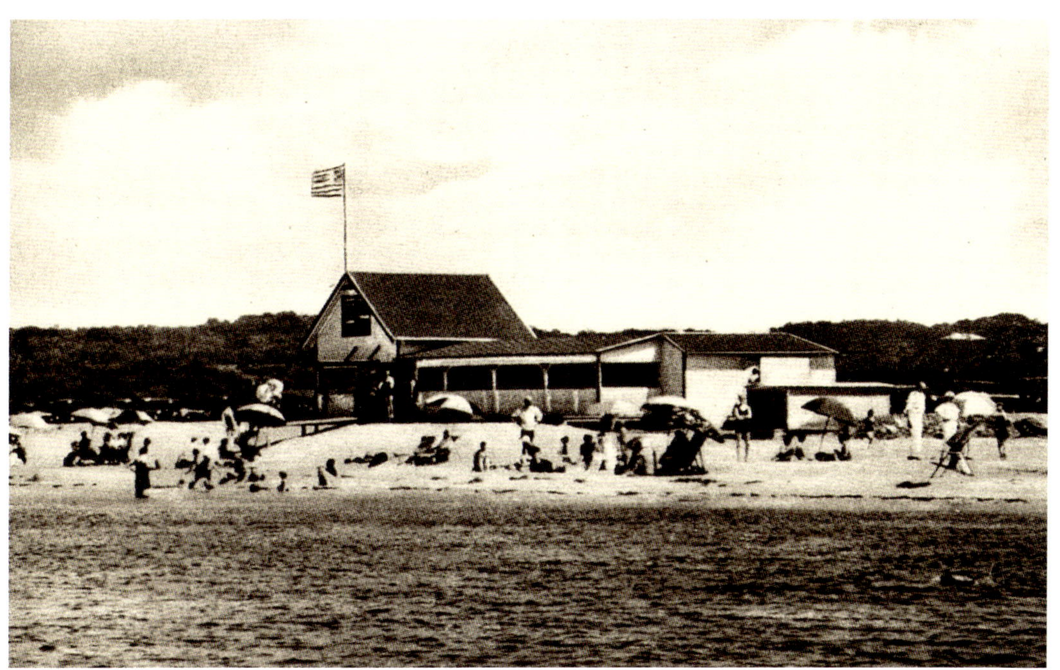

BEACH FACILITIES: A concession stand has been a part of Cedar Beach since the 1930s, offering a variety of foods and non-alcoholic beverages. The original building was destroyed in 1938, but rebuilt to include facilities such as bathrooms and bathhouses. This postcard shows the pavilion in the 1950s. Recently the Town has rented the concession to a full-service restaurant and bar which is open during the warm months.

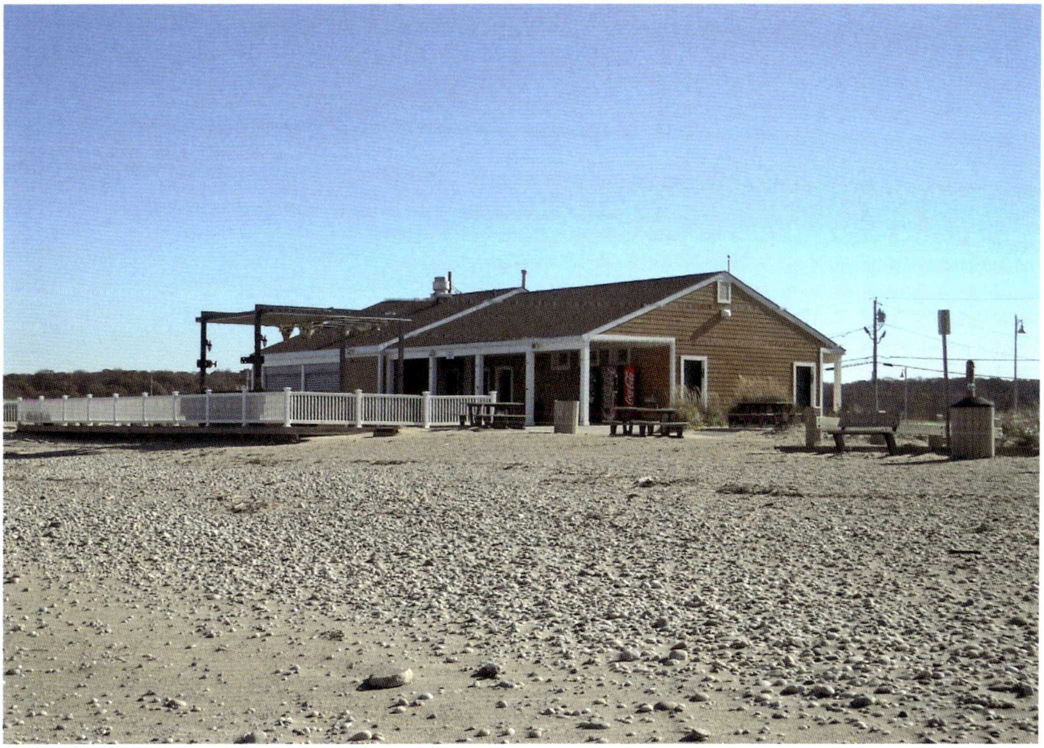

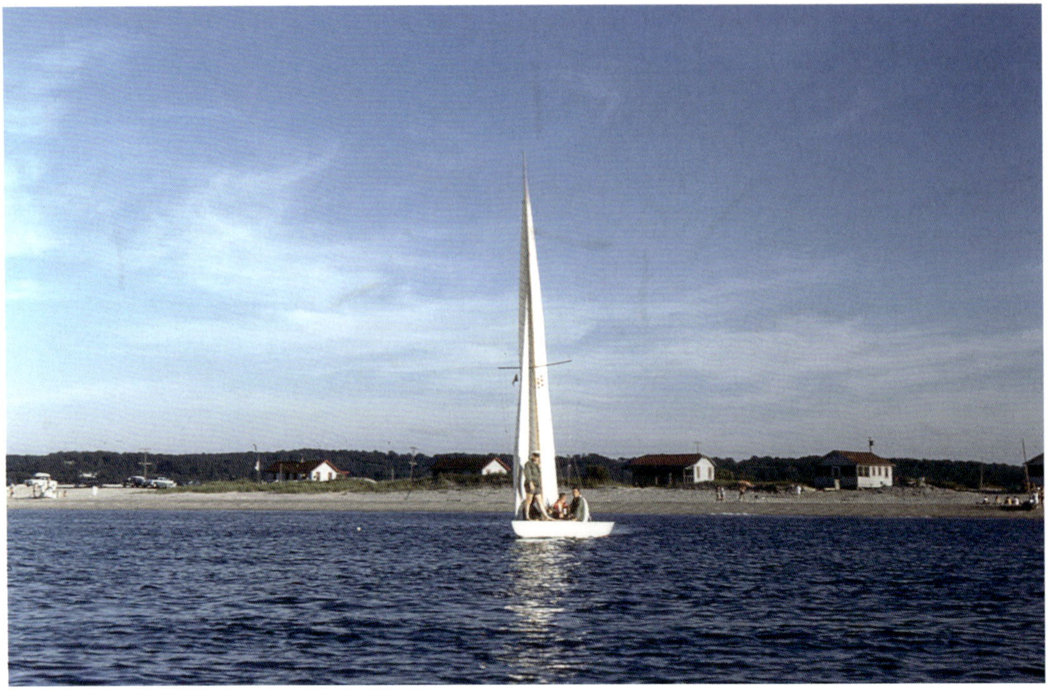

BATZ CABINS: Most private beach houses were to the east of Cedar Beach, but these five cottages owned by Mrs. Charlotte Batz were adjacent to, and west of the beach. She rented these out to various individuals and groups. Eventually the Town of Brookhaven took over the remaining cottages, removed them and added to the public beach. The beach itself was expanded, a basketball court and playground added, with the remainder of the property allowed to return to the wild.

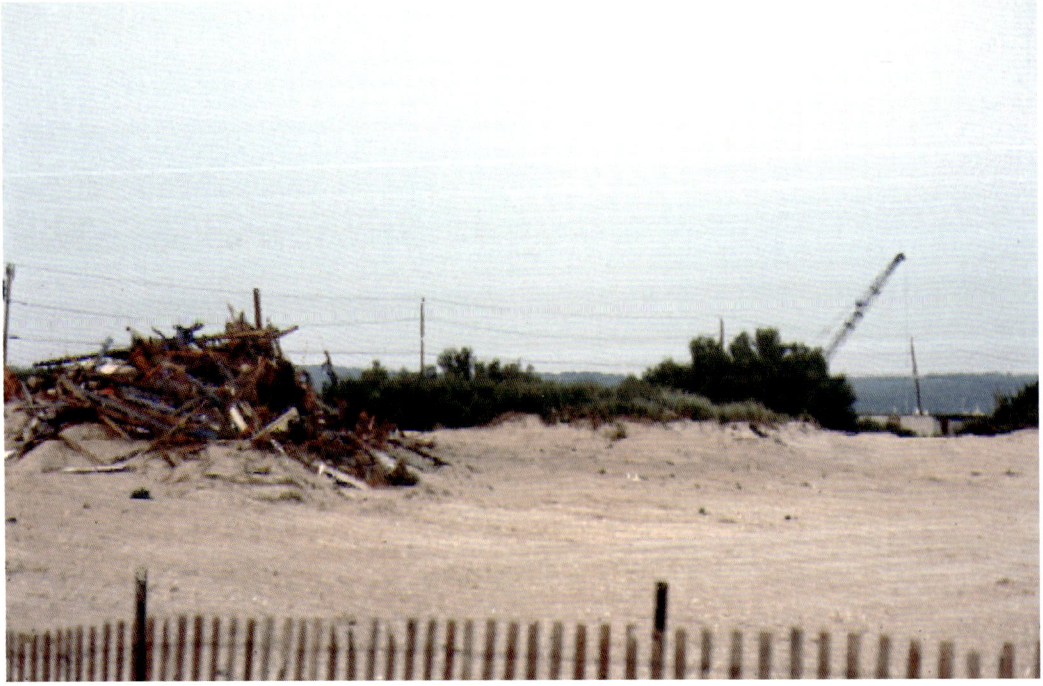

HAGERMAN PROPERTY: The family, from Rocky Point, purchased beach property from James C. Davis, the last owner of property given to his family in the 1600s. James Ray Hagerman built his house and moved his family in in 1961. Life on the beach was something few people could imagine possible at that time, and the water was a big part of family life. They housed pets of all varieties, including a burro, monkey, and dogs. Once the Town of Brookhaven obtained the property the house became the Marine Environmental Stewardship Center. Deterioration of the building led to its closure, but descendant Randy Hagerman has been restoring it.

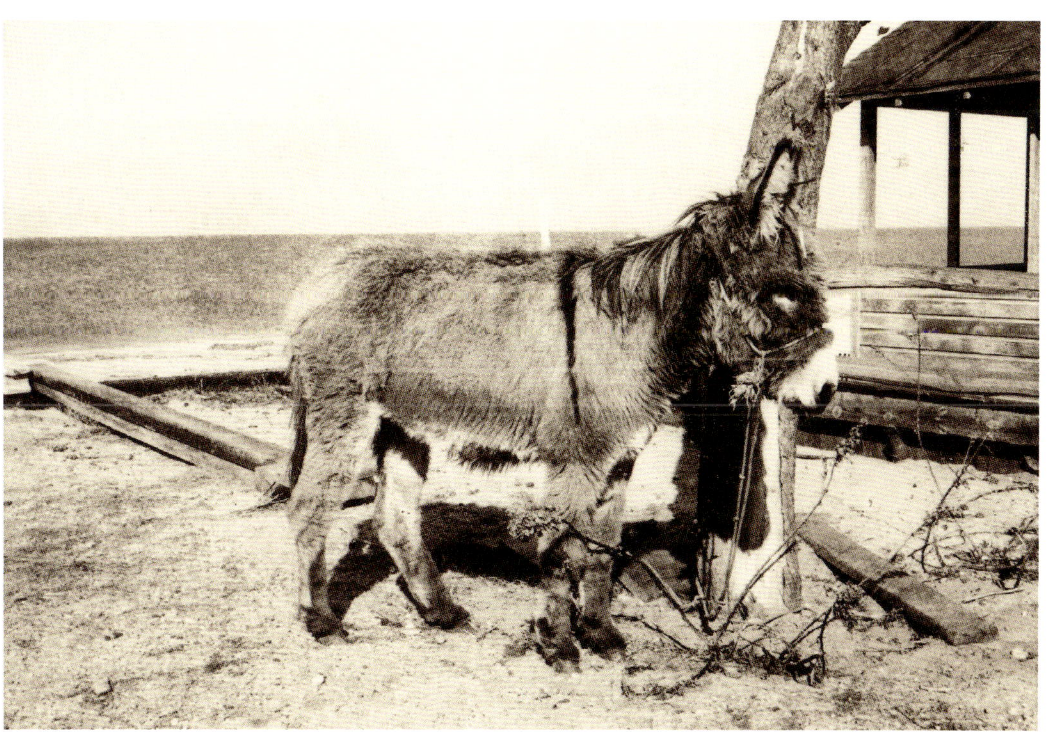

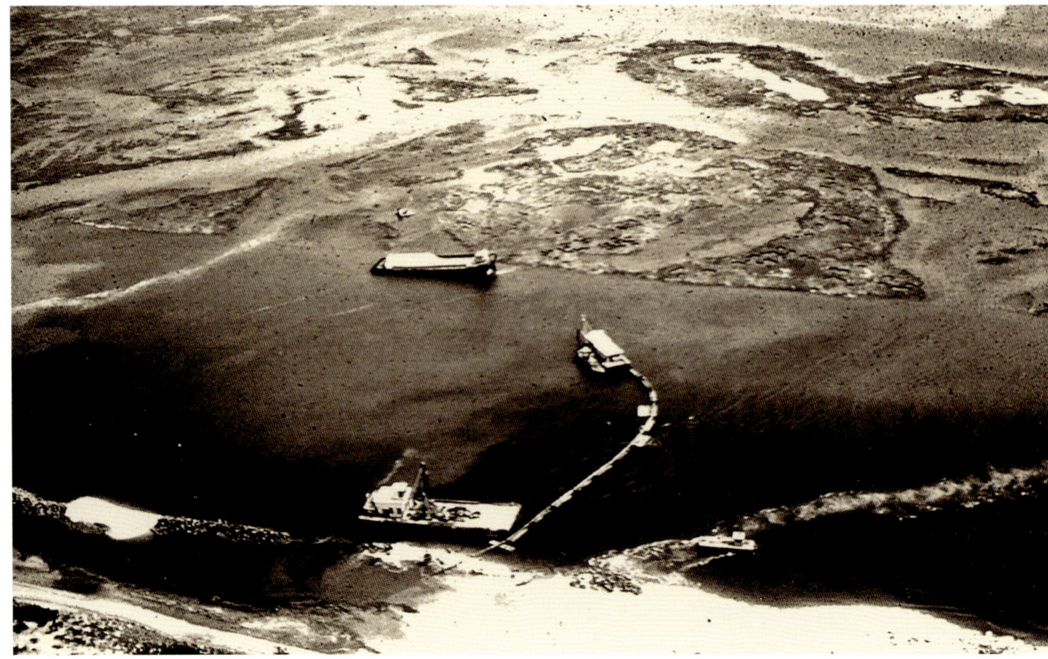

SAND MINING: Mount Sinai Harbor has been mined periodically since 1900, and in the 1950s a dredging project was started directly behind the beach along the north side of the harbor. The dredge removed marshland and mud flats creating a channel which would remain navigable during any tide. This highly controversial project extended the channel from the harbor entrance nearly to Pipe Stave Hollow Road. The creation of the channel allowed the Town to add launching ramps and put in floating docks for the ever growing population of boat owners. In the winter the Town removes most of the floating docks from the water.

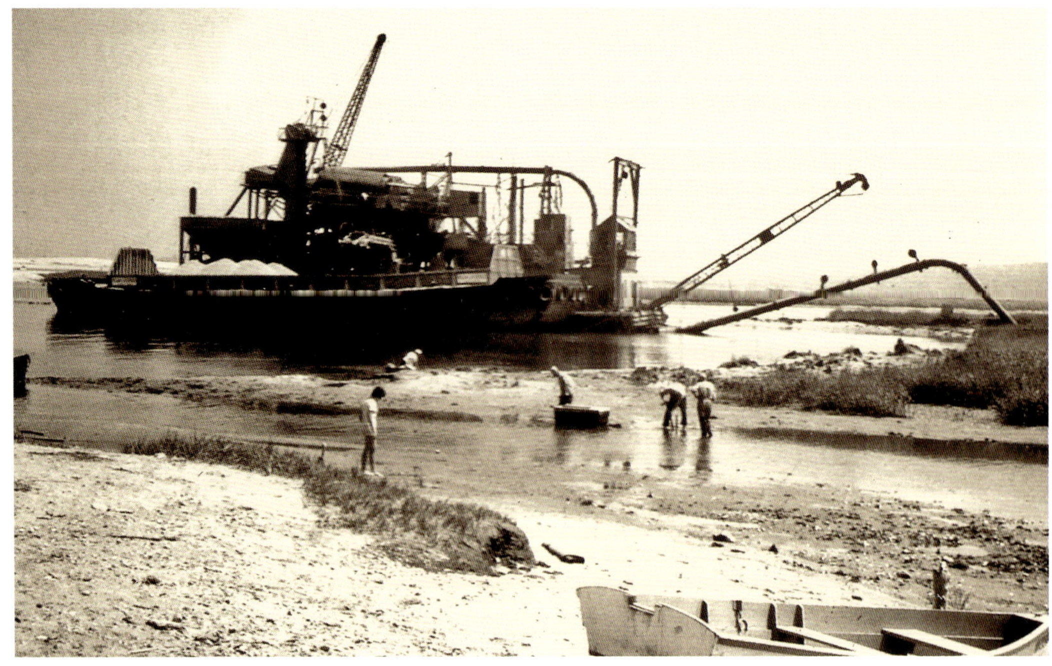

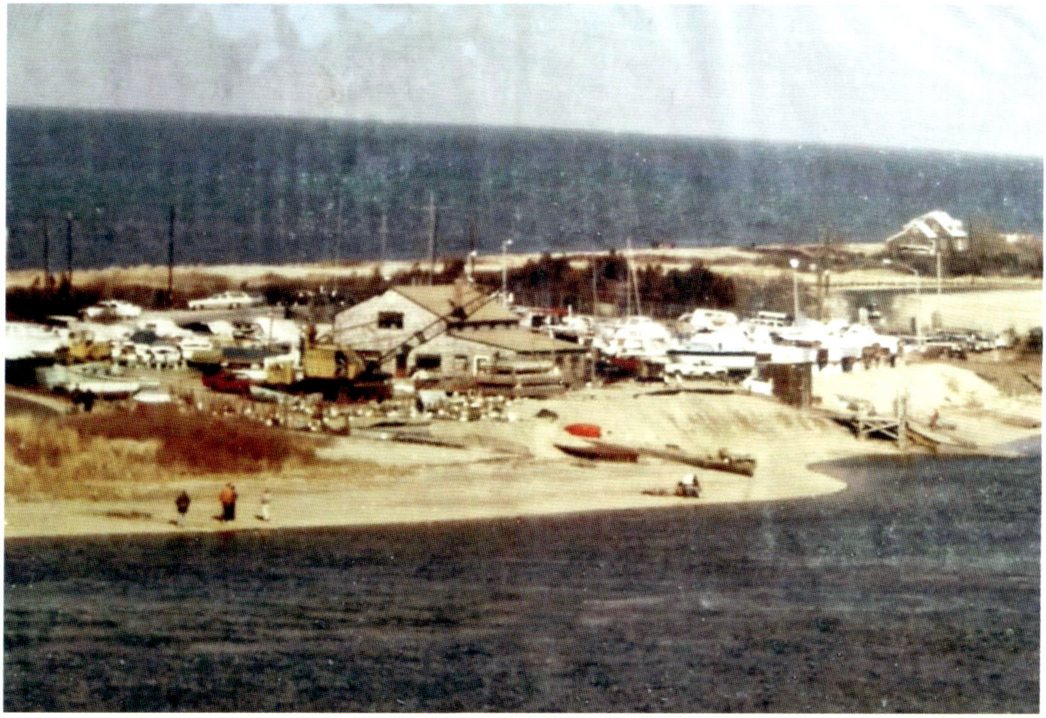

RALPH'S FISHING STATION: Moved to the north side of Mount Sinai Harbor in 1977, having been established in 1961, allowing access to boats of all sizes regardless of the tide. Ralph's has changed to meet the growing needs of the boating community. The aerial shot above shows the fishing station shortly after the move. During the winter months the building is totally obscured by the many boats in storage.

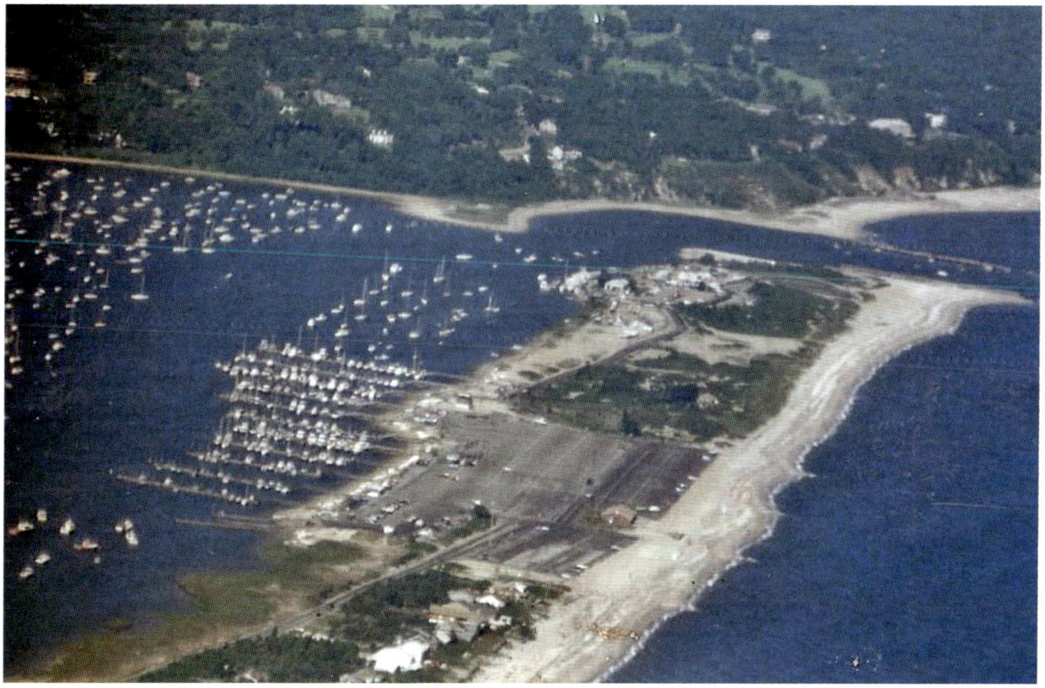

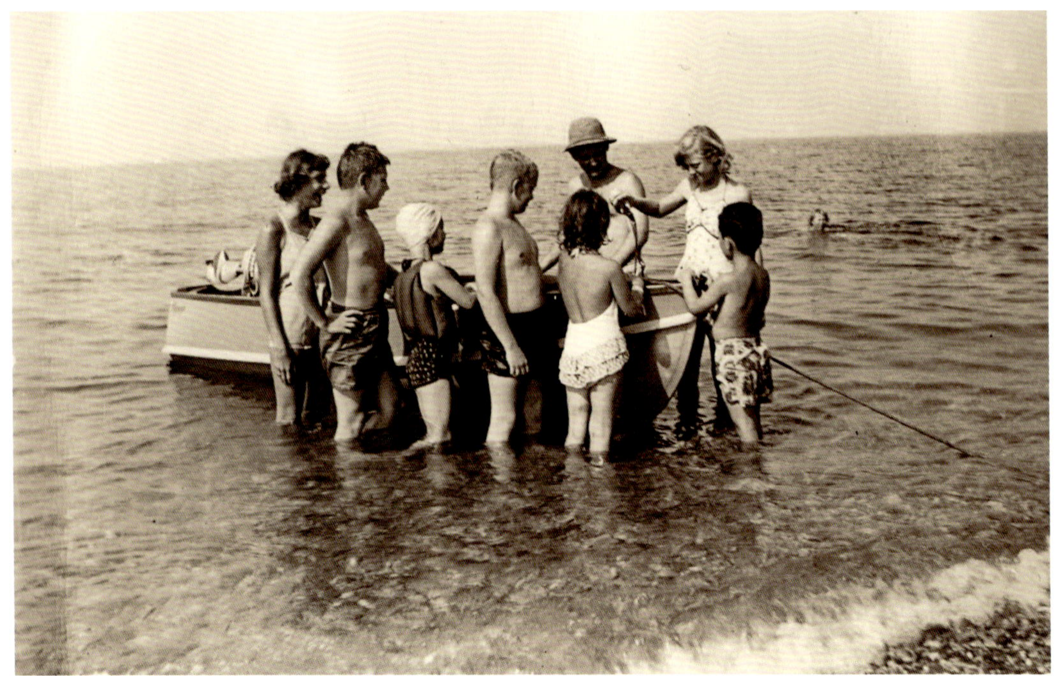

CRYSTAL BROOK PARK: Land along the Sound side of the spit of land was developed beginning in the early 1900s. Individuals and organizations purchased beach properties of varying sizes for recreational use. The communities of Crystal Brook Park, Mount Sinai, and Cedar Beach Manor, Miller Place all acquired beach front property during this period. Above, Margaret Doscher "christens" the boat while her brother Klaus, friends Sally and Ron Rienisch and others observe. Crystal Brook Park maintains a private beach next to Town-owned Cedar Beach, and the bathhouses which once stood on the property are gone.

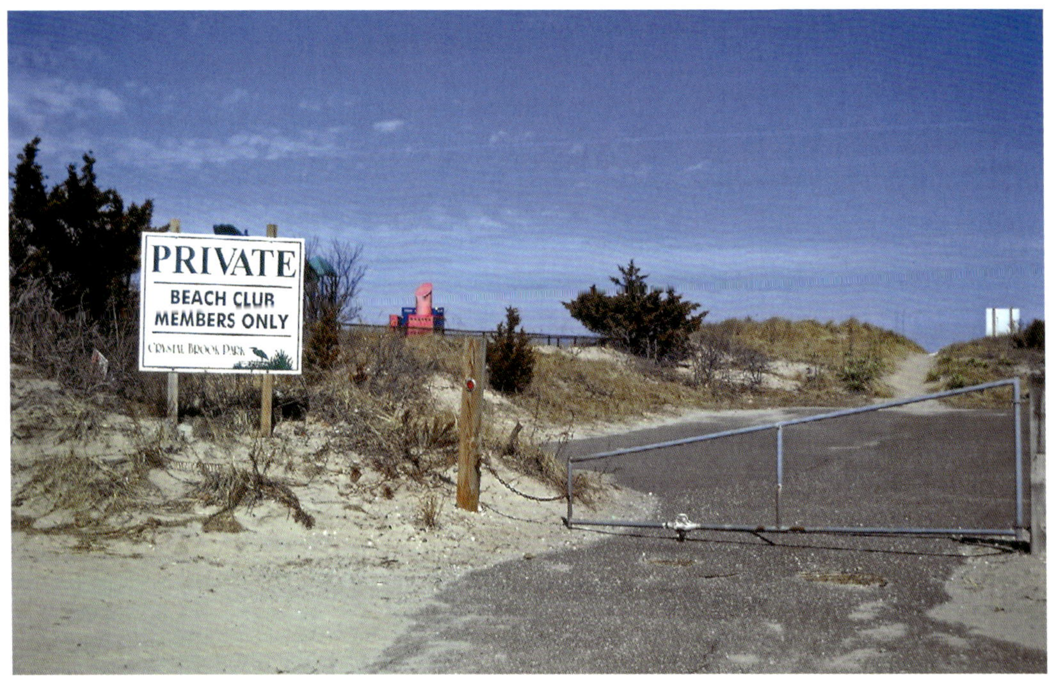

Chapter 5

Commercial Activities over Time

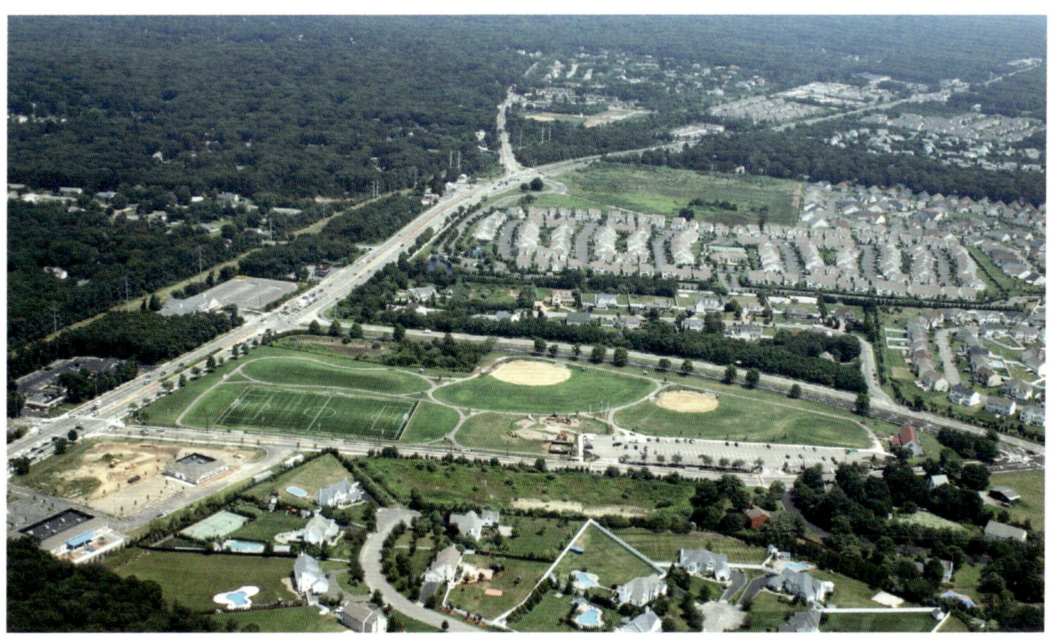

Aerial view of Wedge: This 2009 view looks east toward Miller Place, and includes housing developments and a view of the Rose Caracappa Senior Citizens Cultural and Wellness Center on the north side of Route 25A, just before Echo Avenue.

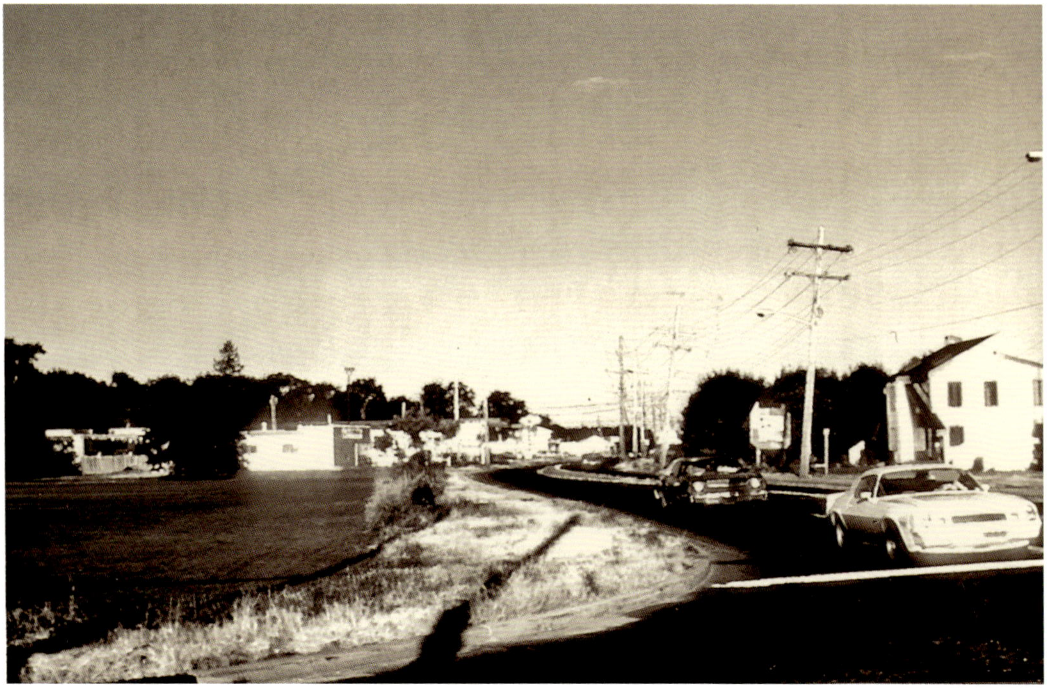

McGovern sod farm: This 1976 view of New York State Route 25A was taken at the intersection of Mount Sinai/Coram Road. The McGovern Sod Farm is on the left, with the local printing shop at the edge of the grassy area. An office building can be seen on the right side of the picture. This photo was taken before the expansion of Route 25A to a four-lane highway in the 1990s, and complemented by a recent photo, showing the changes which have occurred at this location.

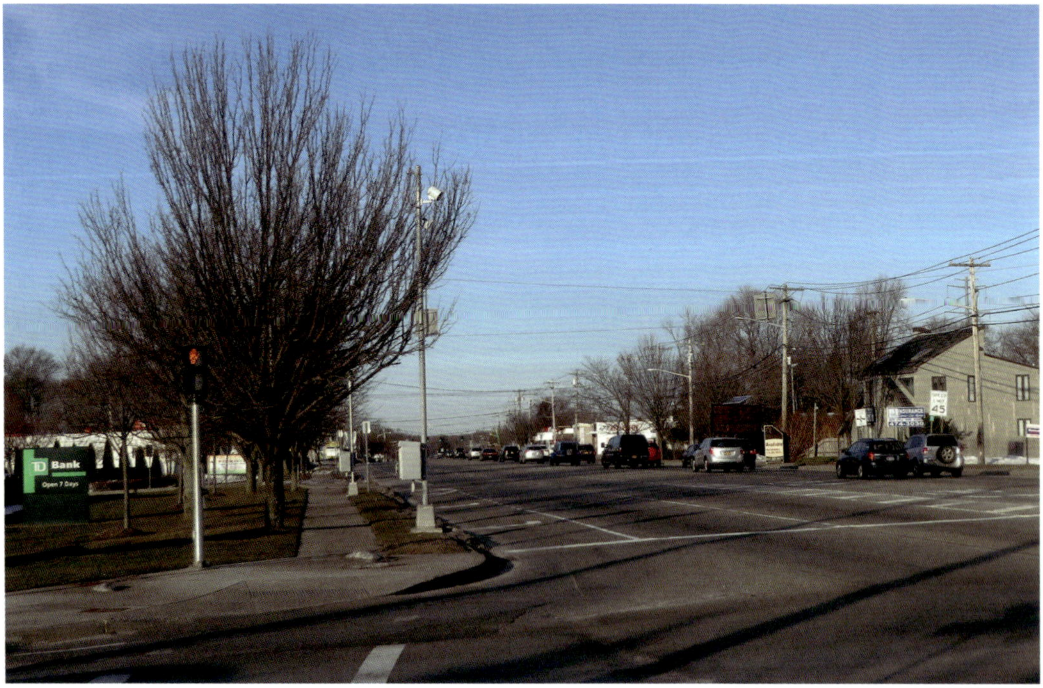

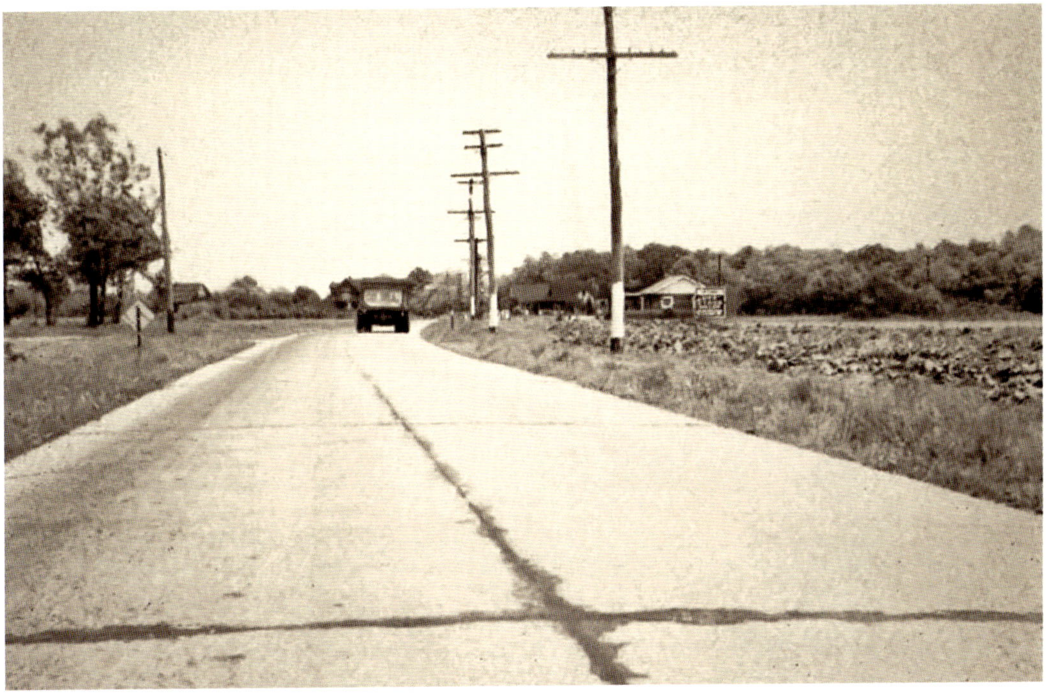

WYLDE ROAD: This May 1938 photo shows that William A. Davis has plowed up to the shoulder of Route 25A. A dump truck with the company name of Colonial is heading east. The sign on the right advertises log cabins available on Pipe Stave Hollow Road. The building just behind the sign was a log cabin and stood until the 1990s. There are three other buildings east of the log cabin, one of them is the present day office of Parkside Fuel.

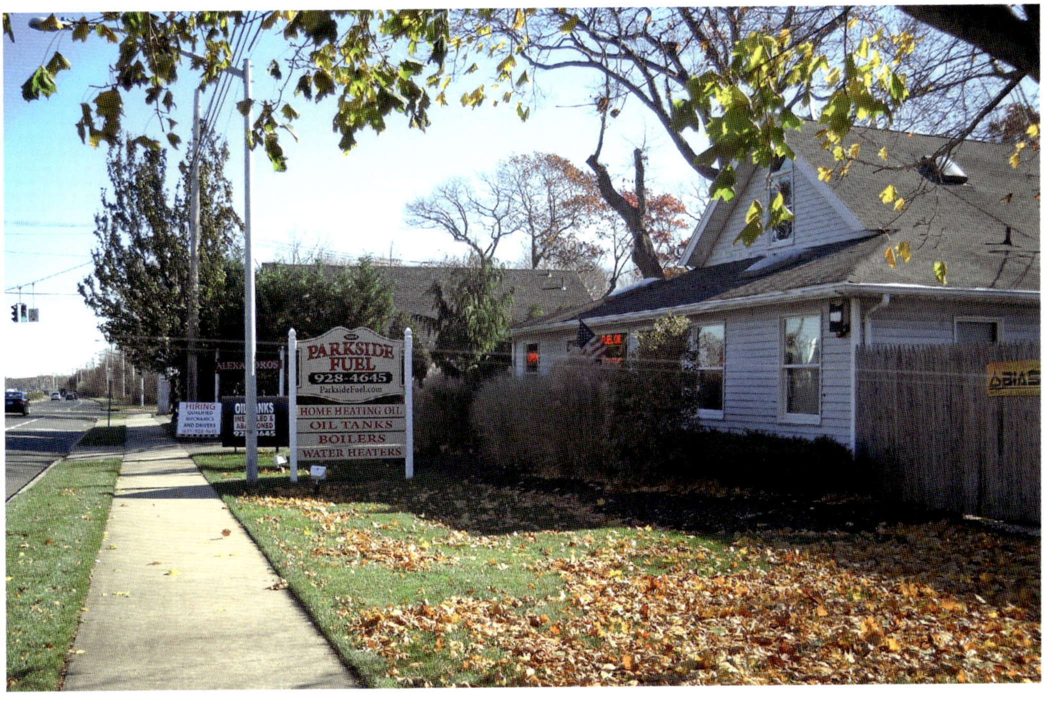

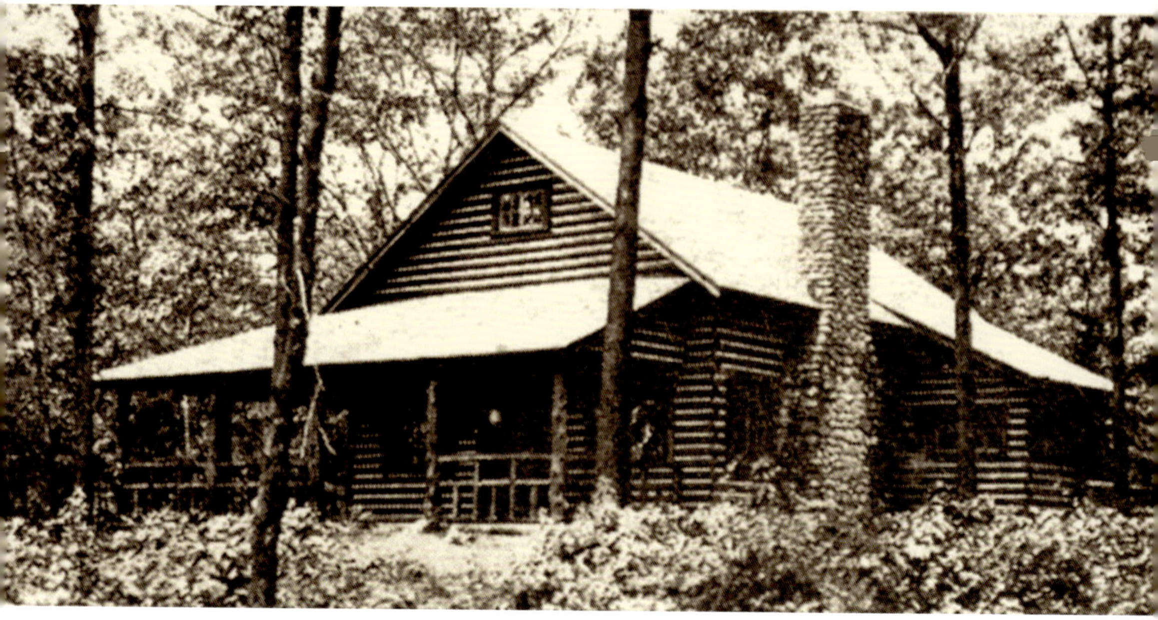

Captain Roman's Inn: In the 1930s Jack Heyser opened a real estate office on the corner of North Country and Pipe Stave Hollow Roads. His wife, Catherine, had a small Tea Room in another part of the building. By 1934 Peter Panagakos and his wife converted the building to a full scale restaurant and called it Captain Roman's Inn. The Savino family opened an Italian Restaurant called Savino's Hideaway in 1976 which operated continuously until 1999, and the family re-opened the restaurant in 2012 after renovations.

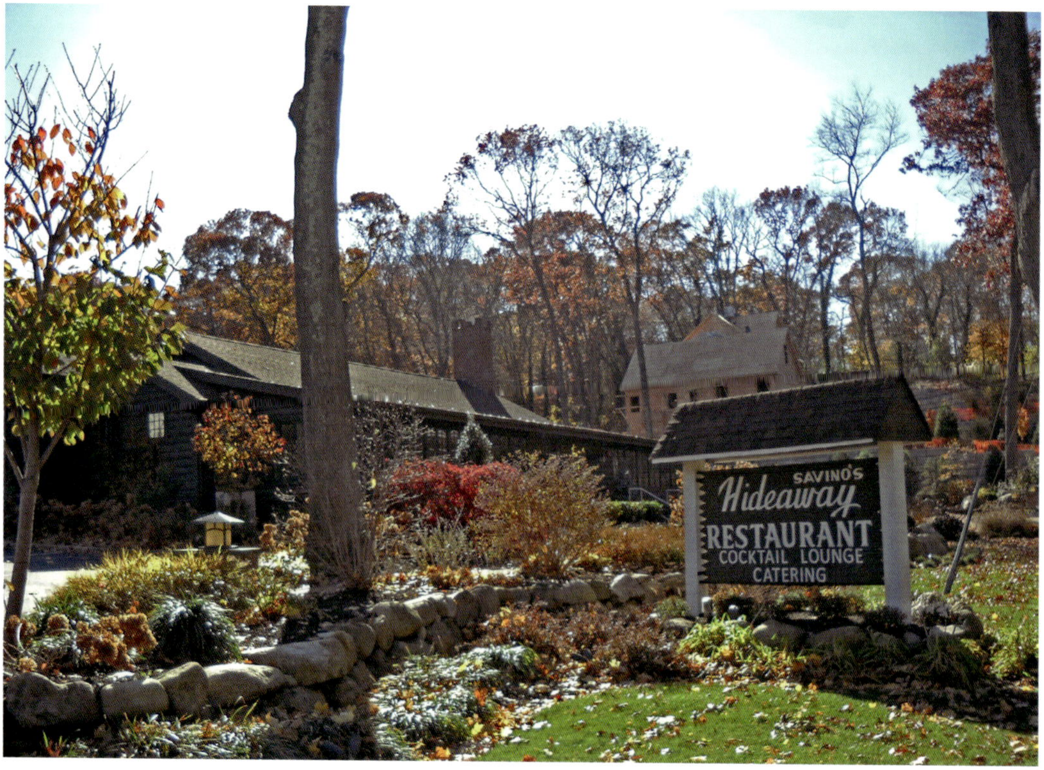

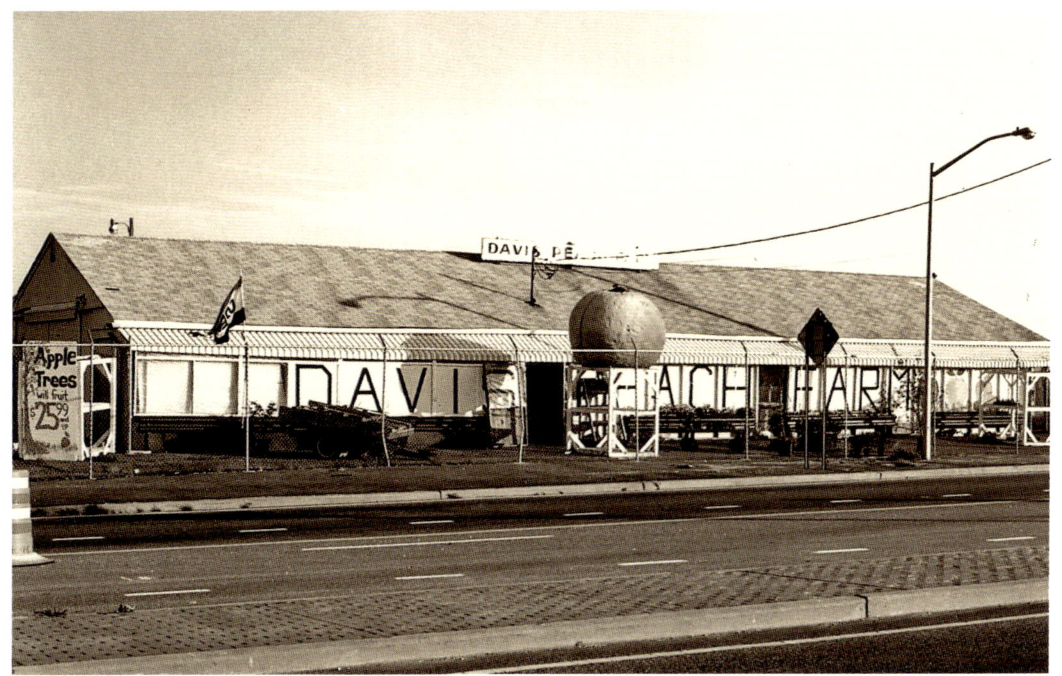

DAVIS PEACH FARM: A Mount Sinai institution, located on the east side of Mount Sinai/Coram Road south of County Road 83, since Archer Davis began growing and selling peaches in 1920s. The Davis family owned a considerable amount of property in Mount Sinai, including the land where housing developments on Peach Tree, Apple and Cherry Lanes were built. The roadside stand, located where the "Ranches" development is now, closed in 2000, and the orchard is slated for development as a Continuous Care Retirement Community.

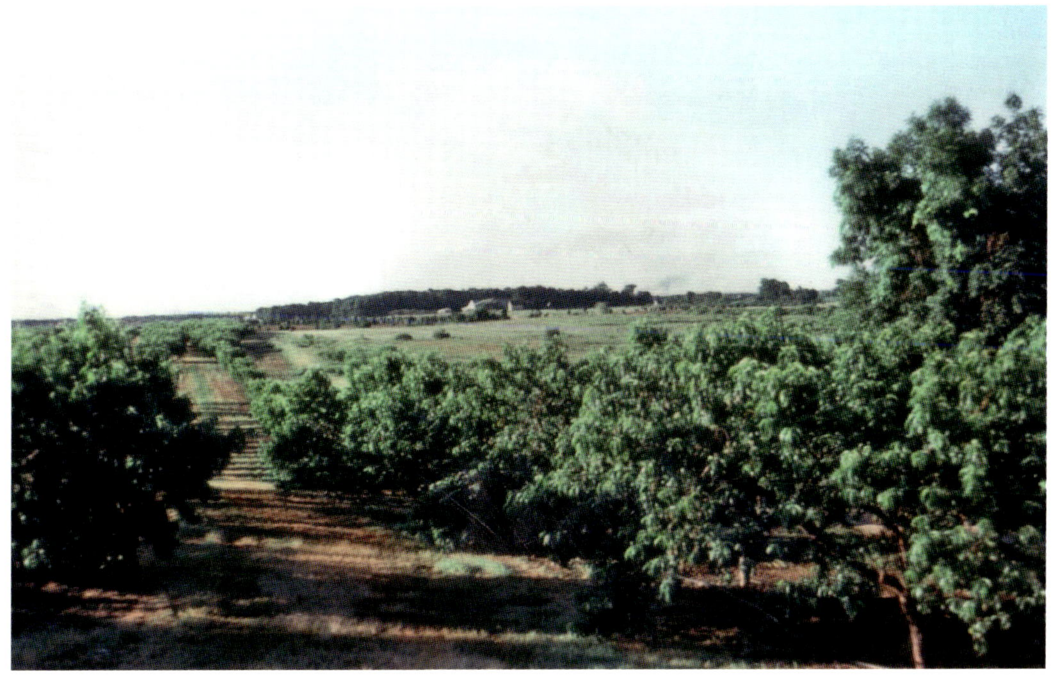

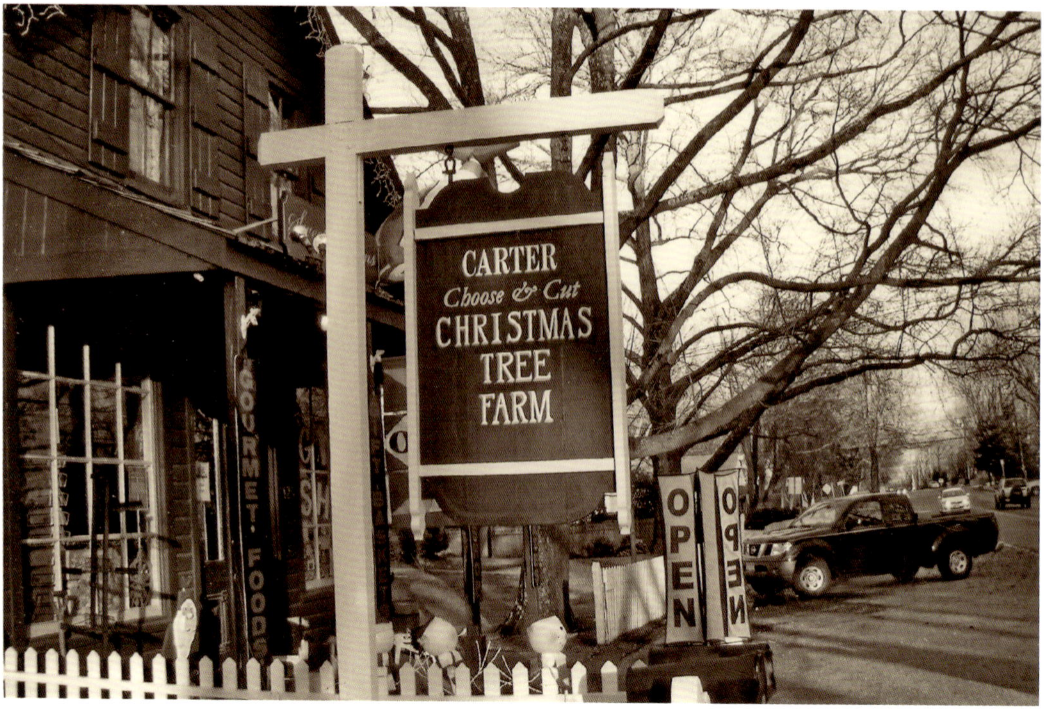

CARTER'S CHRISTMAS TREE SHOPPE: This Miller Place Christmas tree farm continues a family tradition as Ann Carter started and continues to run the business on property originally owned and farmed by her ancestor, Captain Alfred M. Davis. In 2015 it is the only local farm remaining north of Route 25A in either Miller Place or Mount Sinai.

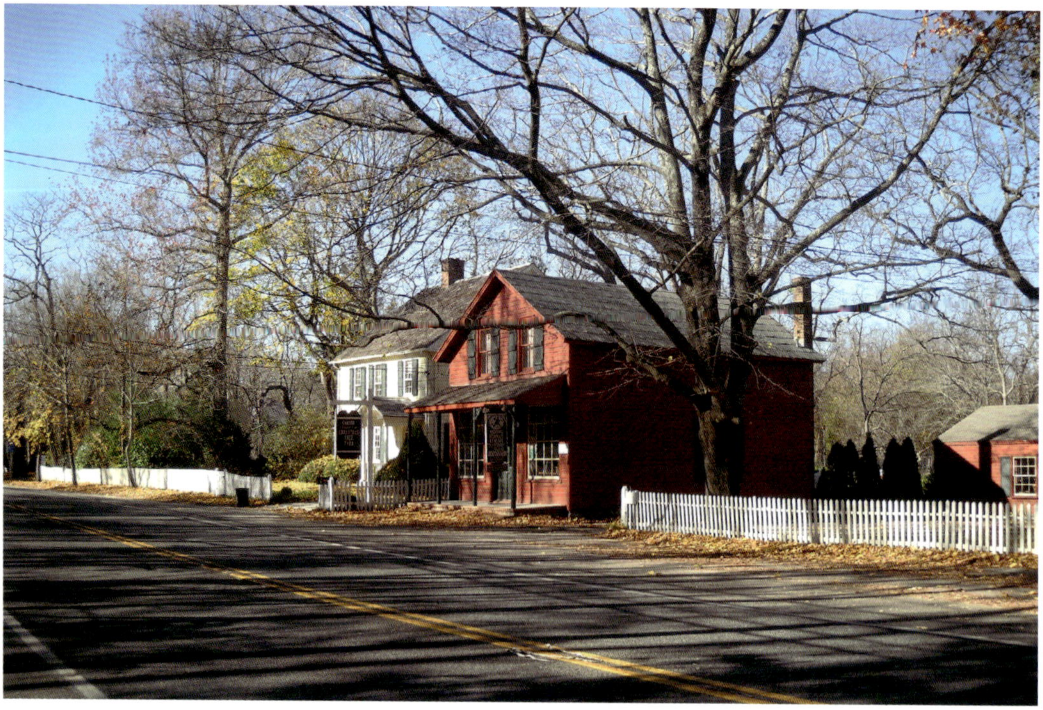

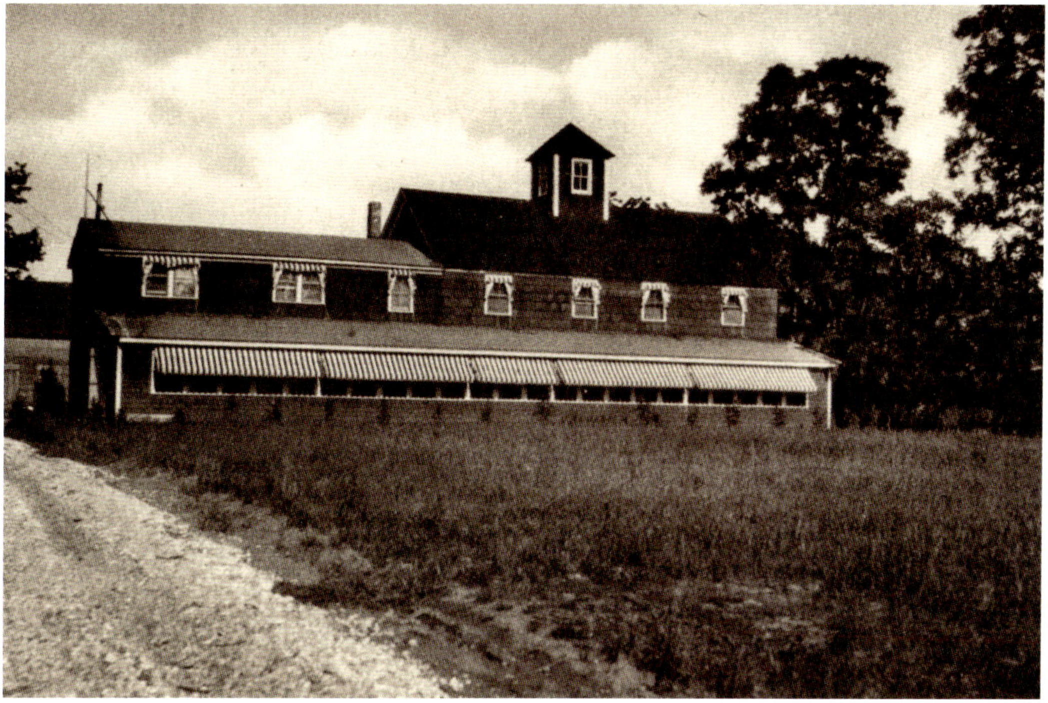

MILLER PLACE INN: Charles A Seifert purchased the Joseph Rowland farm, combining the barns, opening an inn and restaurant in the late 1920s. The inn has had several proprietors and in the 1960s was renamed the Dolphin Inn. It has been rechristened as the Miller Place Inn and is in use as a catering hall, specializing in weddings.

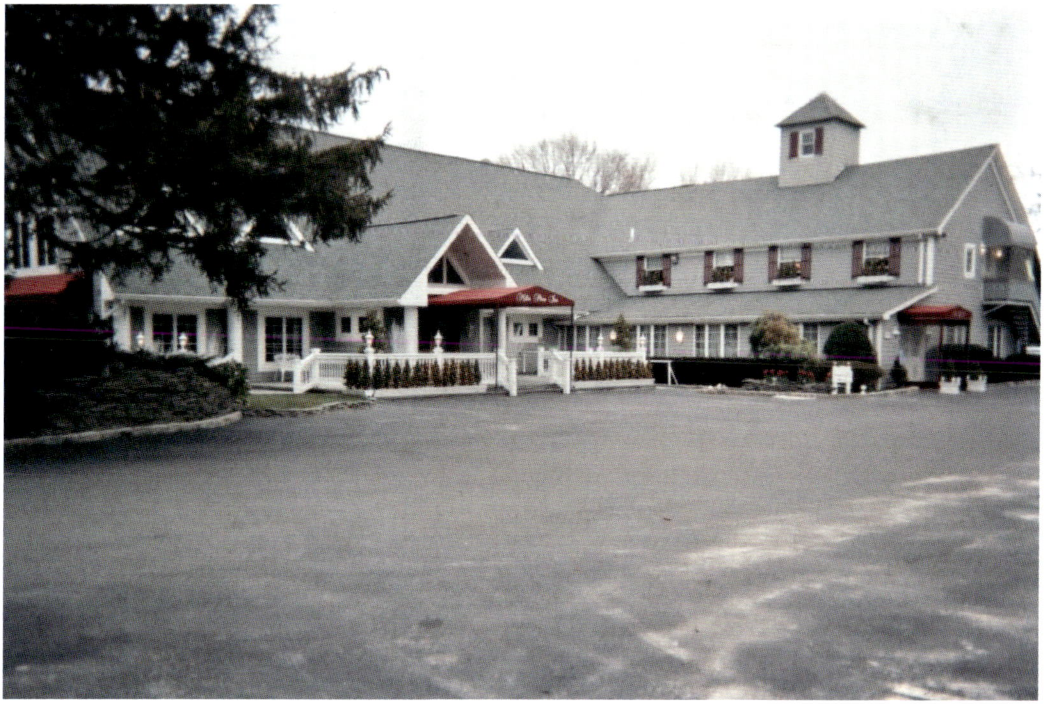

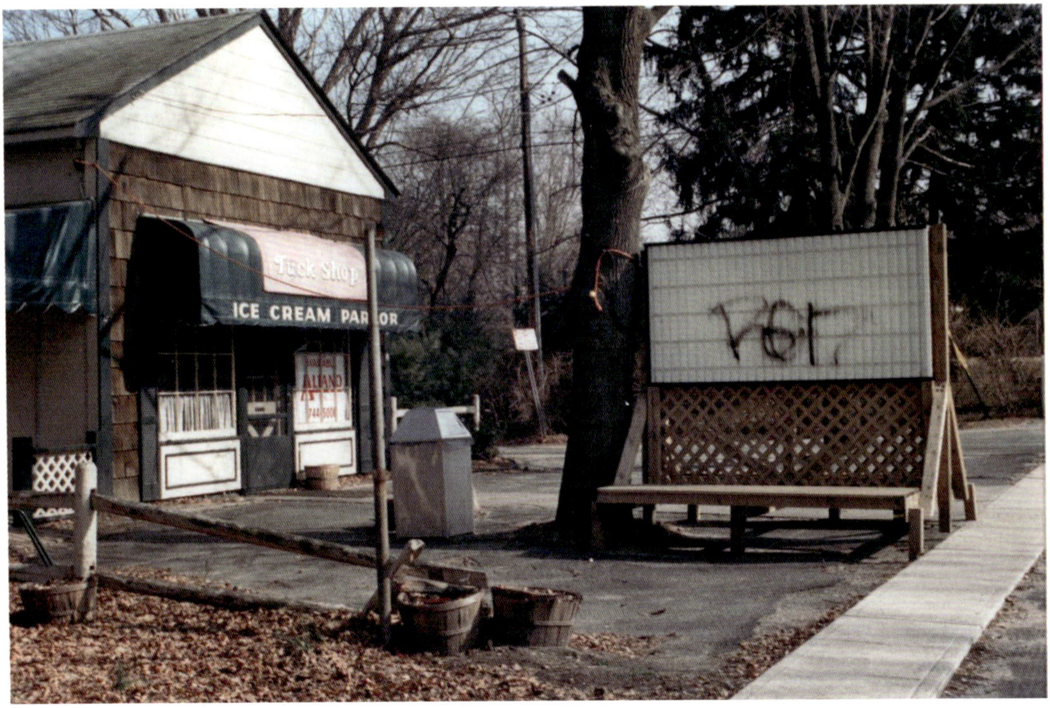

McNulty's Ice Cream Parlor: In the 1950s Stanley Kuczenski built a small commercial building on his property at the corner of North Country Road and Sylvan Lane. Tuck Inn Ice Cream Parlor was one of a succession of businesses that used the building. In 1992 Gail and Jim McNulty opened their Ice Cream Parlor. McNulty's has been a gathering spot for locals and out-of-town visitors since then.

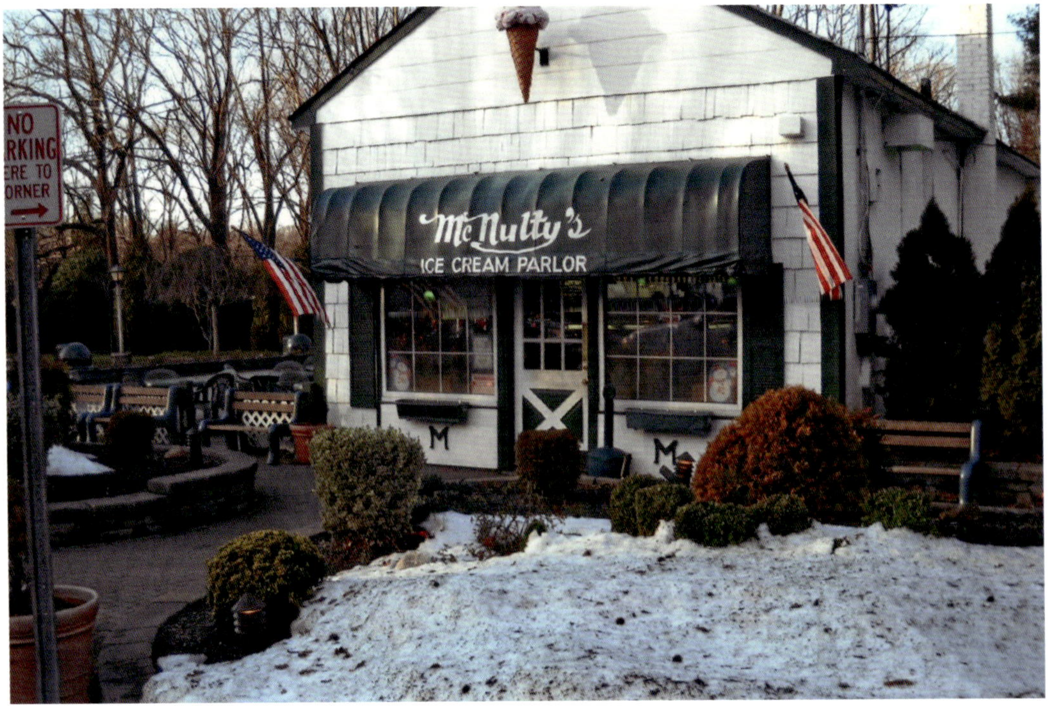

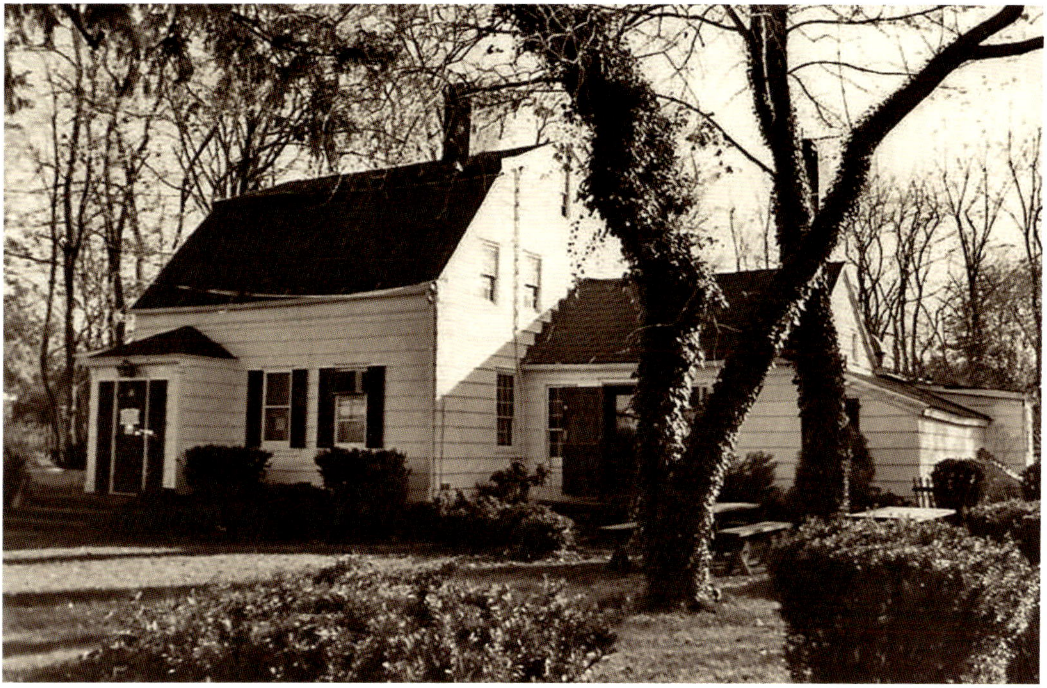

SECRET ROAD INN: The Daniel R Miller house was converted into this restaurant in the late 1950s. Elaine and Wesley Hoffman owned and operated a restaurant on this location from 1963 to 1967, when Guy L'Heureux became proprietor, and the unusual opportunity to taste French cuisine became popular with local residents as well as visitors. This site has seen a number of different restaurants, and was expanded in 1980. Orto's, serving Italian food, is operating at this location in 2015.

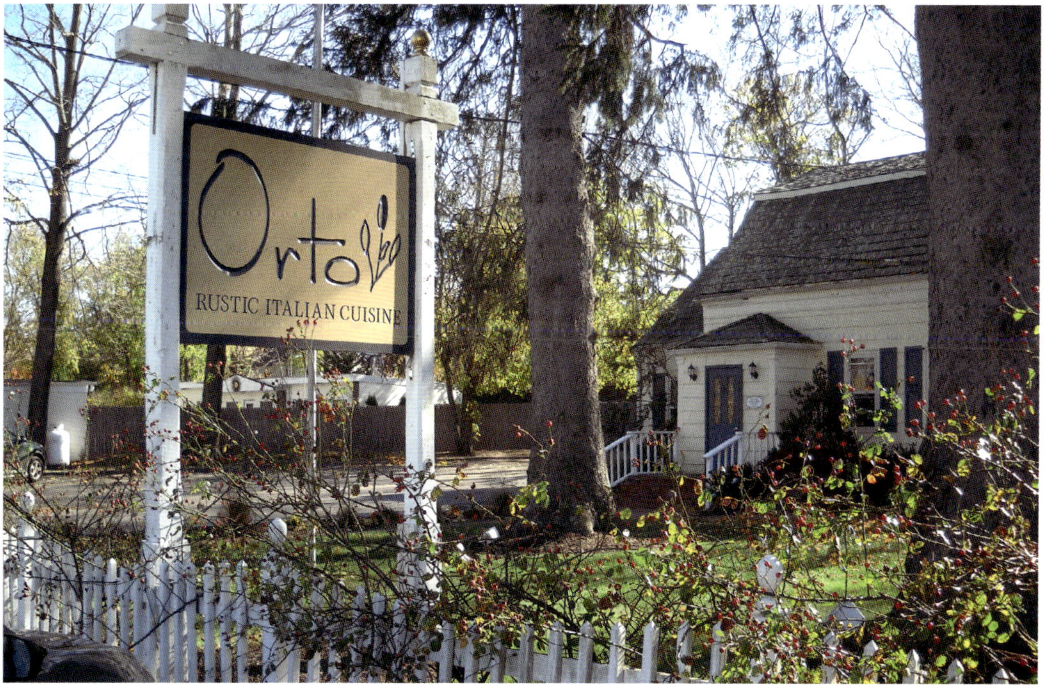

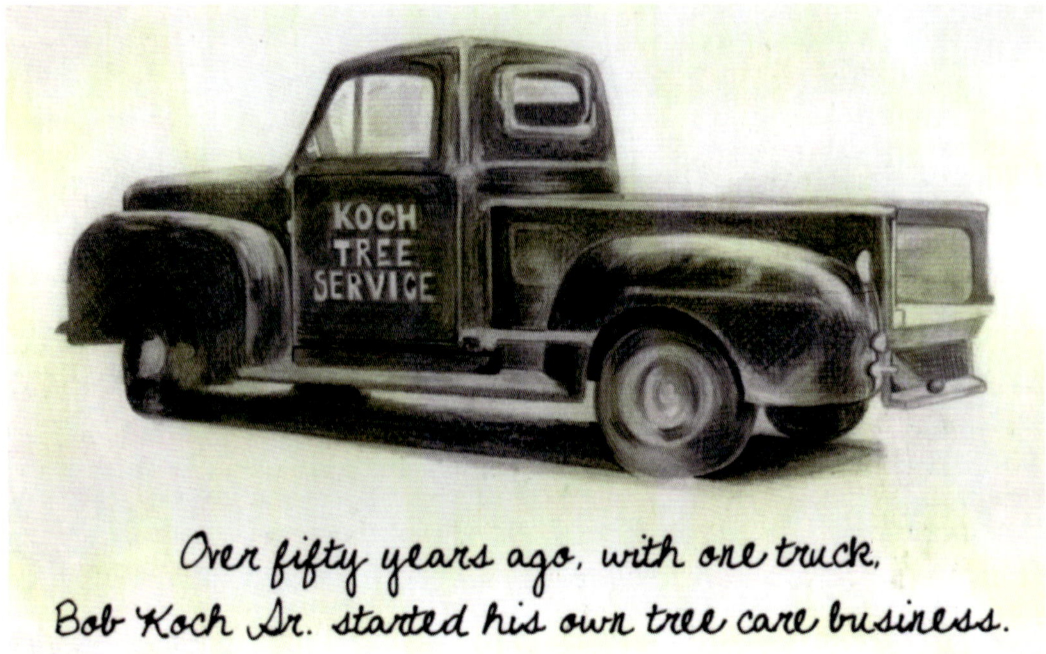

KOCH TREE SERVICES: Bob Koch Sr. moved his business to Mt. Sinai around 1960 after having established it in Setauket in 1958. While he performed all phases of tree work, Koch was never just interested in tree removal, but was considered a tree surgeon. Bob Koch Jr. took over the business in 1988-1989, having worked with his father since a young age. He has since become a certified arborist. As with other locations on Route 25A, when the road was widened the small house on the property was removed. Bob donates time to the Heritage Park to maintain and preserve the park.

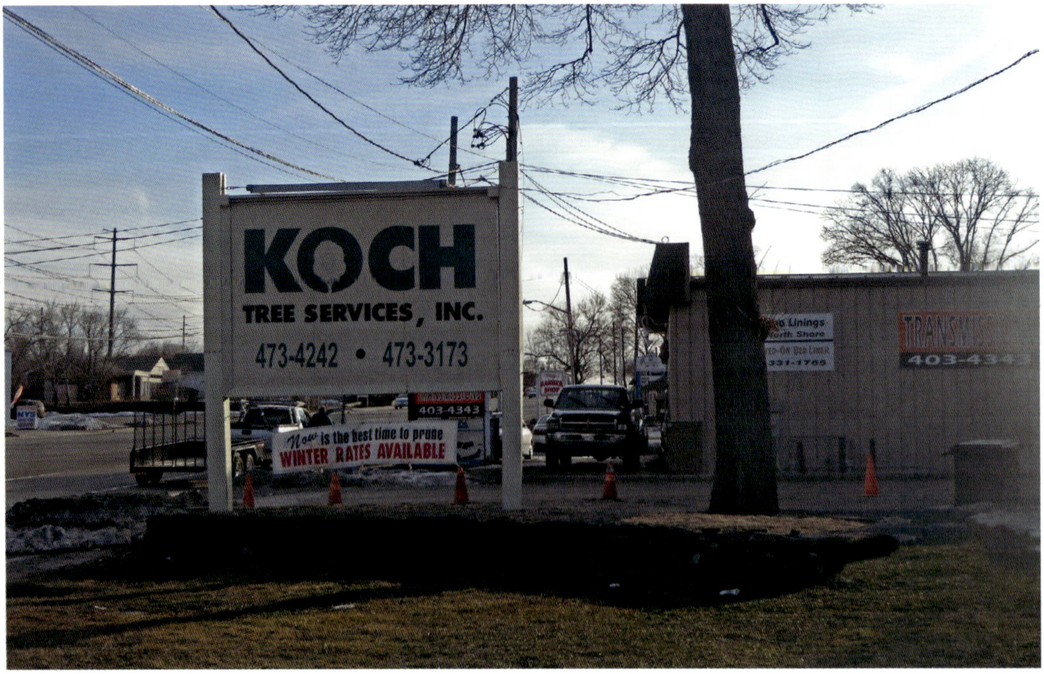

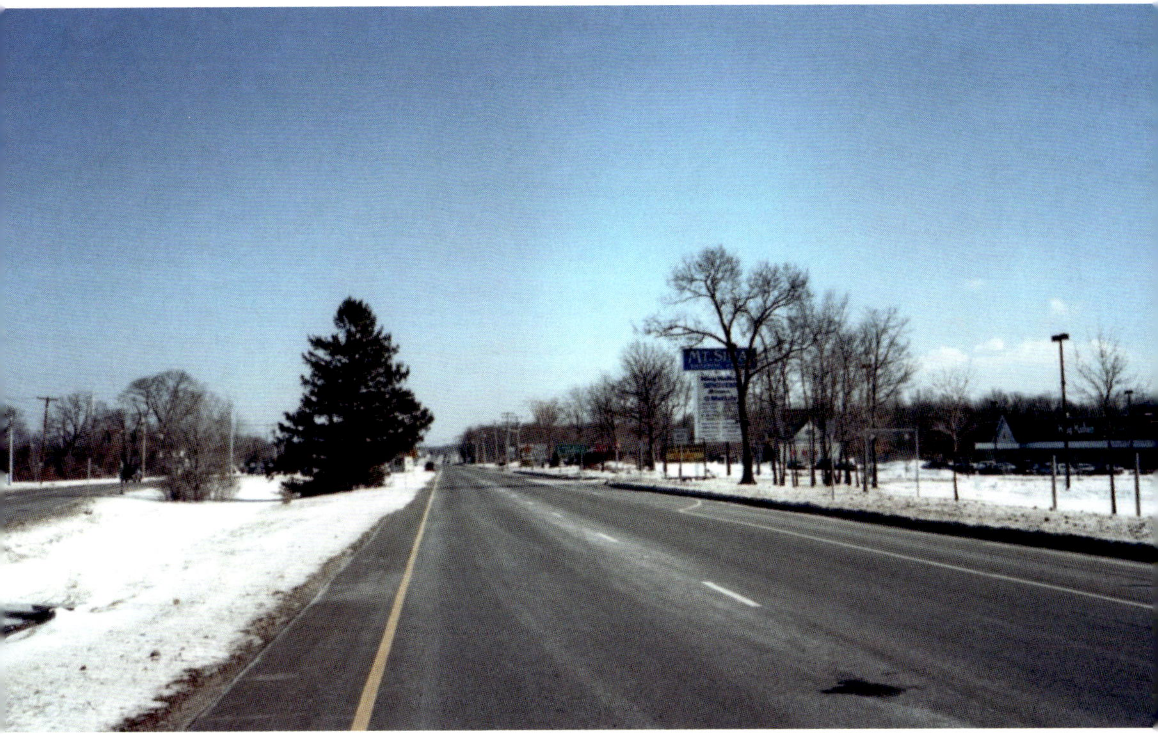

KING KULLEN: This shopping center and supermarket opened in the 1980s and is still an active shopping destination for local residents. The earlier view is from 1996, before the widening of Route 25A.

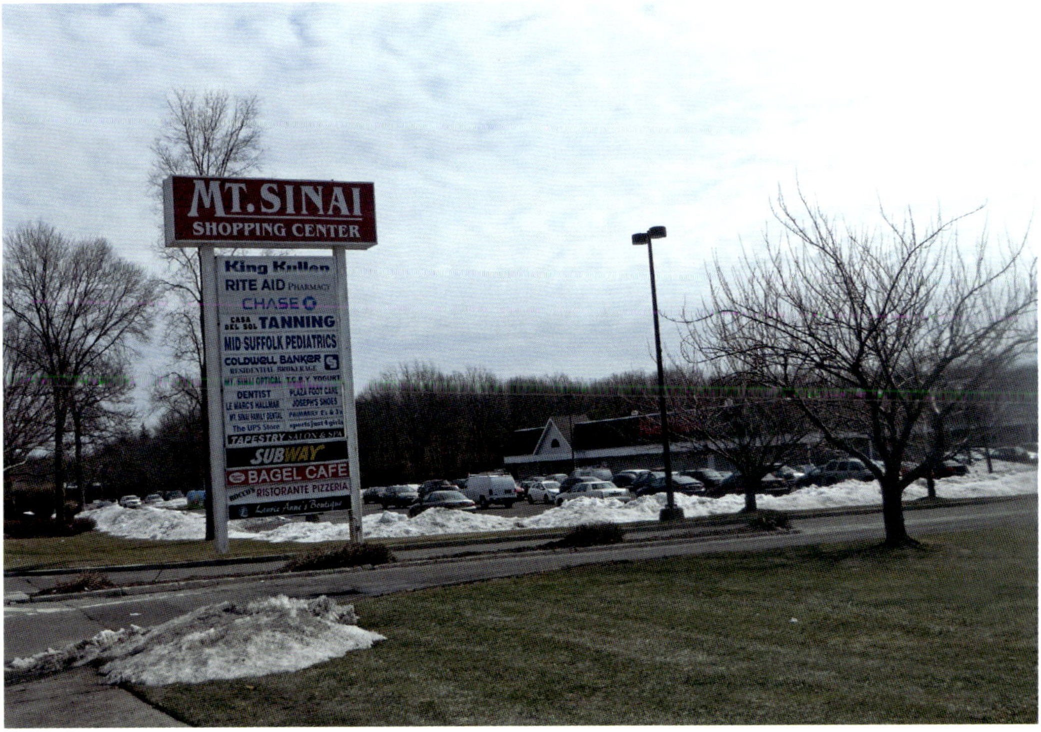

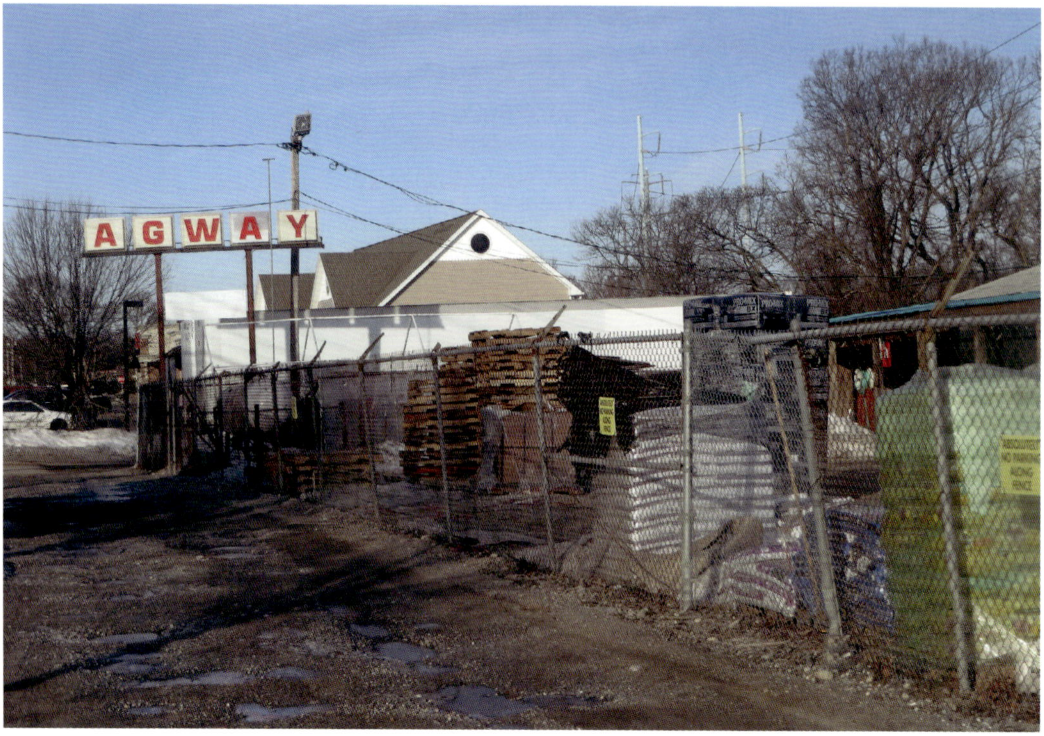

AGWAY: This lawn and garden supply store was founded in 1965, and continues to operate at its location on the north side of Route 25A. The Turning Point Commons shopping center opened in 2014.

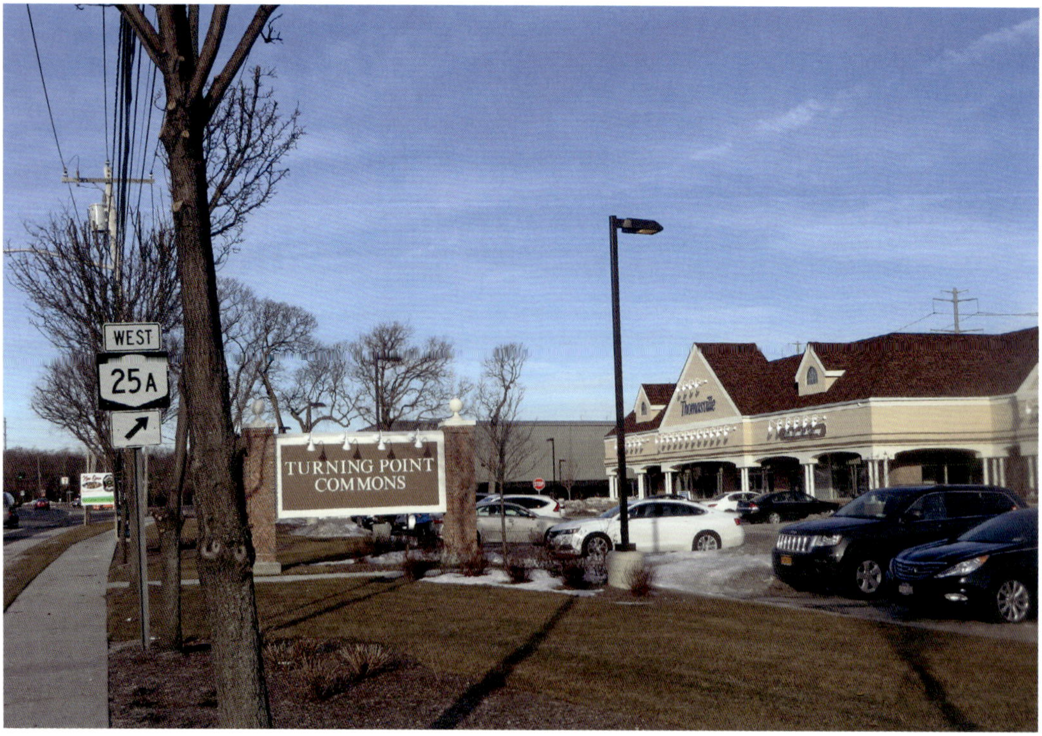

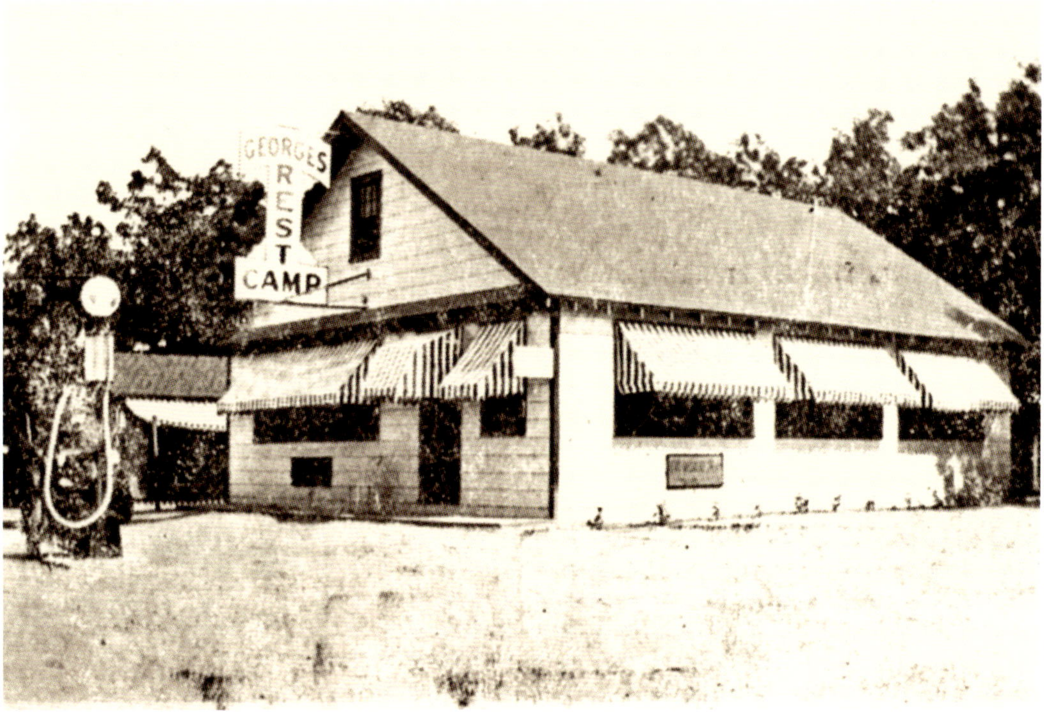

ALLESANDROS: A rest camp with picnic grounds opened on Route 25A, east of Wylde Road during the 1920s. Note the gasoline pump in front of the building. This building still houses a local restaurant called Allesandros in 2015.

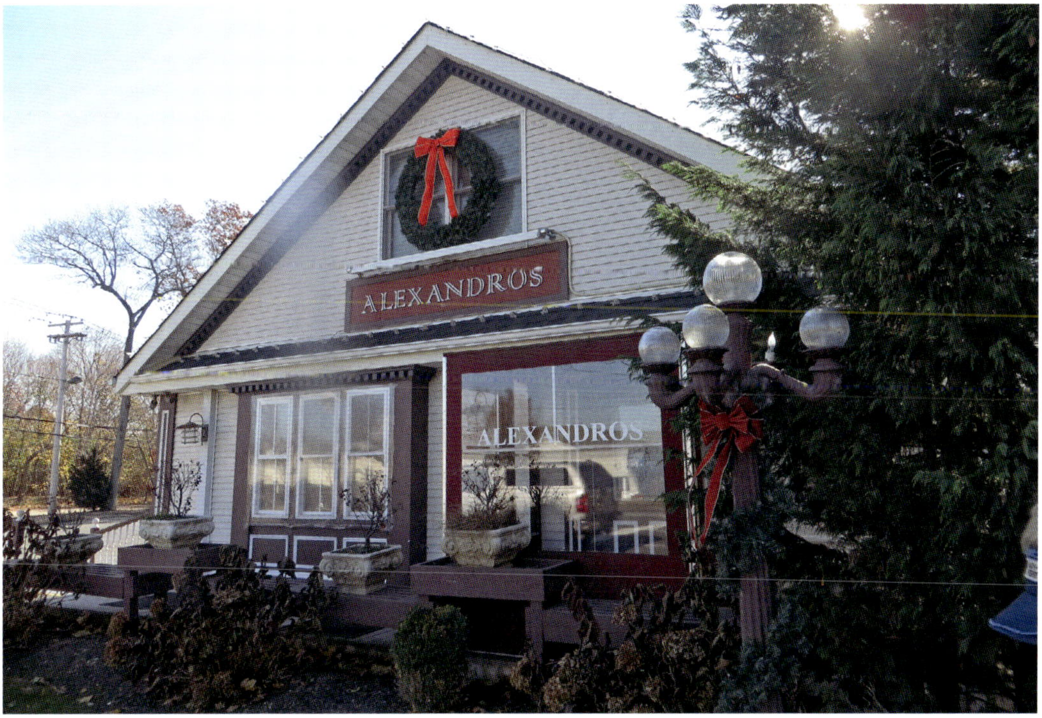

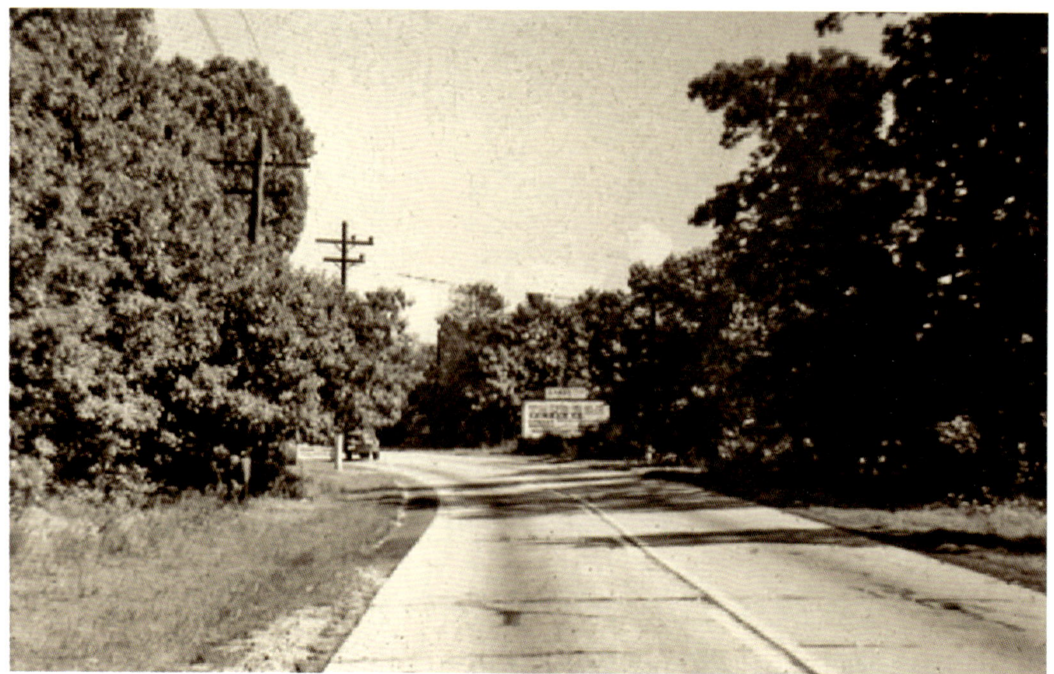

HALLOCK AVE: This road ran from the Port Jefferson-Patchogue Rd (now 112) east to Pipe Stave Hollow Road when the name changed to Echo Avenue. In the 1920s New York State had contracted out for a state highway. The route followed Hallock Avenue until Mt. Sinai-Coram Road when it kept south of the railroad tracks in a straight line. The old picture shows Route 25A in August 1949 somewhere near Crystal Brook Hollow Road, prior to the construction of Route 347. The new picture shows the current widened and commercialized Route 25A.

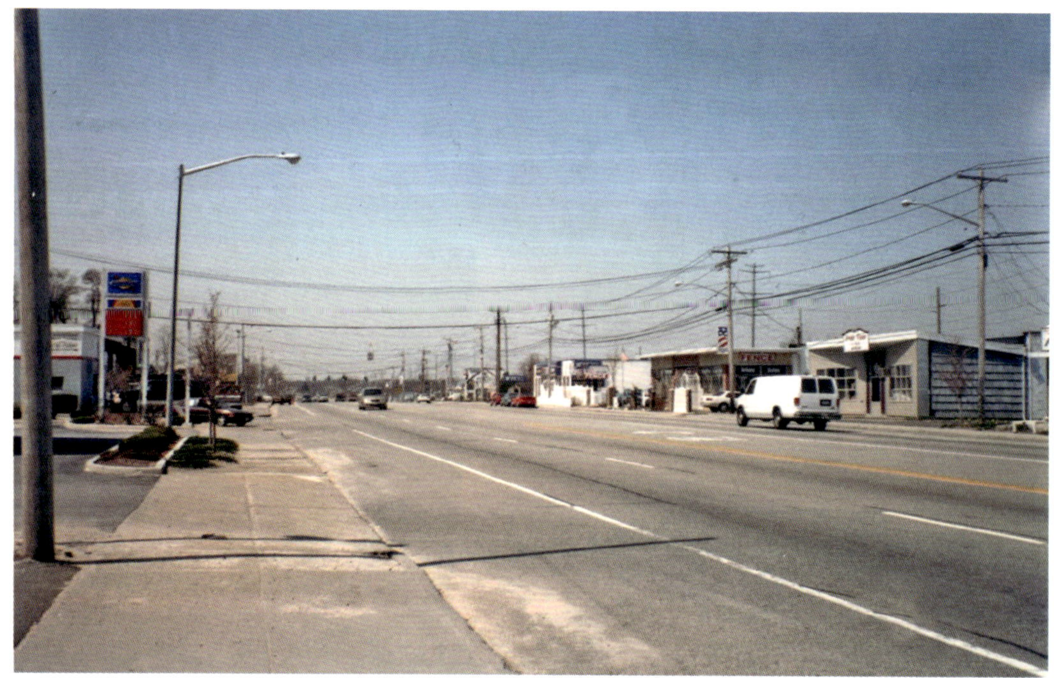

Chapter 6

Celebrating the Future

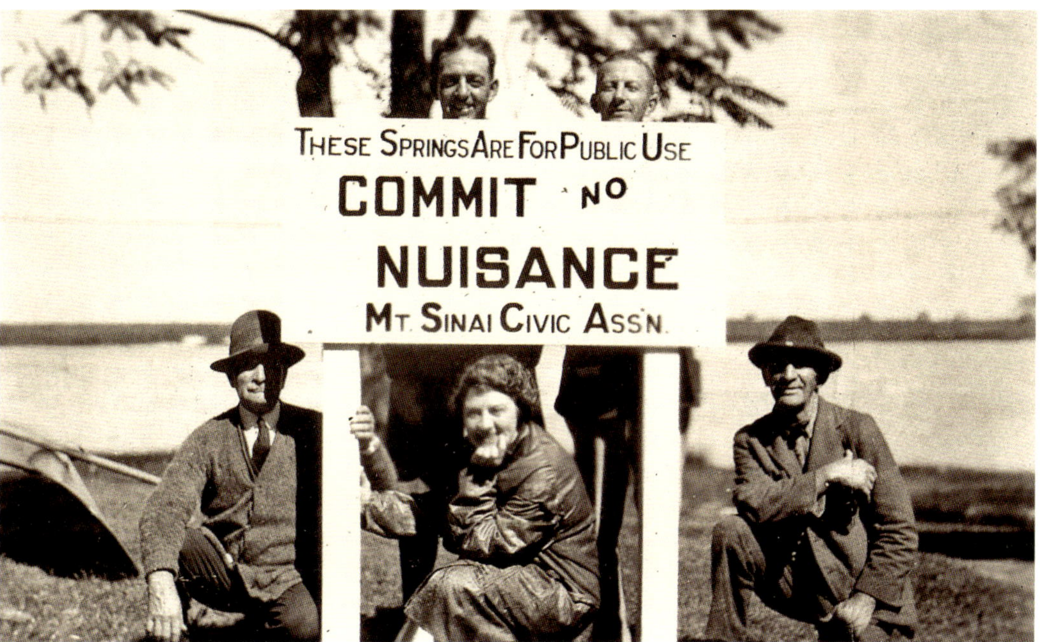

CIVICS: Continuously active since 1916, the Mount Sinai Civic Association was founded by wealthy summer residents from New York City to oppose the dredging of Mount Sinai Harbor. Members of this civic group, which was awarded its certificate of incorporation on October 5, 1916, pose by the harbor.

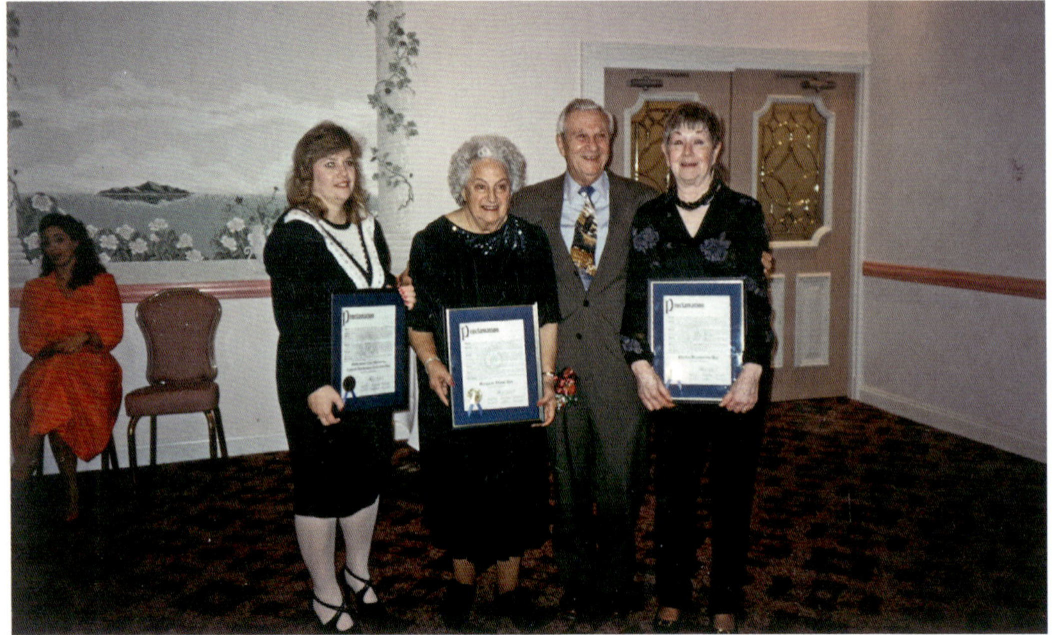

Mount Sinai Civic Association: The Mount Sinai Civic Association celebrated its 80th anniversary in 1996 with a dinner held in honor of longtime activists Margaret Alfano and Phyllis Buschmann, and will celebrate its 100th anniversary in 2016. The Civic has worked diligently to protect the character of the hamlet, and quality of life for the residents of Mount Sinai since its inception. Executive Board members were photographed at the regular meeting in February 2015. Pictured are Town Supervisor Edward Romaine, Treasurer Saranto Calamas, President Ann Becker, Recording Secretary Lisa Pfeffer, Membership Secretary Jennifer Roth, Vice-President and Corresponding Secretary Brad Arrington, and Councilwoman Jane Bonner at the 2015 swearing in of the Executive Board.

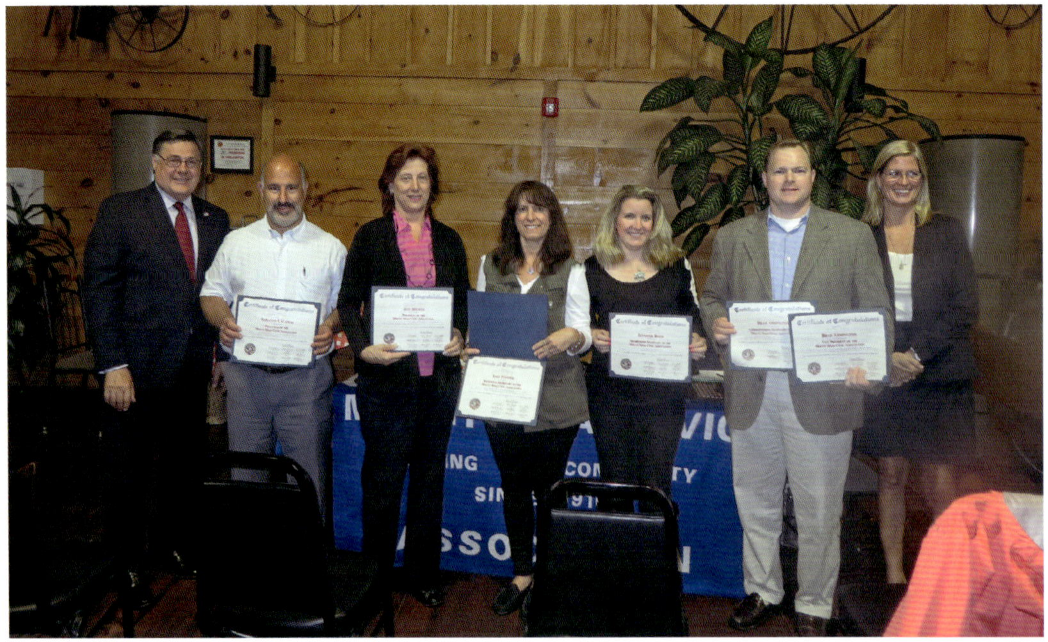

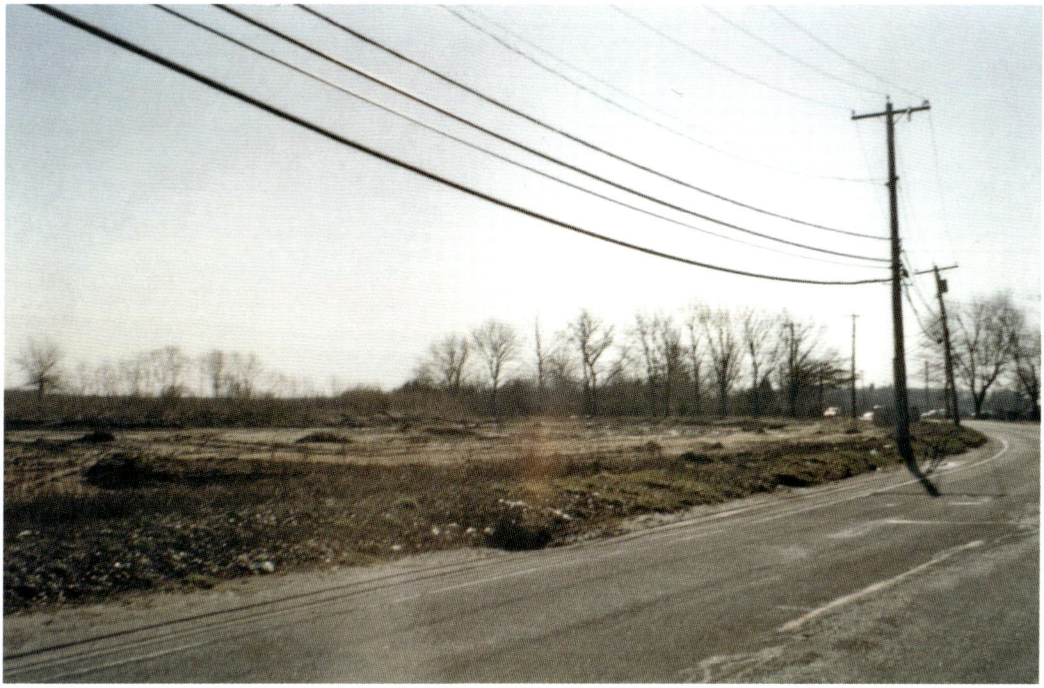

"RIDE FOR A PARK": Local resident and activist Fred Drewes publicized the fight to preserve this property beginning in 1999 with a one-year 15,700 mile bicycle tour of forty-four countries around the world. Honored for his efforts by Brookhaven Town Supervisor Felix Grucci, Fred is surrounded by supporters including Sarah Anker, Deirdre DuBato, Ann Becker, and Town Councilmen Gene Gerrard and John Jay Lavalle. The property served as a sod farm for years before being preserved and developed as active parkland.

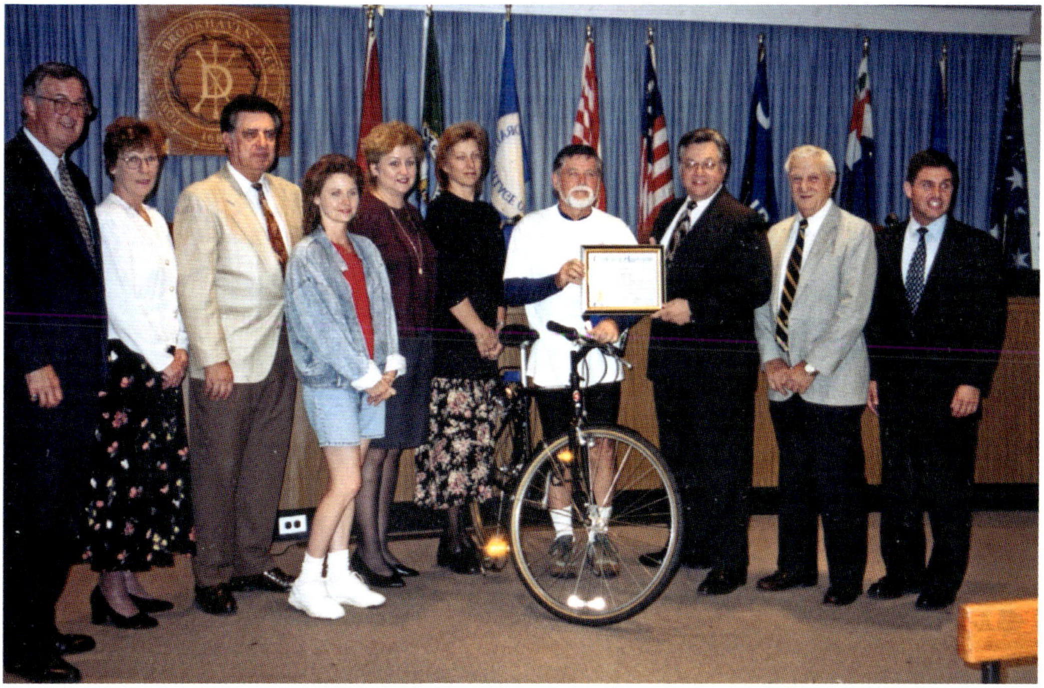

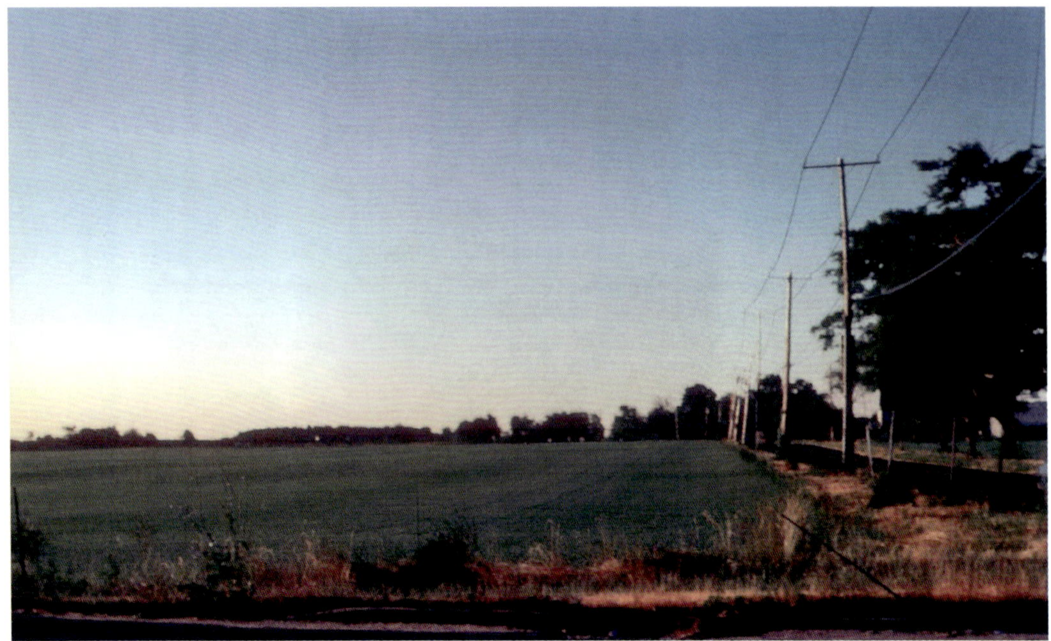

THE "WEDGE": The DeLea Sod farm, pictured here in 1988, operated at this location for many years. This view looks south from Route 25A, with Mount Sinai Coram Road on the right. In 1995, Mount Sinai engaged in a Hamlet Study under the direction of noted planner Lee Koppelman and the Long Island Regional Planning Board. The committee, chaired by Fred Drewes, Eileen Trombino, and later Lori Baldassare, recommended the development of a multi-use park and community center at the intersection of Mount Sinai-Coram Road, County Road 83 and Route 25A, known locally as "the Wedge." However the home improvement store Home Depot contracted to purchase the property from owner Ed McGovern in 2000, igniting a storm of opposition.

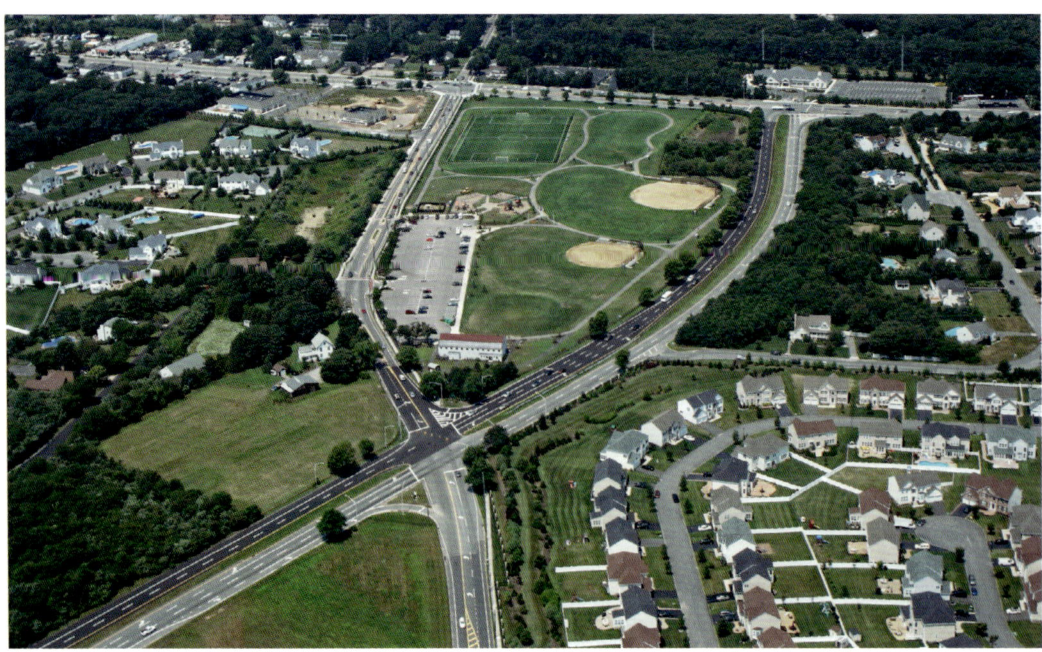

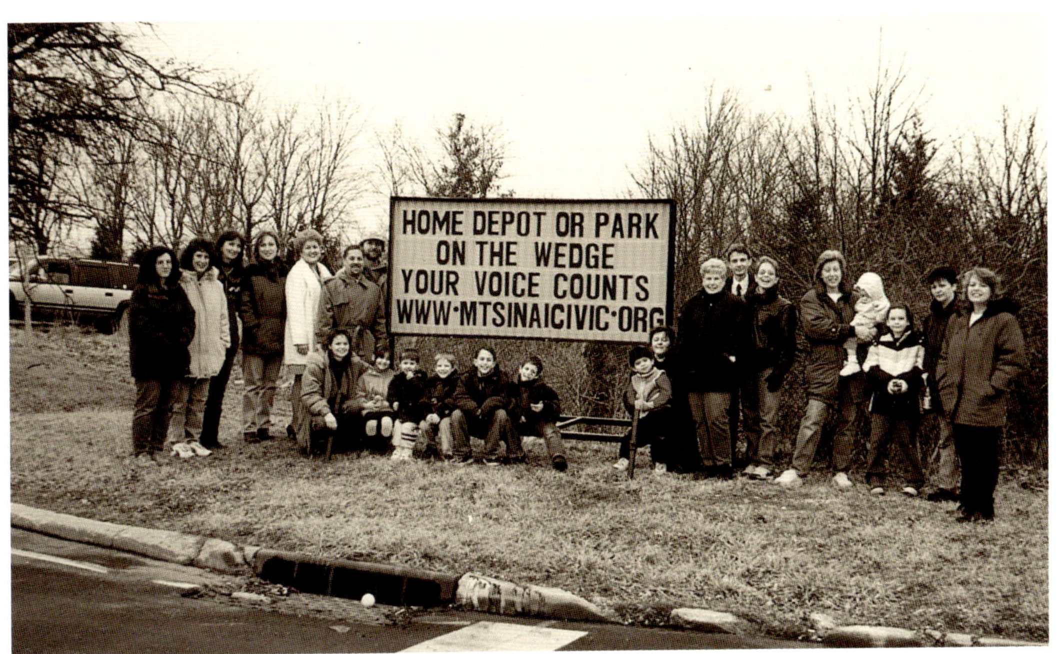

"SAVE OUR FARM": Young resident Alison Becker protests the loss of farmland in Mount Sinai, and residents and local activists who spearheaded the push to preserve the Wedge rally support for the purchase and development of the park. Land preservation efforts were led by the Mount Sinai Civic Association, and advocacy for the park began in 1995, and included a "green ribbon campaign." In 2000 Suffolk County purchased the seventeen-acre parcel, and the park was subsequently developed in partnership with the newly formed non-profit Mount Sinai Heritage Trust. The Civic Association had taken title to a quarter acre of land in 1999, with funding provided by New York State, and later transferred the property to the Heritage Trust.

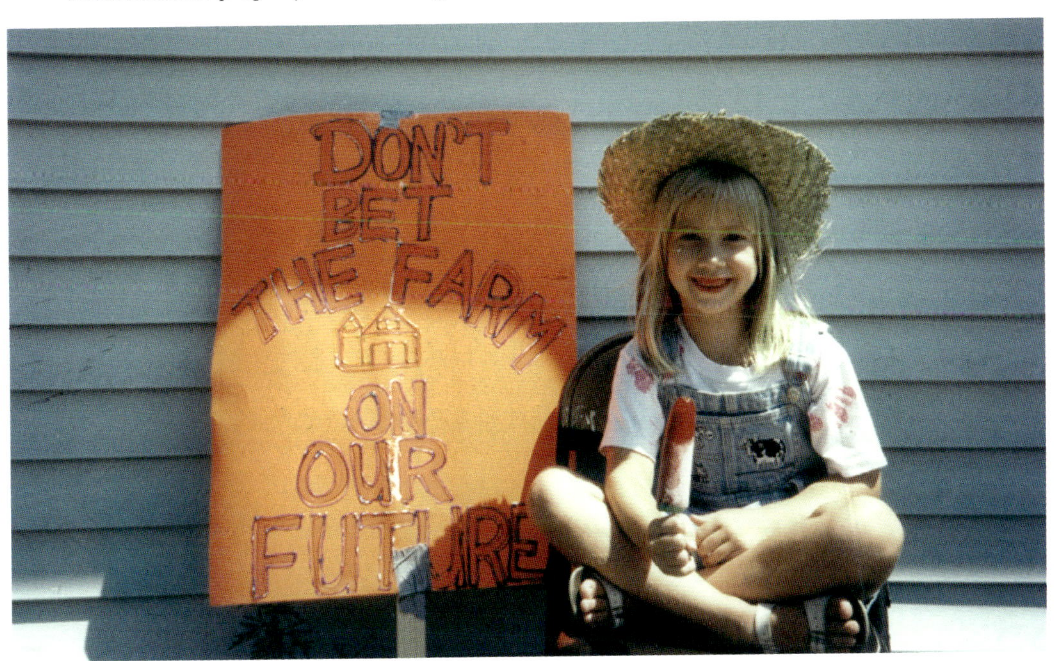

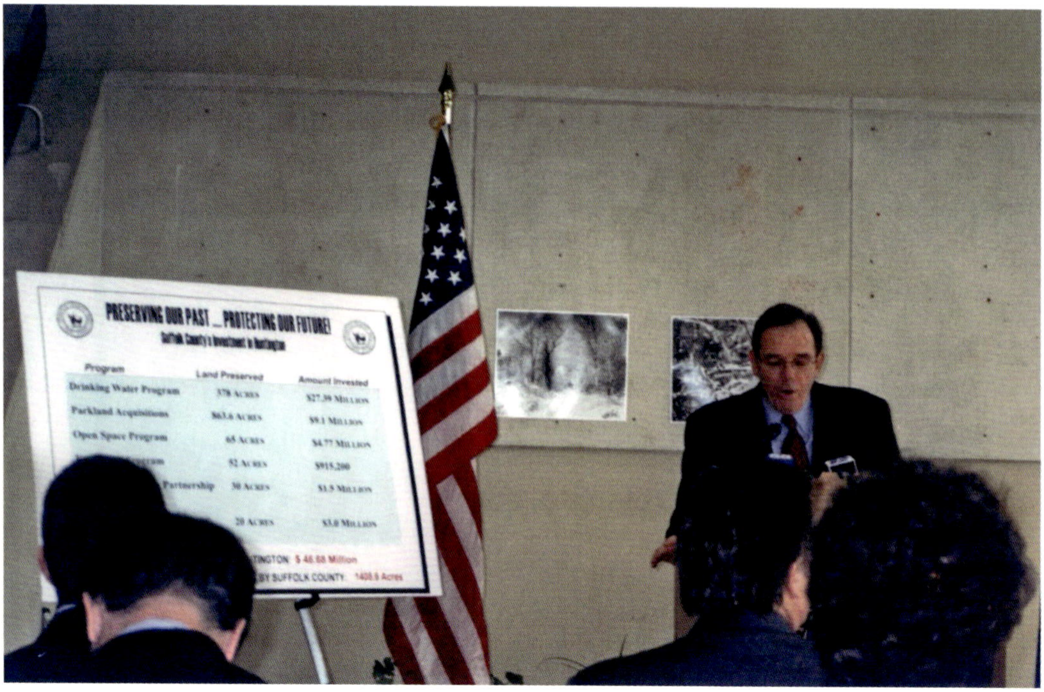

PROPERTY PRESERVED: County Executive Robert Gaffney announced the acquisition of the property at a community event in January 2001. The Mount Sinai Heritage Trust, founded by Lori Baldassare, Tom Carbone and Ann Becker, with the support of Fred Drewes (pictured here with another supporter), continues to partner with the Town of Brookhaven, and provides community recreational facilities and activities for local residents.

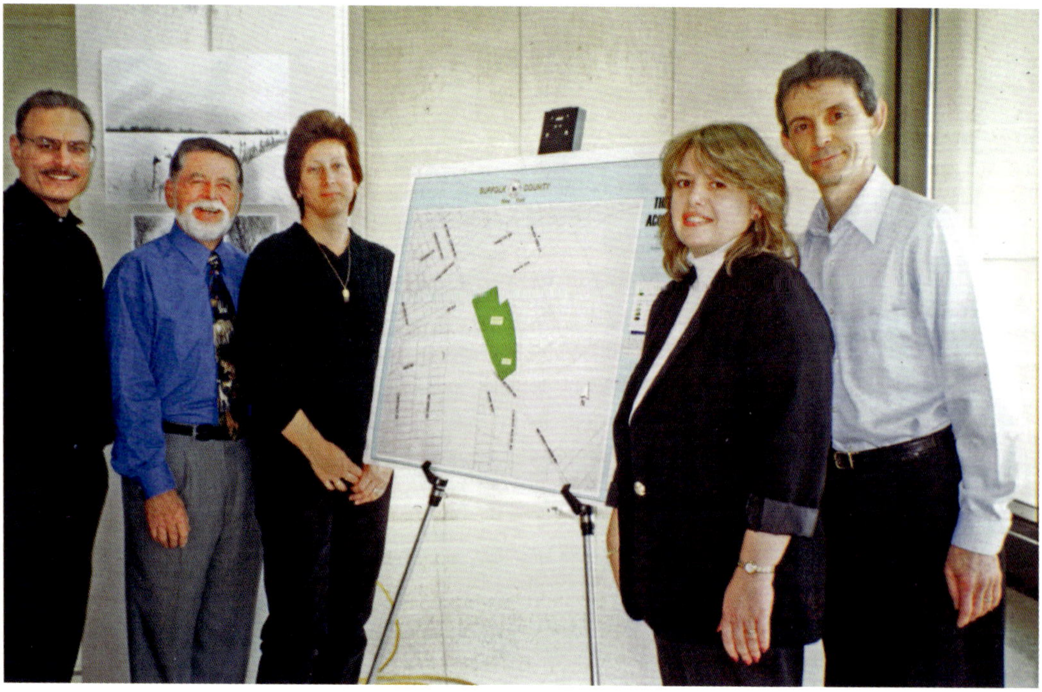

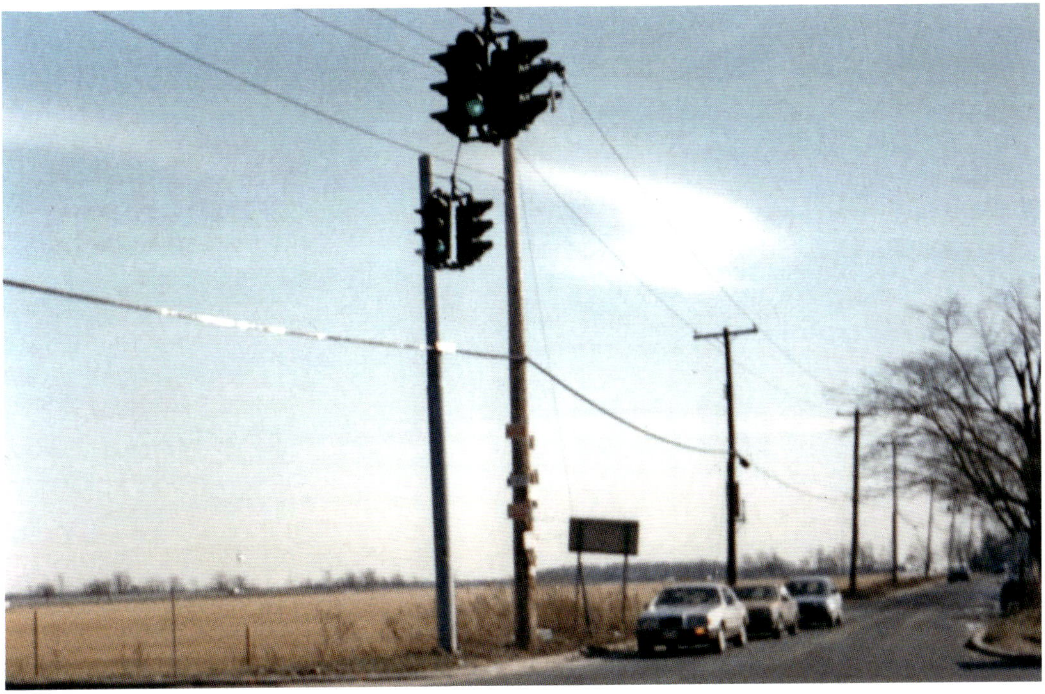

HERITAGE PARK: Construction began in 2003 by the Town of Brookhaven, who partnered with Suffolk County and the non-profit Heritage Trust to develop and maintain the new community park which opened to the public in 2004. Plans included a community center, ball fields, a children's playground, walking paths, and memorial gardens. The community was invited to participate in the planning process; the master plan is being implemented as fundraising efforts permit.

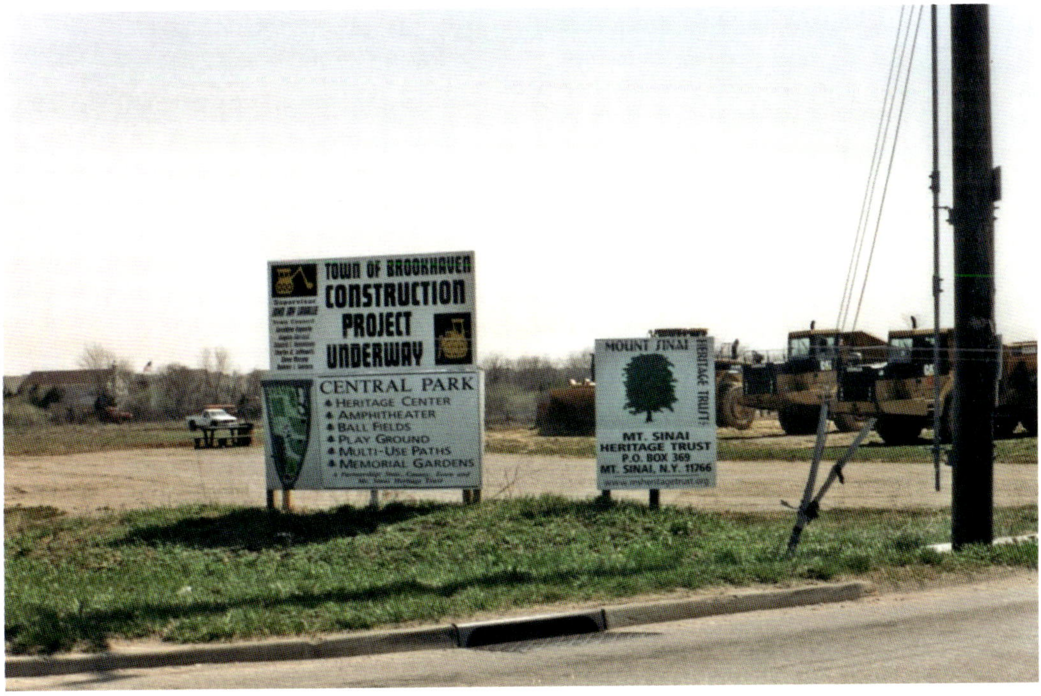

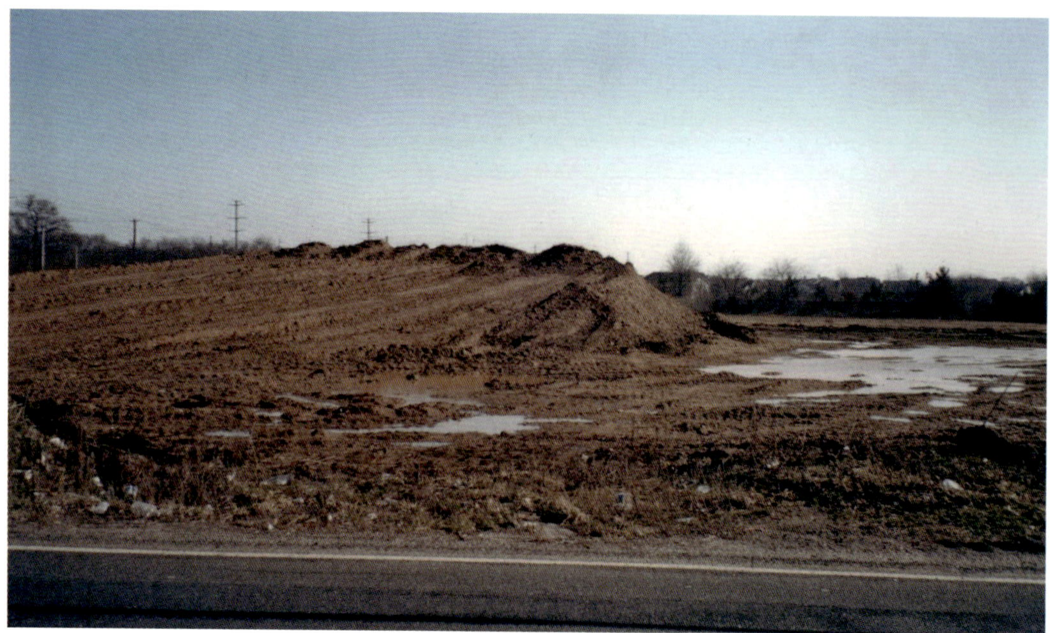

DEDICATION CEREMONIES: In August 2005 Town of Brookhaven and Suffolk County officials joined with the Board of the Heritage Trust, Mount Sinai Civic Association members and local residents to officially open the new park. Flags of the Town of Brookhaven, County of Suffolk, State of New York and United States of America fly proudly in the center of the park. Construction was still underway, but the park provided much needed recreational facilities for north shore residents.

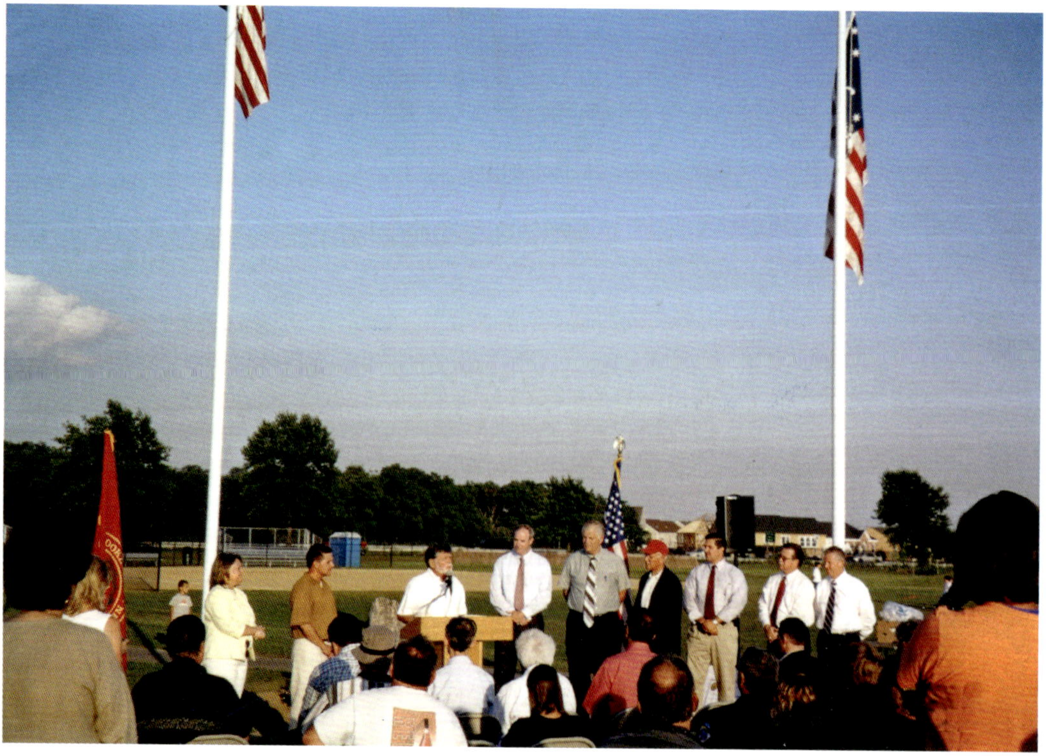

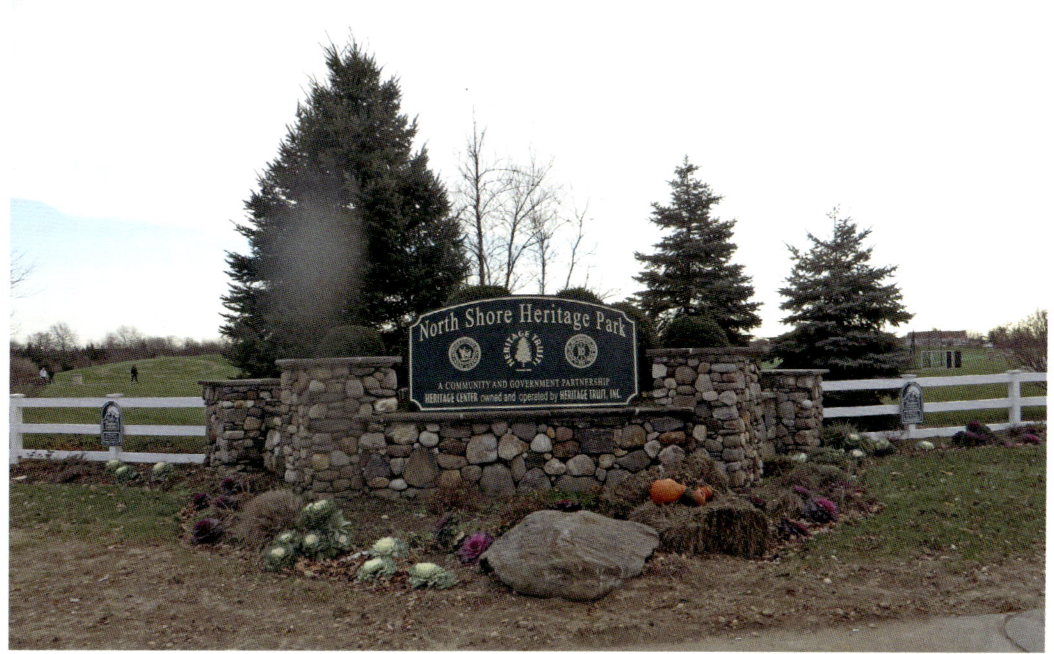

HERITAGE CENTER: This building opened in 2007, and was constructed and is maintained by the non-profit Heritage Trust. The sign located on the northwest corner of the park property at the intersection of Mount Sinai Coram Road and Route 25A was installed by the Heritage Trust, with the landscaping donated and maintained by Kelly Brothers Landscaping, operating in Mount Sinai since 1978. The Heritage Trust continues to partner with Brookhaven Town and Suffolk County to provide the unique features residents have come to enjoy making Heritage Park one of the most popular parks in Brookhaven Town.

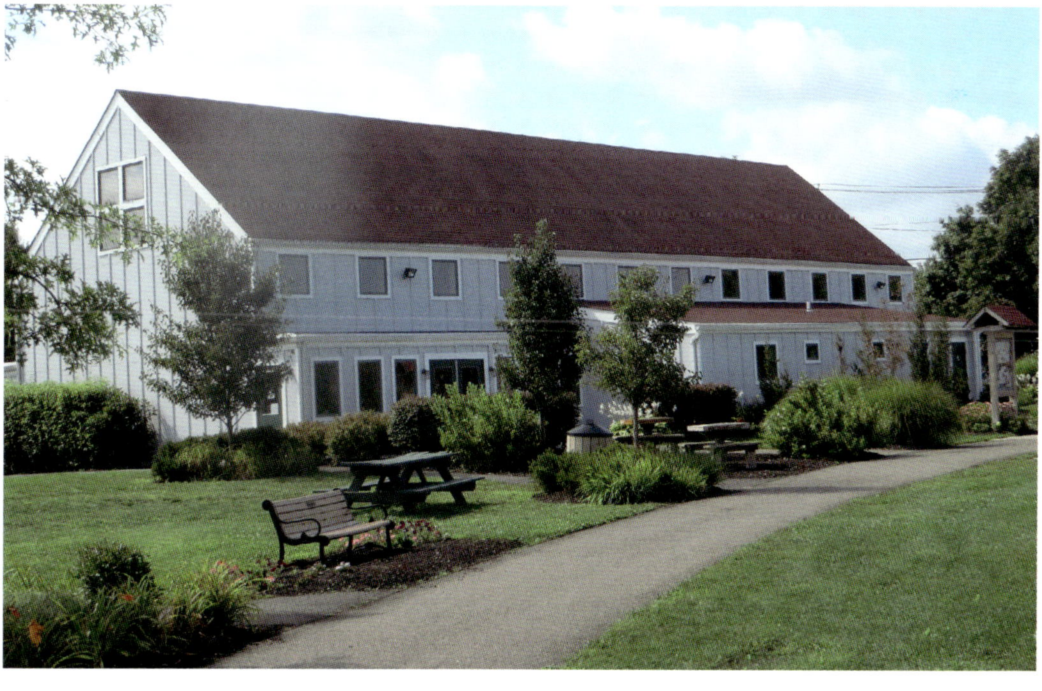

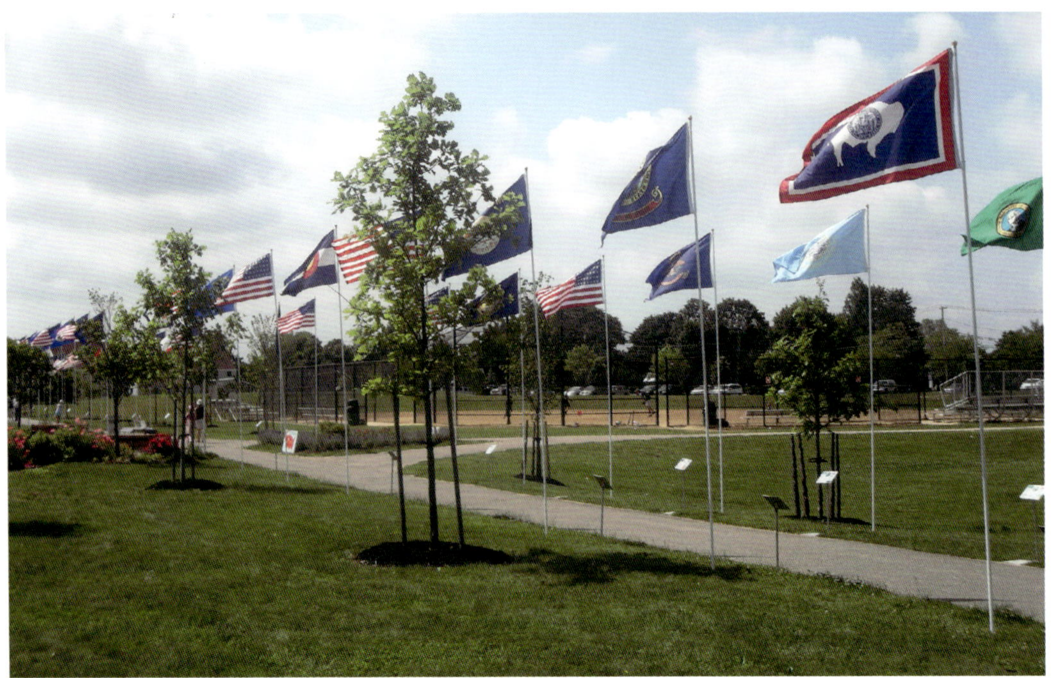

AVENUE AND COURT OF AMERICA: Fred Drewes, longtime community resident and volunteer, along with local businessman Bob Koch, were instrumental in designing, organizing and installing the Parade of Flags display, which is available for viewing on national holidays. Ninety-four state and territorial flags, and fifty-seven signs were included in the first parade, arranged chronologically in the order of admission to the United States. Local Boy Scout troops and park volunteers set up and dismantle the display several times a year. The Court of America was created by Drewes to honor the United States of America.

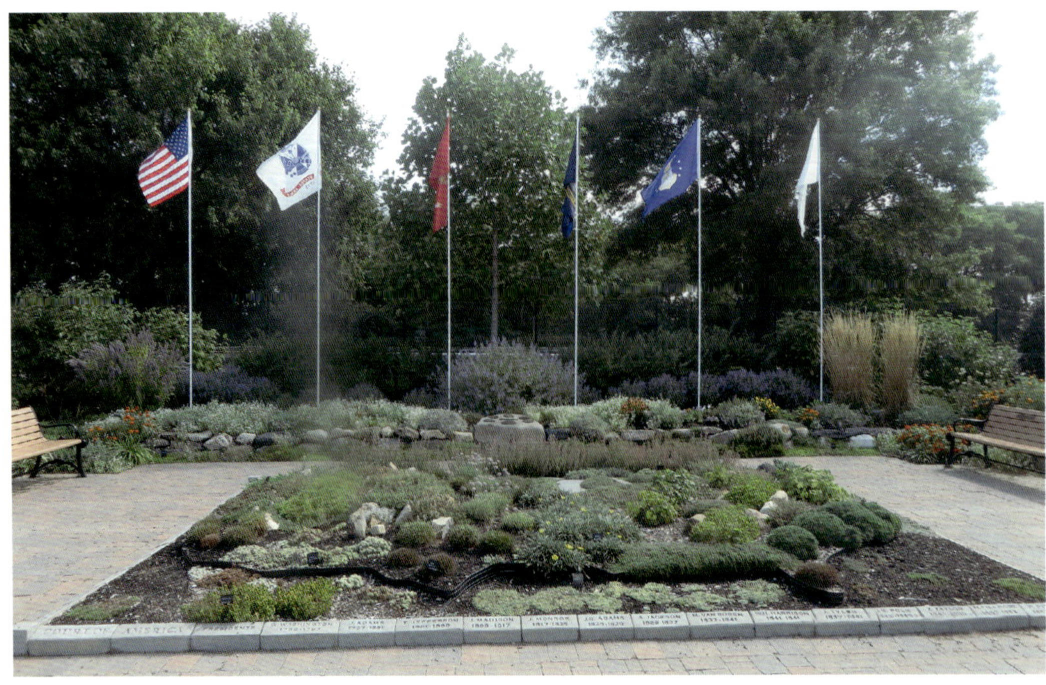

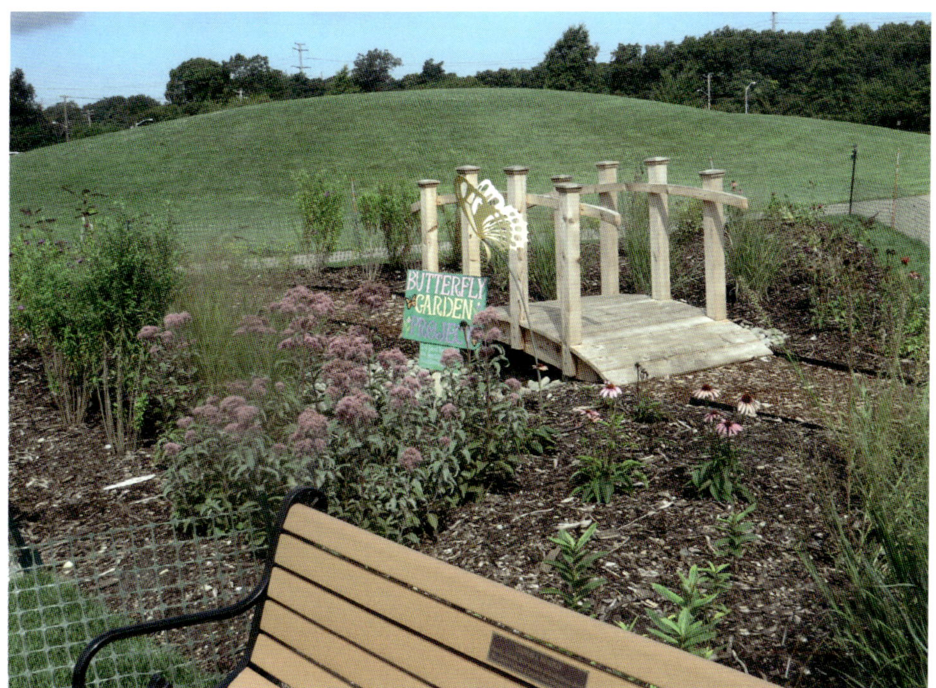

Butterfly Garden: Located near the center of the park, this was designed and donated by a local Girl Scout Troop under the supervision of master gardeners. The "Old Man's Garden" located alongside the Heritage Center, was the brainchild of Fred Drewes, who continues to maintain this garden with the help of volunteers. Gardens behind the building were planted and are maintained by the Mount Sinai Garden Club.

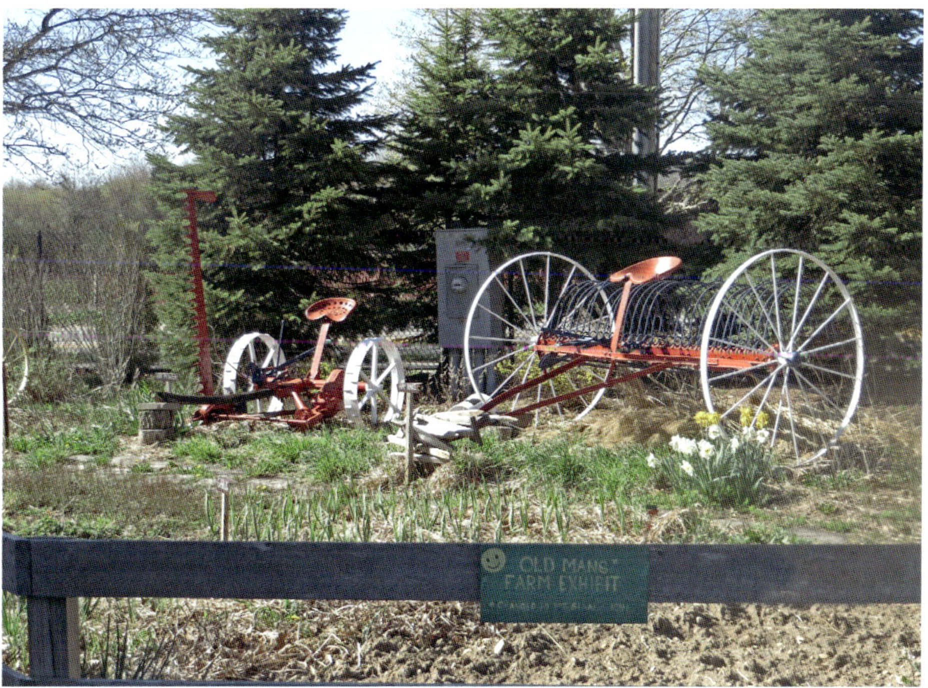

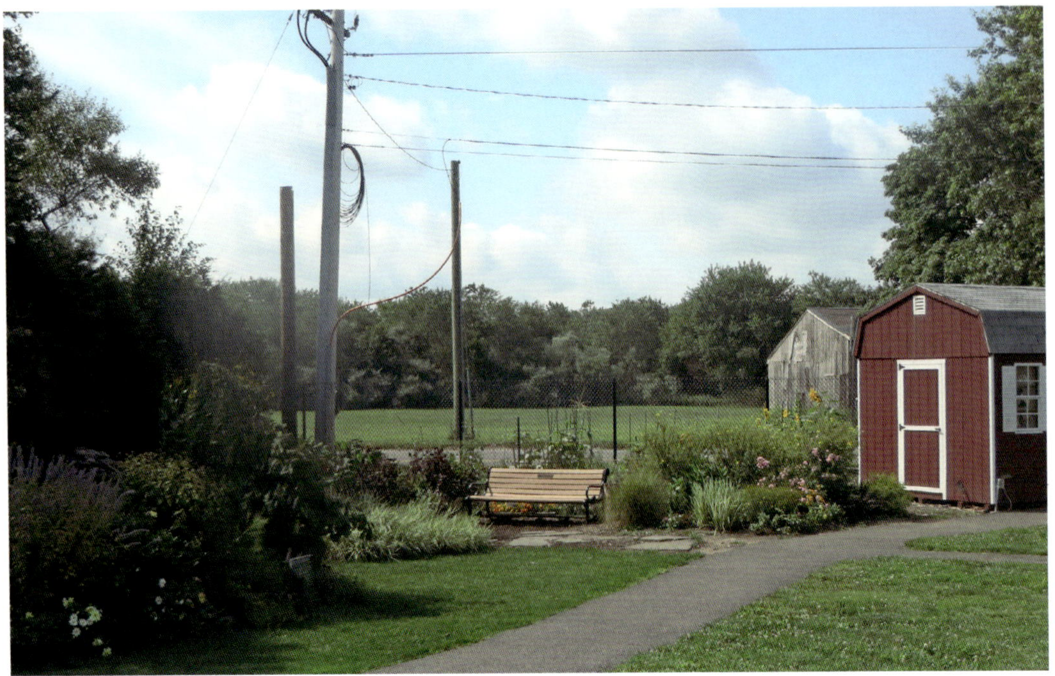

MOUNT SINAI GARDEN CLUB: The Mount Sinai Garden Club was established by Walter Becker and Christine Segal in 2007, with the goal of beautifying the hamlet of Mount Sinai and surrounding communities. The Club has worked extensively in Heritage Park, and offers community garden plots to residents. Various local businesses have donated labor and materials including a pond and sod at the park. This memorial bench is one of four constructed by Mount Sinai High School students and dedicated to the memory of Karen Graham, who taught at the high school and died in 2013.

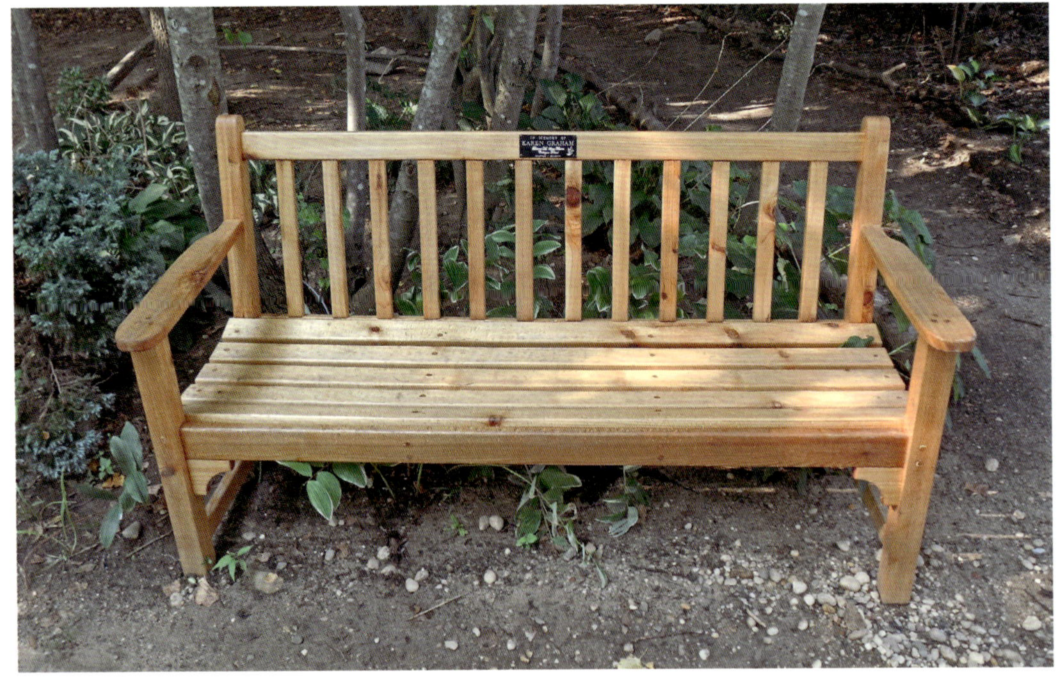

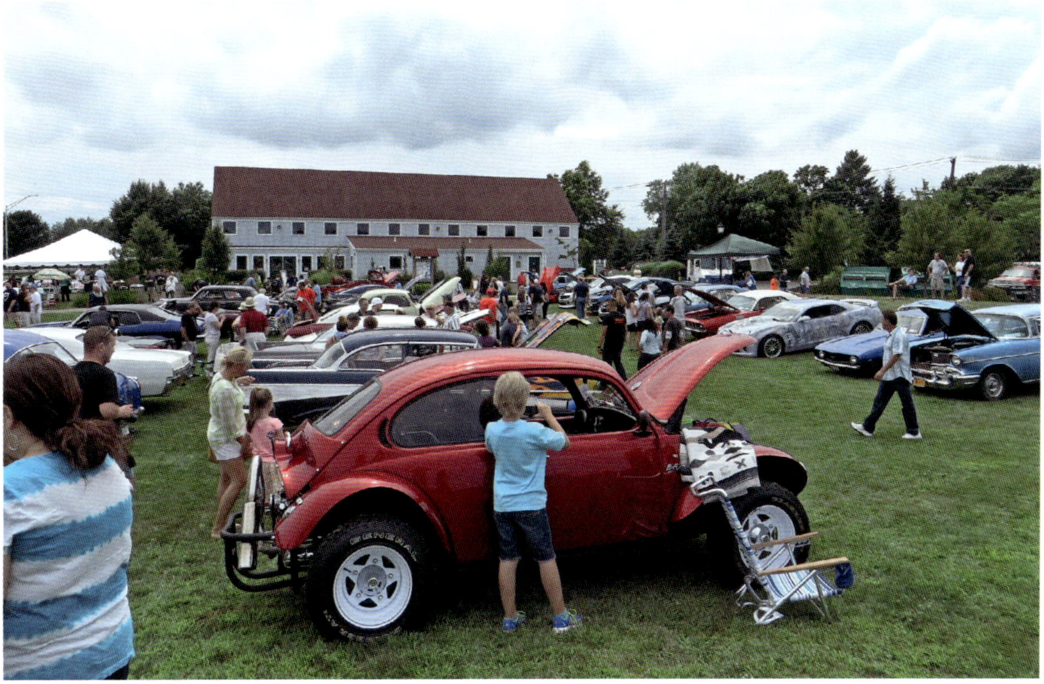

CAR SHOW: The Heritage Trust sponsors many community activities and fund raising events throughout the year. The first Car Show was held in July 2014, and residents Walter and Ann Becker helped organize the raffle for prizes donated by local businesses. Future goals for the park include the donation of an amphitheater, splash pad, putting green, fossil scavenger hunt stones and much more, all funded through donations from local residents and businesses, grants and fundraising efforts by Heritage Trust volunteers.

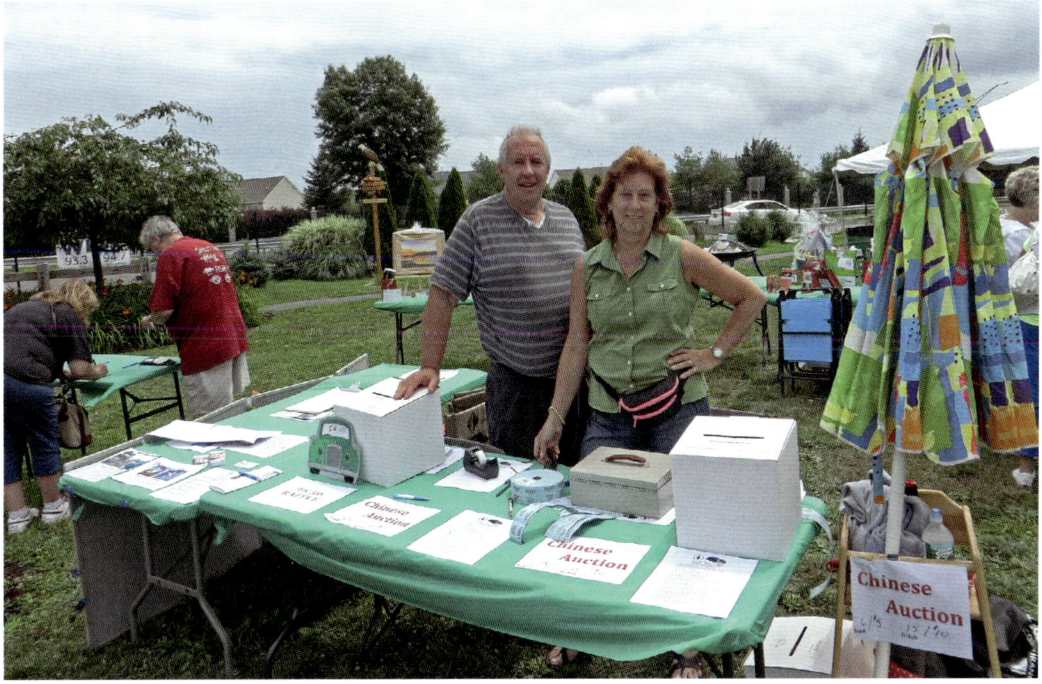

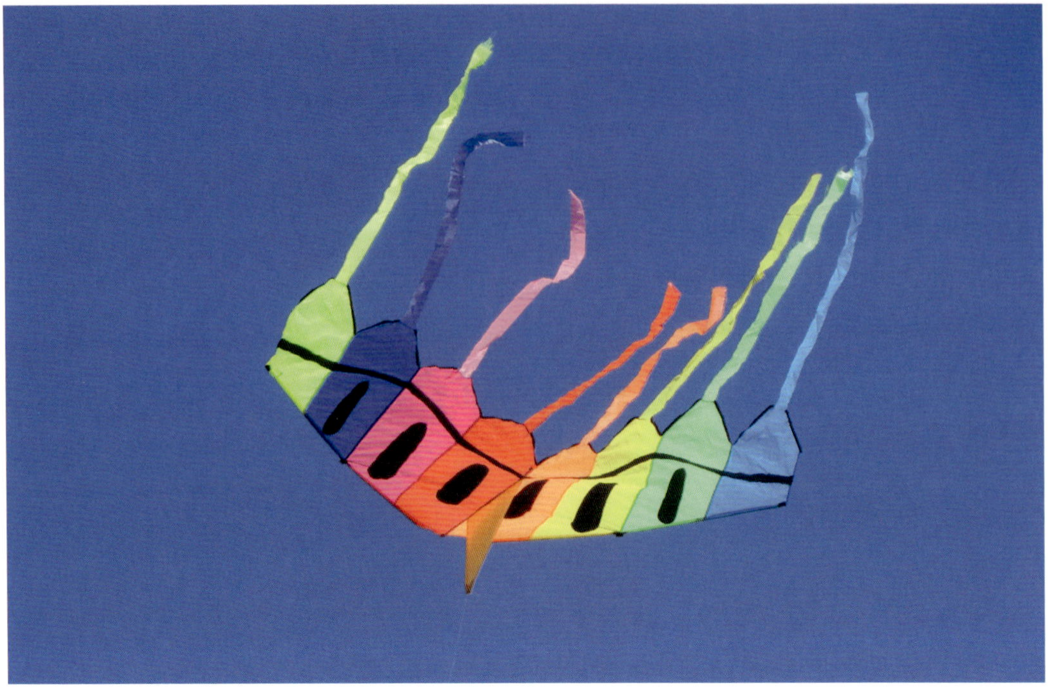

SMILEY FACE: Created in 2012, community volunteers, under the direction of Fred Drewes, planted three thousand daffodil bulbs on the northwest slope of the play knoll of Heritage Park. When in bloom, the daffodils form a smiling face, visible from within the park as well as from the east bound vehicles on Route 25A. The annual Kite Day celebration offers an opportunity for local residents to enjoy a wonderful springtime activity.

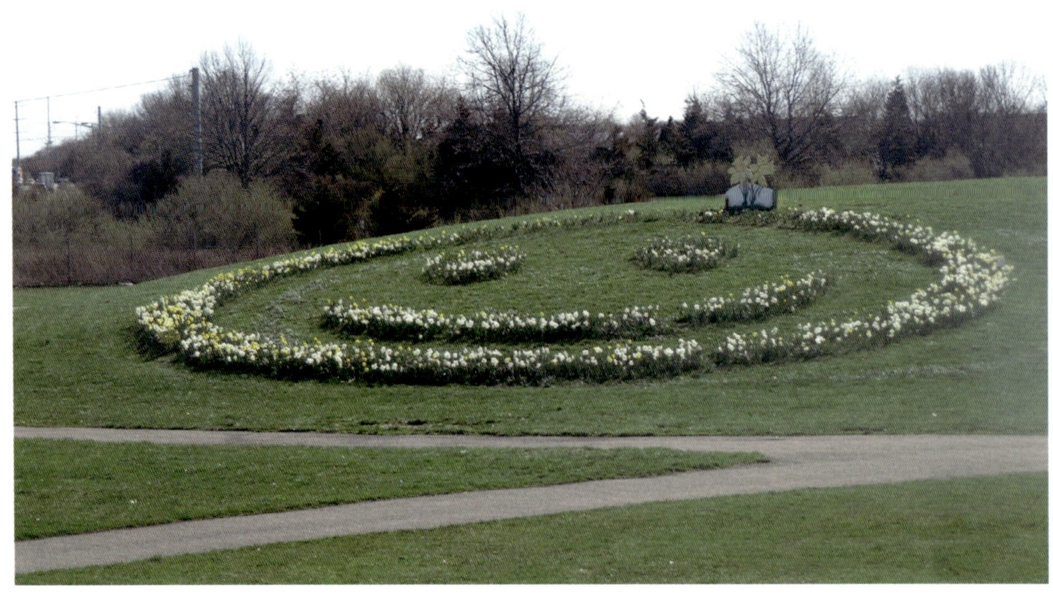

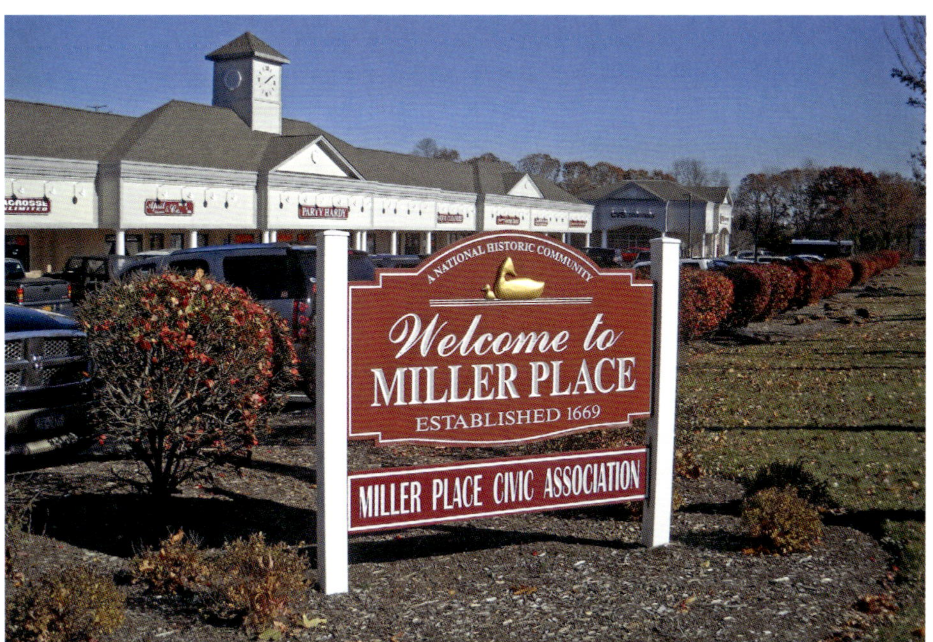

WELCOME SIGNS: Welcoming visitors to Mount Sinai as they travel east along Route 347 at the corner of Crystal Brook Hollow Road, this sign was erected by the Mount Sinai Civic Association in 1999 with funds obtained from the Suffolk County Legislature. The sign inaugurated the Civics' beautification campaign that year. The gazebo was donated by Gera Gardens and dedicated to the memory of Eileen Trombino, past president of the Civic who died in 1995. The landscaping around the sign and gazebo were donated and maintained by Kelly Brothers Landscaping. This Miller Place community welcome sign, installed by the Miller Place Civic Association, is located on Route 25A near the intersection of Pipe Stave Hollow Road.

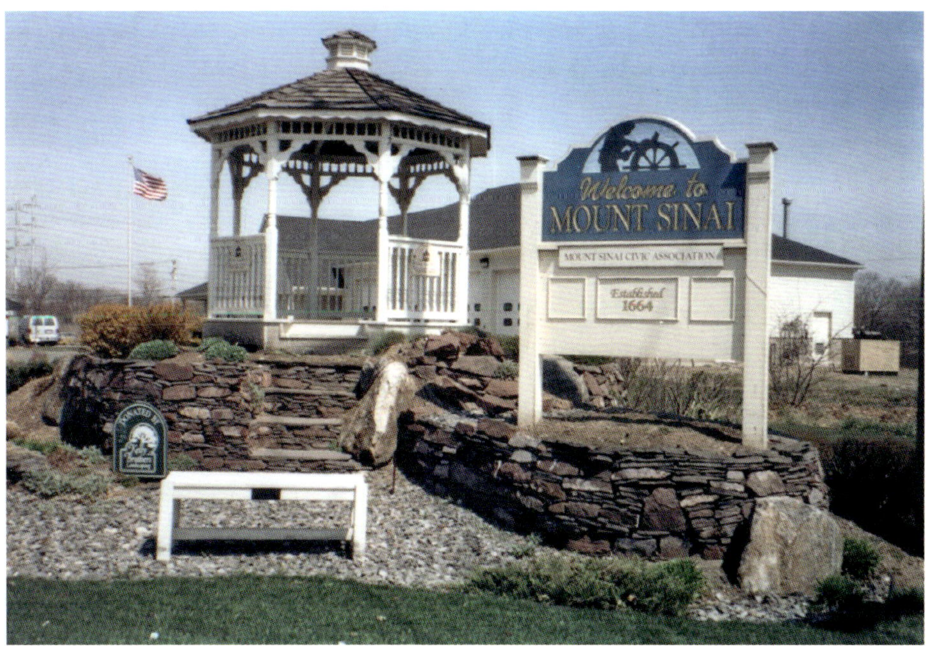

Acknowledgements

We would like to thank the many people who contributed photographs and/or information for this book. The number of photographs available made it difficult to select which to use, and we are very grateful to all who offered to share their images and memories with us. Each and every person contributed information which has added to the knowledge of the rich history of Mount Sinai and Miller Place, and this information has also led to more avenues for research.

We especially thank Fred Drewes, who contributed a large number of photographs as well as detailed information about his extensive community activism and volunteer work. Barbara Russell, Brookhaven Town Historian, generously shared the Town's collections with us, and volunteered to scan a number of photographs, many of which were used in the book. Brian Lenz provided the wonderful aerial views in the book, and we appreciate his willingness to allow publication. In addition, we would like to personally thank the following people and organizations for their willingness to share: Randy Hagerman; Barbara Davenport; Margaret Davis Gass; Rev. Dr. Diane (Samuels) Cangelosi, minister and Jane Davis Carter, historian for the Mt. Sinai Congregational Church, the United Church of Christ; Harry Randall; Alfred Kopcienski, the Miller Place Fire Department; Henry Knoernschild, the Mt. Sinai Fire Department; Laurie (Giffen) Higgins; Mark Larson; Rob Fitton; Bob Koch; Jill Connors; Bethany Porcaro; Kristin Nyitray, Stony Brook University Special Collections; and the Miller Place-Mount Sinai Historical Society Collections. In addition, both authors shared our personal collections as well.

The authors would also like to thank their husbands, Steven Giffen and Walter Becker, for their patience, support and appreciation of our love of history and our desire to inform the public.

While we have worked hard to present accurate information, we take full responsibility for any factual errors which may appear.